Ripped Apart

How Democrats Can Fight Polarization to Win

Also by Steven Stoft

Global Carbon Pricing: The Path to Climate Cooperation
(edited with Peter Cramton, David JC MacKay, Axel Ockenfels)

Dépasser Copenhague: Apprendre à coopérer
(translated by Mathieu Thomas)

Carbonomics: How to Fix the Climate and Charge It to OPEC

Power System Economics: Designing Markets for Electricity

Ripped Apart

How Democrats Can
Fight Polarization to Win

Steven Stoft

PolyScience Press

Berkeley, California

.

Cover art: partially by James Larkin

PolyScience Press
2910 Elmwood Court
Berkeley, California 94705

Notes and Documentation can be found at RippedApart.org.

Ripped Apart: How Democrats Can Fight Polarization to Win
Steven Stoft.—1st ed. (rev. 1.0.3)
ISBN 978-0-9818775-2-5

Dedicated to the strategic liberals
who took back the House in 2018

In theory
there is no difference between practice and theory.
In practice, there is.

—Yogi Berra

CONTENTS

Part 4. Mythology Traps

Part 5. Identity Politics

Part 6. Wrap-up and Overview

Sidebar Pages

Preface and Acknowledgments

Mario Savio, fresh from civil rights work in Mississippi, took his shoes off and climbed on top a police car in the middle of the U.C. Berkeley campus to lead a sit-in. That was Day One of the free speech movement in 1964, and I was stuck in high school waiting for my freedom. But by the next year, I was in Berkeley myself, protesting the Vietnam War, and the year after that I was canvassing to put Ron Dellums on the Berkeley City Council (he would later cofound the Congressional Black Caucus).

Soon after, in 1968, 17-year-old Black Panther Bobby Hutton was killed by the Oakland Police after taking part in an ambush of the police (back then we heard the police ambushed the Panthers). I was arrested for posting an invitation to his funeral, but they could think of nothing to charge me with.

That summer, on a black-and-white television, I watched as Mayor Daley's Chicago police attacked nonviolent demonstrators protesting the rigged 1968 Democratic Convention. As the protesters chanted "The whole world is watching," I felt sure the country would finally see the establishment for what it was, and we might even stop the war. This was the height of the 1960s revolution.

With the best of intentions, we had launched the second great polarization of America. The first had led to Abraham Lincoln, the Civil War and the end of slavery. No one in 1968, could imagine the consequences unfolding today. And no one knows now where they will lead.

That year I voted for the Black candidate from Chicago for president—Dick Gregory. He was a wonderful activist-comedian, but the radical left's disdain for liberals probably handed the presidency to Richard Nixon. After that, McGovern rejiggered the nomination process, which allowed him to unseat Mayor Daley's delegation, win the nomination, and lose the election by a landslide.

That's when I realized we had committed revolutionary suicide. How long would it take to clear out all the crazy ideas? Not the goals of peace and equality, but the crazy self-righteous utopian "strategies" that took no account of the real world. Having a math and astronomy background, I tried to calculate. My generation of activists would need to be replaced and that would take 20 to 25 years.

Biding my time, I taught middle school for a year, did my alternative service as a conscientious objector and wandered around Europe reading Marxist economics and quantum mechanics. I returned to Berkeley for a Ph.D. in economics, started the newsletter for Berkeley Citizens Action to hold the group together between biennial elections and advised City Councilwoman Ying Lee Kelley regarding the CETA federal job-training program. I had met Ying when we were both arrested at an antiwar demonstration. Fourteen of us won our suit for false arrest against the Alameda County Sheriffs.

Bill Clinton did show up 20 years after I made my calculation, but where was the progressive movement?

Then, after I'd given up hope, out of the blue, there was Barack Obama. After 36 years. And there was a movement of progressives right behind him. They were not a reflection of the late '60s radicals. They were a little more like I had imagined the civil rights movement, Year One of the free speech movement, and the start of the antiwar movement—thoughtful and dedicated but with a new upbeat sense of humor. I thought I'd died and gone to heaven.

But even before he was elected, I was driving with friends to a movie when the guy in the back seat, an old '60s radical, began ranting about how Obama was just a corporate shill, as bad as the Republicans. My heart sank. I knew what this meant. I went online, and there they were, the baby-boomer radicals and their political descendants, all foaming at the mouth.

As the election neared, I found myself pacing the floor, asking myself: Do I want him to win? There was no question I'd vote for him. But I knew the radical left. It would take them a while, but they would make life hell for him. I couldn't bear the thought. I had some idea how much support he would need as our first Black president, facing a well-oiled, ultra-right-wing media machine.

At a MoveOn meeting after his first midterm election, the few radicals there were crowing that they had given him a few dollars but had not worked for him—he was "such a disappointment." Right. In two years, all he'd done was prevent another Great Depression, save the auto industry and pass Obamacare, the first big addition to FDR's agenda since 1965.

Just before his second midterm election, Michael Moore summed up the radicals' view: "Mr. Obama, when the history is written of this era, this is how you'll be remembered: 'He was the first Black president.'

Okay, not a bad accomplishment, but that's it. A big disappointment." No Republican could have been more damaging than this inside hit job.

As his second term ended, the radicals shifted into overdrive, and after eight years of sabotage, we lost by a hair. And they may well do it again. The remnants of the baby-boomer radicals had passed down to later generations their self-righteousness. It was a repeat of how I'd seen the "red-diaper babies" corrupting the political movements of the early '60s.

Watching this unfold, I did my best to figure out how a small group of dedicated, well-intentioned politicos could repeatedly stymie the very changes they wanted. Yes, it was due to overreach on their part. It was believing righteousness beats thinking. But why do they get away with it? Why don't we dedicated liberals and radical liberals speak up? And most important, how can we stop Trump and get back on track?

There was only one way to find out. I'd done this twice before, once for electricity markets and once for climate policy. I knew it would work and only take about three years. I'd write a book … and explain it to myself. I enjoyed all the eye-opening surprises I found along the way. I hope you do, too.

For almost three years, Arlin Weinberger has been my constant sounding board, constructive critic, and light-handed copy editor, all of which has made the process of discovery far more enjoyable, and the difficulties of writing, less daunting.

My copyeditor Karel Kramer took on the nearly impossible job of turning a mountain of excess detail into something readable and, when I let her, into something enjoyable. And many thanks to my proofreader Bob Cooper who brought consistency to my experimental approach to all things grammatical. Remaining errors are due to my late changes.

Thanks also for many helpful comments and pointers from James Weinberger, John Ballard, Judi and Hardy Dawainis, Carl Fuchshuber, Charlie Carlson, Pete Ordway, Dick Cheville, Nic Wood, and Tim Aaronson.

Defined Terms
(just for reference)

Political labels are constantly shifting, mean different things to different people, and are highly contentious. But they are necessary for any intelligent discussion of politics. The best I can do is pick labels that have some intuitive appeal and then define what I mean when I use them. Of course, these definitions are still fuzzy because people are complicated.

Radicals, the radicals left—Roughly, the left-most "tribe" as defined by More in Common.* That's about 8% of the population. In Part 6, I define this group more precisely as those following the utopian ethic.

Liberals—Democratic voters who are not part of the radical left. In Part 6, I redefine this group to those following the strategic ethic.

Radical liberals—Those favoring radical change but who understand that making strategic incremental changes is usually the fastest way to make fundamental change, so they follow the strategic ethic.

FDR liberals—Essentially the same as "liberals" but emphasizing that they agree with FDR, who captured the term "liberal" from the Republicans and redefined it. Not a classic (libertarian) liberal and not socialist. Includes modern views on civil rights.

Progressives—All Democrats except the most conservative.

Socialists—Those who believe capitalism and the profit motive must be replaced by collective economic institutions.

Democratic socialists—Any socialist since 1900 (except communist socialists). When in quotes, this means a confused FDR liberal.

Political Trap—A delusion that causes issue polarization.

Moralistic Trap—A delusion that causes emotional polarization.

Us / We—FDR liberals and radical liberals (these groups overlap almost completely).

---

* The *More in Common* survey is explained after Chapter 1.

Introduction:
How Delusions Spark Polarization

The first principle is that you must not fool yourself—and you are the easiest person to fool.

—Richard Feynman
(physicist, second only to Einstein)

"An incendiary bomb, a thermite bomb, fell behind our house and burned with a terrible, white-hot heat ... my brothers carried pails of water to [my father], but water seemed useless against this infernal fire—indeed, made it burn even more furiously. ... Meanwhile, the bomb was melting its own casing and throwing blobs and jets of molten metal in all directions."

Oliver Sacks, the renowned neurologist and author, published a memoir of his childhood in 2001. He had grown up in London during World War II, but it was a memory he would not "hesitate to swear on in a court of law and had never doubted as real."

After his account of that night was published, an older brother assured Sacks that: "You never saw it. You weren't there." Sacks was astonished. Despite all his training, his own mind had deceived him.

As his brother explained, "We were both away at Braefield at the time. But David [our older brother] wrote us a letter about it." When Sacks carefully compared this manufactured "memory" to an equally old and validated memory, he could find no difference in quality between the two.

$\sim$

We know that millions can be deceived by political propaganda, but we believe this happens because those being duped are biased "low-information voters" like we believe our political opponents to be. We are equally sure that our team, whoever they may be, can be trusted to have accurate information, at least on any point of significance.

But what if that's wrong? What if all our minds are designed to make us feel far more certain than we have any right to be? Then our side may also be subject to delusions. Could such delusions, masquerading as certainties, cause the infighting that's polarizing Democrats and adding to the national polarization that is the lifeblood of Trumpism?

As I will show, this is our plight, and the reason we will lose again unless we take corrective action.

To solve a problem, first admit there is a problem, then comprehend its magnitude. Most of us have peeked at these delusions, but we still fail to recognize them when we ourselves are most in danger.

So let me show you some hair-raising examples. Some are believed by millions of good Democrats yet cause untold damage to our cause. Skeptical about this? Good. Skepticism is your friend in this battle, but it's not enough. We need evidence.

When I started researching this book, I had recently read a review of *On Deaf Ears: The Limits of the Bully Pulpit*—a book by political scientist George Edwards, based on 10 years of research, showing that presidents nearly always fail in their attempts to persuade the public. And not infrequently, presidents speaking from their "bully pulpit" have even had the reverse effect of what they intended.

For example, Edwards found that support for "regulatory programs and spending on health care, welfare, urban problems, education, environmental protection and aid to minorities all *increased* rather than decreased" during the presidency of Ronald Reagan. Known as "the great communicator," he had opposed all of these programs from his bully pulpit. And he had favored increased defense spending yet support for that decreased.

However, I soon came upon an argument by someone I trusted who seemed to be staking his political reputation on the contention that the bully pulpit works wonders. Because he was an economist, as I am, I suspected he might not be up on his political science. So I decided to check. What I discovered was a political version of the manufactured thermite-bomb memory.

What the Expert Said

Robert Reich has long been one of my minor heroes because he exposes socioeconomic problems simply and with humor. Furthermore, his credentials as a policy expert with hands-on political experience are unmatched. He served under Presidents Ford and Carter, became Clinton's Secretary of Labor, and was part of Obama's transition team. He is the Chancellor's Professor of Public Policy at U.C. Berkeley's Goldman School of Public Policy and has taught at Harvard's John F. Kennedy School of Government. He has been a contributing editor of *The New Republic, The American Prospect, The Atlantic, The New York Times,* and *The Wall Street Journal.*

Given his leftward leanings and his expertise, it is no great surprise that he became Bernie Sanders' most illustrious and astute surrogate and interpreter. And unlike many of Sanders' supporters, he treated Hillary Clinton fairly, possibly because their political backgrounds overlapped, and they had become friends.

Reich kept a cool head in the Sanders-Clinton war even when he explained in a 2016 op-ed why Clinton would make the best president for the status quo, but Sanders would be the only president who could bring about fundamental change.

His argument was simply put and powerful: Sanders was the one who would use the "bully pulpit" of the presidency to lead Americans to stand up for positive social change. Clinton, like Obama, would only be a "dealmaker-in-chief." That's a persuasive argument only if the bully pulpit really works. And Reich knew that.

To prove it worked, he used the example of how Teddy Roosevelt had achieved four miraculous progressive changes by using his bully pulpit:

1. "A progressive income tax,
2. Limits on corporate campaign contributions,
3. Regulation of foods and drugs, and
4. The dissolution of giant trusts."

All that from His Presidential Pulpit?

I had heard the usual things about Roosevelt, so I was not surprised by the list of his accomplishments. But *On Deaf Ears* had me doubting that all this was mainly the result of Teddy's preaching. I read what is considered the best biography of Roosevelt, *The Bully Pulpit*, and then double-checked a few more sources. Here is what I found:

1. The income tax. The Democrats passed the first federal income tax in 1894, and it *was* highly progressive. But the next year it was declared unconstitutional, and it remained so until the 16th Amendment to the

Constitution was ratified in 1913. Teddy Roosevelt was president from 1901 to 1909. So he had nothing to do with "getting a progressive income tax." He didn't even push for it.

What was Reich talking about?!

It seemed incredible that such an experienced and esteemed policy expert could be so completely wrong about something so central to his politics and so easily checked. And he was spreading this myth to tens of thousands of his devoted followers.

To top it off, the real story shows the exact opposite of Reich's theory—we got the income tax through, you guessed it, exactly what Reich said Clinton was best at, political dealmaking! President Howard Taft championed the 16th Amendment and secured its ratification. According to Doris Kearns Goodwin, author of *The Bully Pulpit*:

> As he pursued his tax agenda with [Senator] Aldrich, Taft engaged in "some pretty shrewd politics." He met individually with members of the Finance Committee and "committed them separately" to [backing the 16th Amendment].

That's not using a bully pulpit. That's back-room dealmaking, and that's how we got a progressive income tax.

2. Campaign contributions. In his first run for president, in 1904, Teddy Roosevelt and the Republicans were caught taking enormous corporate campaign contributions. The most radical of the era's famous progressive journalists argued privately that he should give them back. Roosevelt refused and argued that it was "entirely legitimate to accept contributions, no matter how large," provided they were freely given. Finally, under mounting political pressure, he signed a bill, written by his archenemy, "Pitchfork Ben," limiting contributions—but lacking an enforcement mechanism.

I was prepared for Reich to overplay the bully-pulpit myth, but I was totally unprepared to discover that Reich had misled me about which side of an issue Roosevelt was on.

As I describe in Chapter 26, Reich's last two points are also misfires. Food and drug regulations were largely spurred by Upton Sinclair's book, *The Jungle,* and public sentiment for trust-busting was whipped up by Ida Tarbell's book, *The History of Standard Oil.* These books were so powerful that both are still in print today.

Sadly, Roosevelt's most well-known "accomplishment" preaching from his bully pulpit had the unwanted consequence that his favorite progressive investigative journalists (especially Ida Tarbell) were ridiculed as "muckrakers," severely damaging their credibility.

Yes, just as *On Deaf Ears* had alerted me, using the bully pulpit is unreliable at best—even when used by Teddy Roosevelt himself. Fortunately, Roosevelt was an excellent dealmaker-in-chief (and proud of it), and he really does deserve his place on Mount Rushmore.

Don't Blame Robert Reich

Everything that I checked turned out to be backward or at least sideways. Yes, the developments cited by Reich did happen but not because of Teddy's preaching, and sometimes against his will or when he was no longer president. How could an advisor to four presidents and a renowned professor at the nation's top two policy schools possibly be so completely wrong about the political topic he cared most about? I was flummoxed.

It seemed impossible that he could be *that* wrong, and I was just as sure he wasn't lying. Then I remembered Oliver Sacks. Reich probably didn't check any source because his memory was so vivid that he would not, as Sacks put it, "hesitate to swear on it in a court of law."

Exactly what he "remembered" I cannot say, but I myself had "remembered" enough about Roosevelt that I did not doubt Reich's four mistaken "facts" about what Roosevelt deserved credit for; I only doubted that Teddy's bully pulpit was the force behind these accomplishments. The bully pulpit myth is, however, so well established that most people still believe it. Before George Edwards wrote *On Deaf Ears*, pretty much the whole political-science community believed it, as well as most presidents.

I feel certain that Reich had heard many things over many years so, as Sacks put it, this could have led to "subsequently constructing a 'memory' that became more and more firmly fixed by repetition."

Why it Matters

Both sides, Republicans and Democrats, believe they have personal qualities that protect them from political delusions. To some extent, that's true. We don't fall for most of the nonsense that surrounds us. But what we do fall for can do us great harm. Because I'm interested in protecting and strengthening the liberal side, I pay more attention to our myths and delusions than to conservative ones.

That's why I've chosen the bully pulpit example. It shows, beyond a shadow of a doubt, that the characteristics we all assume will protect us—concern for the public good, intelligence, education, and political experience—are insufficient, even if we possess them in abundance, as does Robert Reich. So we should not be surprised to find that political myths and delusions are the main drivers of politics, even on our side.

Delusions are common, but are they so damaging? Consider the bully-pulpit myth, which has long been widespread. Reich tells us that Obama failed to use his bully pulpit, and so he "allowed powerful interests to cash in" to the tune of "about $16 billion a year" paid to the drug industry. This turns what seems to be the harmless, feel-good bully-pulpit myth into the beginnings of polarization.

No one can know that using his bully pulpit would have worked, and Edward's research shows it's quite likely Obama could *not* have done what Reich assumes would have been a sure bet. Taking Reich's advice could have even made things worse. Of all people, shouldn't Obama have been considered innocent until proven guilty? Especially when the only evidence against him was baseless speculation.

Convicting Obama. In fact, Obama was not just convicted of making a mistake. The radicals convicted him of intentional harm with malice aforethought. This transforms a discussion of issues into moralistic judgments, which are the basis of "emotional polarization." That's the kind ripping us apart.

At a MoveOn meeting that I attended after the Democrats "took a shellacking" in his first midterm elections, two radicals who had worked hard for him in 2008 said they hadn't worked at all on the midterms—they had only come to the meeting to carp about how Obama had deceived us about who he really was.

Their view was common among radicals, and it had set in early. To mark his first 100 days in office, Katrina Heuvel, the radical editor of *The Nation*, had warned that if Obama did not win the public healthcare option, that would show that he had *not* been making "necessary compromises" but had instead been unnecessarily "watering down policies to appease for-profit special interests."

Heuvel, a fan of the bully-pulpit myth, was sure that Obama could win the public option if he really wanted to. She was so sure Obama knew this—that if he didn't use his bully pulpit and succeed, then he must be corrupt, an appeaser of "for-profit special interests." Most of the radical left agreed.

She too was led toward emotional polarization by the bully-pulpit myth. Such polarization weakened Obama and the Democrats for eight years. Then the bully-pulpit myth was used to damage Clinton in the primaries, and that had a lingering effect when she ran against Trump.

The 'New Jim Crow.' It's worth looking at one more dramatically wrong example of a delusion that's still polarizing the Democrats and helping Trump win.

The 'New Jim Crow' myth claims that mass incarceration of Blacks was a substitute for the Jim Crow laws, which were overturned by the 1964 Civil Rights Act. It further claims that the Democrats were to blame and did it for racist reasons. That's about the worst accusation you can imagine being leveled against the Democrats—that racist Democrats put about a million blacks in jail while trying to pick up a few Southern racist votes.

Again, this was coming entirely from the radical left of the Democratic Party. *The Nation* published "Why Hillary Clinton Doesn't Deserve the Black Vote" just as the 2016 primaries were getting started. It was written by Michelle Alexander, author of *The New Jim Crow,* which spent three years as a *New York Times* bestseller. About that time, Clinton was accused on MSNBC of calling Blacks "superpredators" to help pass the 1994 crime bill. *The Atlantic* published the same claim and linked to the same video of Clinton that was shown on MSNBC.

Oddly, no one noticed that every frame of the video clearly showed the date was 1996 (not 1994) or that Clinton was not talking about Blacks or the crime bill. And the problem is much deeper than that. The 1994 crime bill had the support of the majority of Blacks, especially Black leaders (Ch. 5). Of course, the radicals never mention that, although it's an easy fact to find. Like Robert Reich, they are so sure they're right that they don't feel any need to check.

This polarizing racial smear against Clinton was used by Trump and Russian trolls on the internet and by Trump in the debates. Undoubtedly, it cost Clinton votes among Whites as well as Blacks, and it certainly helped elect Trump. Such radical myths (fake history) should not be taken lightly.

Negative Partisanship and National Polarization

National polarization—hating the other political party—naturally causes people to get out and vote for their side, even if they don't much like their own candidate. That's called negative partisanship, and it now dominates national politics.

With people thinking like that, the best way to get out the vote is to tell frightening stories about how evil or crazy the other party is. And that's just what social media and some of the press often does.

That's why the more extreme elements of the Democratic Party are so helpful to Trump. They take positions that fire up his base and turn out the Republican vote. Of course, this effect is tremendously amplified by the likes of Fox News and even more-extreme, right-wing news outlets. The more flamboyant their "crazy Democrats" story, the better.

For example, the Madison, Wisconsin school district adopted a rule barring the use of the n-word regardless of circumstances. After much racist harassment, when a Black playground attendant finally said "Don't call me nigger" he was fired! (Ch. 29). Of course, the right uses this to confirm the right-wing belief that no one can escape the left's politically-correct charges of racism, not even a well-loved, cautious, Black playground attendant. That polarizes Republicans against Democrats and fires up Trump's base.

Then there's the idea that democratic socialists are not socialists, just as Bartlett pears are not pears (whatever). This is wrong, and it also needlessly ties the Democratic Party to "socialism," by far the most polarizing label in politics.

There are many more of these nationally polarizing myths, believed by millions. All of them play into the culture war and feed the right-wing media, which uses them to galvanize Trump's base using negative partisanship, something that radicals seem happily oblivious to.

At a time when negative partisanship is driving politics, this naivete could quite possibly hand Trump a second term. And that could bring us to our democracy's tipping point.

Who Won the 2018 Midterms?

Of course, the radicals want to win and have theories of why their radical actions and language will win more voters for Democratic candidates. But let's take a look at what just happened.

In the 2018 midterm elections, the Democrats flipped 43 House seats from red to blue, saving us from two more years of completely unchecked Republican power. Who did that?

There were three explicitly Berniecrat PACs in that race, and one had vowed to run 400 candidates, Republicans and Democrats, all of whom would swear allegiance to Sanders once elected. This would give us a 'Brand New Congress.' Between them, they made 117 endorsements, but not a single candidate that they endorsed flipped a seat from red to blue.

Had we depended on the radicals, it's virtually sure Trump would have had control of both houses of Congress. That's nearly unthinkable. But all the swing-state Democrats live in fear having to run on a radical ticket in 2020.

Depolarizing the Democrats

As Chapter 1 explains, emotional polarization, not issue polarization, is the kind that's ripping us apart. Most often that means hating one's opponents and that comes from viewing them as immoral. Usually this is based on a mistake, and most often it's based on a myth or some form of groupthink that takes a simplistic view of the world. For example—the view that presidents can get what they want with their bully pulpit.

If radicals believe that's so obvious that everyone knows it's true, then when a president doesn't achieve some radical goal, they are sure he could have but just didn't want to. That means he's immoral. And that leads to polarization and hatred. The same dynamic causes national polarization. This typically means polarization grows out of myths and delusions, which cause people to see others as evil when they are only badly mistaken.

The way out of such a trap (seeing mistaken people as evil) that catches most of us at one time or another is simply to realize how common it is for people to believe political myths and delusions. Part Two proves exactly that and shows some astounding examples, just in case you weren't convinced by Robert Reich.

This is not a new idea. It's the idea behind the civil rights movement, which in my view, is the best political movement in our country's history. More recently, this idea has been popularized by Michelle Obama with her maxim, "When they go low, we go high." Going low is caused by some of the dreadful delusions people fall prey to. And going high is treating those who've been misled as if they were mistaken (which usually is the case) and not ridiculing or cursing them because we see them as immoral people. This depolarizes us, avoids triggering polarization in our opponents, and can even encourage them to depolarize.

My hope is that arming readers with the facts behind the radical myths will make them braver about taking a stand against such polarizing delusions, even if they don't use the facts to engage in arguments. I have seen people speak up and state their position, without arguing, simply because they've become more certain of what they already believed.

Knowing that enough people disagree with these radical myths can provide the social pressure needed to stop and reverse the spread of polarizing ideas. Failing this, we will lose again in 2020 with unimaginable consequences.

To save our party and our democracy, we must, without hostility, reject the radicals' magical thinking, polarizing anger, and mistaken condemnations. The attitude we must express is this: Welcome to the Party, but Please, Check Your Guns at The Door.

PART 1

What Polarizes Us?

Political Traps suck us in and target our specific weaknesses just like advertising does. That's why some traps are set for Democrats and some for Republicans.

There's no one formula for avoiding them, so our only hope is to learn to "know them when we see them." These traps just lead to *issue* polarization—not our biggest problem.

More dangerously, Political Traps lead us into the purity trap, a Moralistic Trap that causes us to see others as immoral or evil and then hate them. This is emotional polarization, the kind that is ripping apart the country and the Democratic Party.

Chapter 1. The Perils of Polarization. In which Monty Python helps explain emotional polarization.

Chapter 2. Clear and Present Danger. Democrats are pursuing two polarizing strategies that endanger the 2020 election.

Chapter 3. How Polarization Develops. The radical left took the place of the civil rights movement, a big step toward polarizing the country.

Chapter 4. How to Depolarize a Cyclops. Daryl Davis actually did this, but first, he depolarized himself.

Chapter 5. Three Political Traps. Charisma, populism, and political myths produce the most potent Political Traps.

Chapter 6. The Crime Bill Myth. The anatomy of the most vicious political myth currently plaguing the Democrats.

Chapter 7. The Purity Trap. Political Traps lead to the purity trap, which causes emotional polarization.

CHAPTER 1

The Perils of Polarization

O, yes,
I say it plain,
America never was America to me,
And yet I swear this oath—
America will be!

—Langston Hughes, 1935
"Let America Be America Again"

Not so long ago, America was great, and we knew it. The far left will say, "No, America was badly flawed." And it was. But greatness does not require perfection. The right will agree that the country was great but will forget why that was so. True greatness displays courage and generosity. It is not just about making better deals.

Greatness is moving forward together, which requires keeping emotional polarization and recriminations to a minimum. That doesn't mean our views converge. It means we can talk across divides—with civility. Instead, we are now gripped by the most vicious polarization since the Civil War—the second great polarization. Even the Democratic Party has polarized. That only amplifies Trump's polarizing efforts. Such hatred endangers our democracy itself.

Back when Americans were patriotic, during World War II, we rescued Western Europe at the tragic cost of 400,000 brave American lives. Then we educated eight million returning GIs, helped three million buy homes, and insured millions against unemployment, all under the U.S. government's GI Bill of Rights. Next, we jump-started Europe with the Marshall Plan, which cost the equivalent in today's economy of $2,500 per person. In 1964, we launched the first successful mission to Mars and soon passed the Soviets in the race to the moon. The same year, Martin Luther King Jr. won the Nobel Peace Prize.

But the biggest surprise, as we look back from the jaded present, is that 80% of the Republicans, in both the House and the Senate, voted for the 1964 Civil Rights Act, as did 69% of the Democrats in the Senate and 63% in the House. Neither the parties themselves, nor America, were particularly polarized, and the outcome was decisive. We got things done.

When America was great, politics was bipartisan. We were tackling our social problems at breakneck speed: legislation on civil rights, voting rights, women's rights, health care, and the war on poverty, all passed in a two-year period. So what went wrong?

What is Emotional Polarization?

Polarization began ripping our country apart in the late 1960s, and it's just gotten worse. Only when we truly understand what polarization is can we begin to fix it.

It always takes two forms. **Issue polarization** is the one most often measured, and the one we tend to think is fundamental. But what really worries people, and rightly so, is **emotional polarization** (academics call this "affective polarization"). Understanding the difference provides the key to the dangers of our present situation.

It may surprise you to note that positions on political *issues* are no further apart now than in the Great Depression. In the early 1930s, we had no unemployment insurance, no Social Security, no Medicare, no safety net at all, and Franklin Roosevelt (the liberal candidate) won the presidency on a balanced budget platform with a campaign theme song of "Happy Days Are Here Again." The Republicans, of course, ran somewhat to his right. Meanwhile, Huey Long, the wildly popular, populist Louisiana governor and then-U.S. Senator, was demanding wealth redistribution that makes Bernie Sanders and Elizabeth Warren look like Tea Party candidates.

Despite this high degree of issue polarization, Congress never voted along strict party lines, and the public trusted government far more than it does today. Issue polarization was greater, but emotional polarization was far less.

Perhaps it seems obvious that issue polarization and emotional polarization should go hand in hand. But, as Gershwin wrote in *Porgy and Bess*, "It ain't necessarily so." Here's why:

"Listen," shouts the angry but unintentionally hilarious leader of The People's Front of Judea (PFJ), "the only people we hate more than the

Romans are the fucking Judean People's Front" (JPF). That's from Monty Python's film, *Life of Brian* (set in 30 AD). Of course, in the film, the two political sects, the PFJ and the JPF, are almost identical. But each hates the other more than they hate their real enemy, the Romans. They are almost perfectly aligned on their only important issue—they have no *issue* polarization. But through infighting, their *emotional* polarization has gone through the roof.

(Full disclosure: In 1968, I voted for the Freedom and Peace Party, not to be confused with the Peace and Freedom Party! Such hairsplitting is a real talent of the radical left.)

Another way to look at the difference between types of polarization is that with emotional polarization, we view our political opponents as enemies rather than adversaries. We hate our *enemies* and seek to conquer or destroy them as in war. Although we want to defeat our *adversaries*, compromise is still possible, even honorable. Trump is our enemy; Obama voters who voted for Trump should still be our adversaries. Emotional polarization is turning America into a nation of enemies.

The danger to the party. In 2016, the Democrats showed once again how infighting causes emotional polarization. To an impartial observer, the differences between Hillary Clinton's and Bernie Sanders' positions on issues were insignificant when compared to the differences between either of them and the Romans … er … the Republicans. Issue polarization was minimal. Yet rivalry led to vilification (mainly by Berniecrats), then to conspiracy theories and mutual hatred. The Democrats ended up more emotionally polarized than at any time since 1968 when the antiwar movement forced LBJ not to seek a second term.

No one knows if party polarization caused Hubert Humphrey's loss in 1968 or Hillary Clinton's in 2016. But both are possible, as is the chance that the Democrats' polarization in 2020 will reelect Trump.

Polarization: The Danger to Democracy

According to Steven Levitsky and Daniel Ziblatt in their 2018 book, *How Democracies Die*:

> If one thing is clear from studying breakdowns throughout history, it's that extreme polarization can kill democracies.

They add that today's polarization is "deeper than at any time since the end of Reconstruction [1877]." That was the first great polarization.

They also argue that polarization has been leading to increased "breaking" of democratic norms since the Republican attacks on Bill Clinton in the early 1990s.

Vicious circles. Once emotional polarization becomes intense enough to threaten democracy, it can also amplify itself by generating two distinct vicious circles. The first ricochets between the opposing bases; the second plays out in Congress.

Within each base, the extremists have the loudest voices and do their best to vilify the entire opposition. Each extreme's vilification provides "evidence" that the other extreme uses to increase polarization on its side. This does not mean the two sides are equally guilty, but in a vicious circle, both sides participate.

In Congress, when one party breaks democratic norms to gain an advantage, the other party feels pressure to do the same. When society is sufficiently polarized, each party's base applauds its representatives for breaking democratic norms and justifies this by pointing out that the other side does the same. This vicious circle, which has been gaining steam for about 25 years, is how polarization becomes the greatest danger to democracy.

Conclusion

Trump caps a decades-long drift of Republicans towards polarization as *their* political strategy. A similar tendency has long been found among the radical left. And since 2015, that trend has threatened to take over the Democrats as well.

We now face an urgent question. To fight the Republicans, will we adopt Trump's strategy of polarization? As Molly Ivins once warned us, polarization is good for winning elections but can wreck democracy. Hang on though, it's worse. She was talking about Newt Gingrich and only meant that polarization helps *Republicans* win elections. That's not the half of it. Polarizing our own party, currently the main thrust of the radical left, is the best way imaginable to help Trump.

Trump is polarizing the country to win the election and wreck democracy. He eggs on the radical left so they'll wreck the Democrats and help him wreck the country. That says it all.

- Emotional polarization wrecks democracies, and parties too.
- We should instead choose "the better angels of our nature," as Lincoln urged before the Civil War.

Political Tribes in the U.S.

More in Common is an international initiative to combat threats of polarization. In 2018, it conducted a poll of almost 8,000 potential voters and refreshed it after the midterms. Political attitudes were used to divide the population into a set of "tribes" with closely aligned political views. The statistical analysis suggested seven tribes. To simplify this, I have lumped together three pairs to produce the following groups.

Group	Percent of Population	Percent of Party Vote
Radical Left	8%	23% of Dem vote
Liberal	26%	47% of Dem vote
Moderate	41%	29% of Dem vote
Radical Right	25%	66% of GOP vote

The "radical left." This left-most tribe is 80-percent White, and the richest and best-educated of the seven tribes. They reported feeling safer than the others. They care the most about climate change and inequality. Ironically, out of all seven tribes, they care the least about the more practical issue of jobs. Only 30% think "political correctness" is a problem, while 83% of the rest of America does.

Liberals. More than half of the moderates vote Democratic, and I will include moderate Democrats when I mention liberals, so my definition is broader than just the two liberal tribes and includes about 85% of the Democrats. They are the "we" that I will often refer to.

CHAPTER 2

Clear and Present Danger

I opened the doors to the Democratic Party and 20 million people walked out.

—George McGovern, 1972

Under the mistaken certainty of victory, shared by millions, Hillary Clinton signed a copy of *Newsweek's* commemorative "Madam President" issue for a supporter. The next day, when Trump won the election, *Newsweek's* distributor was forced to recall 125,000 copies that told of a hopeful future that was not to be.

Fifty years ago, Hubert Humphrey, one of our most liberal senators, lost a close election he should have won. Thousands of us refused to vote for him because he represented the Democratic establishment. He lost to Richard Nixon by 0.7%, and Nixon went on, four years later, to devastate the Democratic Party with his Southern Strategy and much help from the radical left. We still have not fully recovered.

Looking back, there's no way to be sure that we radicals made the difference then, and the same is true today. But we do know that 12% of those who voted for Sanders in the primaries voted for Trump in November. Another 12% defected in other ways. (Of course, some of these were just conservatives who tried to mess with the Democratic primaries.)

The first 2020 danger we'll look at is the chance that the parallels between 1968 and 2016 will continue. That would be devastating, but it's entirely within our power to stop it. Then we'll examine two strategic mistakes that are supporting what many predict will be Trump's two central modes of attack during his 2020 campaign.

The Origin of Trump's Base

Just as in 2016, something much bigger than the radical rejection of the establishment was going on in 1968. In 2016 it was Trump and in 1968 it was Trump's doppelganger, George Wallace. That was the start of Trump's base, and that matters because it warns us not to be lulled into thinking his base will soon disappear if we just take back the White House.

Wallace split off from the Democrats to form the American Independent Party and took a large slice of the White working-class with him. Here is Wallace, an avowed White supremacist, talking to the Northern working class in 1968 about a federal government with Democrats in charge:

> They've looked down at the bus driver, the truck driver, the beautician, the fireman, the policeman, and the steelworker, the plumber.

Like Trump, he based his appeal on a culture war. His official slogan in 1968 was "Stand Up for America," and his favorite catchphrase was "law and order" (still used by Trump), which targeted Blacks and antiwar protestors. He implied male hippies were sexual deviants, and he was proud of not being politically correct.

The parallels between Trump and Wallace are uncanny

Wallace was taking advantage of a working-class exodus from the Democratic Party partly caused partly by LBJ's civil rights legislation but even more by school busing controversies. (Four months after passing civil rights, LBJ won an astounding landslide.) But this exodus was amplified by the left's frequent expressions of hostility toward U.S. troops in Vietnam and toward America in general. This culture war is old and durable and will not yield to simple legislative fixes.

How Today's Path Parallels the 1972 Disaster

As Yogi Berra would have said about our present party politics, "It's dé-jà vu all over again." And he would've been talkin' about how Obama, Clinton, and some radical candidate could parallel LBJ, Humphrey, and McGovern.

In 1964, Lyndon Johnson won his historic landslide victory by 23%, striking a decisive blow against the conservatism of Barry Goldwater and ratifying the triumph of the Kennedy-Johnson Civil Rights Bill. But a mere four years later, the 1968 Democratic National Convention paralleled the 2016 Convention in its divisiveness.

By '68, LBJ's Vietnam War was killing more than 1,000 young men a month, so we pushed him aside. But he engineered Vice President Humphrey's nomination without Humphrey running in even a single primary, let alone winning one. The nomination was rigged, and the convention floor was rowdy, to say the least.

After that convention, some of us said, "Good luck without us," as did some Berniecrats in 2016. I voted for Dick Gregory, a radical Black comedian. Humphrey lost the 1968 race to Richard Nixon by a hair.

The breadth and fury of our resistance to Nixon may well have outdone our present resistance to Trump. In November 1969, massive demonstrations were held at the White House and in San Francisco. In May 1970, at Kent State University, four antiwar protesters were killed by the National Guard. Huge May Day protests in 1970 were met with 10,000 troops, ordered by Nixon to join 7,000 police, who arrested 12,000 protesters.

The parallel also holds within the Democratic Party. George McGovern had been one of the antiwar/anti-establishment candidates who lost to Humphrey at the contentious 1968 convention, as Sanders lost to Clinton in 2016. But Humphrey's loss gave McGovern and his young progressives the upper hand in the Party, and they rewrote the Party rules, much like what's been done for 2020. The McGovern forces used their rule changes to win his nomination.

After four years of unprecedented resistance to Nixon, we were optimistic. But McGovern lost in 49 states, ending all talk of "The Revolution." McGovern summed up Democratic losses from 1964 to 1972 with brutal honesty: "I opened the doors to the Democratic Party and 20 million people walked out."

Dangerous Approaches to the Culture War

Besides the danger of McGovern redux, we are helping Trump with his two major lines of attack—immigration and socialism. We like to flaunt the U.S. becoming a majority-minority country, where the majority consists of people of color. And we call ourselves "socialists" although we're not. Both strike fear in the hearts of his base, and both anger them, unify them and make them stronger. That's just as dangerous as our infighting

The most popular political book of 2002, *The Emerging Democratic Majority*, explained that the increase in the Mexican-American population would lead inevitably to a permanent Democratic majority. The 1986 Immigration Act had allowed 2.3 million Mexicans who had immigrated illegally to become citizens, and then we broke our promise of tight border controls, setting up a repeat. Trump's base drew the obvious conclusion: We rigged the system against them to take away the country as they knew it. (No, I'm not saying that was our intention; I'm saying we need to understand how they see it, to avoid adding fuel to Trump's fire.)

Likewise with socialism. Virtually all of the Democrats calling themselves socialists, as we will see later, are really only advocating FDR liberalism—even according to Sanders. So why adopt what amounts to the right-wing definition of socialist and then incorrectly call ourselves socialists as the red-baiters always have? Just to outrage conservatives? Of course, Trump just loves the idea of running against a socialist. (In Chapter 23 we'll discover the real reason behind Sanders' ploy.)

These two dangers were pointed out in early 2019 by presidential biographer Jon Meacham and by Ian Bremmer, a political scientist known for political risk assessment. Both put special emphasis on the "socialism" risk.

My point is a simple one: There's plenty that we care about that they won't like. So why go out of our way to make them feel attacked? Attacks, real or perceived, only increase Trump's base's desire for a strongman. Either we understand this or risk losing.

A House Divided Against Itself ...

The 1972 election was a disaster for many reasons, but the one that is most relevant today is how the Democratic Party treated the White working class.

The radical wing of the party, which supported McGovern, made rule changes before the 1972 convention that cut sharply against working-class representation. State delegations were required to meet quotas for minorities, women, and young people, but the quotas did not require labor or working-class representation. The radical left (and I was among them) distrusted the working class for being generally pro-war and sometimes racist.

McGovern's followers found that Mayor Daley's Chicago delegation did not reflect the new progressive quotas, so they put together their own unelected delegation, which successfully challenged Daley's. The Mayor and his 59 delegates were ejected from the convention and replaced with a delegation led by Jesse Jackson, the leader of what he called the "Rainbow Coalition," a name borrowed from the Black Panthers.

A columnist for the *Chicago Sun-Times* noted, "There's only one Italian there [in the Jackson delegation]. Are you saying that only one out of every 59 Democratic votes cast in a Chicago election is cast by an Italian? ... Your reforms have disenfranchised Chicago's White ethnic [working-class] Democrats." That election was the only time the AFL-CIO did not endorse the Democratic candidate for president and the only time Republicans won the union vote. That was absolutely due to the radical left.

As noted above, *More in Common* identified a group of radical activists who now play a similar role in the Democratic Party to McGovern's supporters. Just as was true back then, today's radical activists are better off and better educated than the average American, and also more ideological and less concerned with jobs and healthcare than any other political tribe, from left to right.

The radical left constantly blames the liberals—calling them "neoliberals"—for losing the White working class. But this is just a divisive cover for their own role. And it's highly polarizing.

Conclusion

Boasting of our eventual majority-minority victory or our radically righteous "socialism" can raise some of our spirits temporarily. But this short-sighted gain is both self-deceiving and self-defeating.

Worse yet are the intra-party attacks, especially those on the party's liberal base. These weaken us and keep us ignorant of the crucial lessons that we need to learn from past mistakes.

This is not the time for grandstanding or for moralistic accusations against our own people. We all share the same broad goals of fairness and greater equality and work hard in ways that match our diverse communities.

To achieve the country we want, we must fight polarization in our party and the country.

- Claiming we're stronger and better only makes us weaker and less deserving of respect.
- All Democrats share the same broad goals. We just have different views on how to get there.

CHAPTER 3

How Polarization Develops

Polarizing people is a good way to win an election, and also a good way to wreck a country.

—Molly Ivins, political columnist

"Other side, nigger," said the teenage wannabe Klansman, as he pointed to a door that said "COLORED." The 19-year-old John Lewis was prepared. "I have a right," he said calmly, "to go in there, on the grounds of the Supreme Court decision in the Boynton case." "Shit on that," came the reply, as the young tough smashed Lewis in the face. It took a few months, but Lewis and the other Freedom Riders, Black and White, won that fight for the Blacks—but really, for all of us.

Lewis was no coward; quite the opposite. Had the Freedom Riders been cowards, they would never have stepped onto those buses. They knew exactly what they were up against, and they had been well-trained and well-practiced in nonviolence. One of his teachers had studied under Mahatma Gandhi in India.

They won without increasing national polarization because of their extraordinary civility. But their bravery was every bit as important. Bravery commands respect. Aggression calls forth retaliation.

The civil rights movement may have been the greatest chapter in American political history, so I will touch on it several times. But here I will use it to show how forceful civility leads to progress rather than polarization, while incivility does the reverse.

The same dynamic that ended the civil rights movement and began polarizing us continues today and is escalating. But it is easier to learn from the past because we are less emotionally involved with it. First, it's important to see what powerful, yet civil, grassroots protests look like because this has been so nearly forgotten that many simply cannot imagine it. Then we'll see how radicalism can destroy the civil forces that brought success.

Freedom Riders: Civil but Powerful

The Supreme Court ruled in 1946 that segregation of interstate buses and their facilities was unconstitutional. But as late as 1961, the year Lewis boarded the bus, Southern interstate busing was still segregated. Less than four months after Kennedy took office, the first Freedom Riders left Washington, D.C., on a Greyhound bus and a Trailways bus with the intention of reaching New Orleans for a conference. There were only six or seven Freedom Riders per bus, about half Black and half White, and two of the Blacks did not sit in back as required by Jim Crow laws in the South.

The results shocked the nation.

The Greyhound bus was met by a mob organized by the Ku Klux Klan in a town not far from Birmingham, Alabama. In anticipation, the whole town came out to watch, but the police arrived 20 minutes late. Two Highway Patrolmen on the bus kept the mob out of the bus, but its windows were smashed and its tires slashed before the police escorted it out of town with the mob following.

When the bus, tires flat, stopped after a few miles to call for repairs, the mob firebombed it and held the doors closed. But something, possibly an explosion, caused them to back off. According to Janie McKinney, who was 12 at the time, "The door burst open, and there were people just spilling out of there. They were so sick by then [from smoke inhalation], they were crawling and puking and asking for water. They could hardly talk." Although White and afraid for her life, but propelled by her Christian upbringing, she found a pail of water and a cup. The first person she helped was an elderly Black woman who was not a Freedom Rider. She gave her water, washed her face and then went on to help the others. Later she learned the Klan had met to decide if they should try her as an adult but decided against it.

The Trailways bus that left an hour later carried John Lewis and other Freedom Riders. They were not so lucky. John Lewis and a friend were beaten by Klan members as soon as the bus stopped in South Carolina. After that, the FBI, the Birmingham Police and the Klan worked in coordination. Birmingham's Public Safety Director, Bull Connor, had assured the Klan they would have 15 minutes to "beat" the Freedom Riders "until they looked like a bulldog got ahold of them" before the police arrived. That's what happened.

Due to more threatened violence, none of the Freedom Riders were able to make it past Birmingham on the buses and instead flew to the rally in New Orleans. Over the summer, more than 300 Freedom Riders were jailed, often for months, under atrocious conditions. Jailed for what? For breaking illegal Jim Crow laws. Attorney General Robert Kennedy had struck a deal with Mississippi's Democratic Senator, James O. Eastland. Kennedy would not interfere in Mississippi's affairs by sending in federal marshals as long as Eastland would guarantee there would be no mob violence.

Impact of the civil rights movement. On June 11, 1963, President John F. Kennedy gave his "Report to the American People on Civil Rights," a speech delivered on radio and television in which he proposed legislation that would later become the Civil Rights Act of 1964.

Martin Luther King Jr. sent a telegram to Kennedy stating, "Your speech was one of the most eloquent, profound, and unequivocal pleas for justice and freedom of all men ever made by any President. You spoke passionately for moral issues." This, and a lot of politicking by LBJ, led to the passage of the 1964 Civil Rights Act by an overwhelming majority in both houses of Congress, and then to the war on poverty and to legislation for Medicare, Medicaid, food stamps, VISTA and more.

Incivility Leads to Polarization

Black radicals. As early as 1963, in his famous "Letter from a Birmingham Jail," King was feeling trapped between two forces. One was the force of complacency and the "other force is one of bitterness and hatred, and it comes perilously close to advocating violence." He was pointing to the Nation of Islam (which would murder Malcolm X two years later). By 1966, Black radicals on the left were rejecting King's nonviolent approach. Stokely Carmichael, the champion of the Black power movement, denounced integration, saying "integration was irrelevant when initiated by Blacks ... this country has been feeding us a [deformity-causing] thalidomide drug of integration." King's popularity plummeted.

The Black Panthers, formed in 1966, declared that "power grows out of the barrel of a gun." In 1968, the Panthers' Minister of Information, Eldridge Cleaver, fled to Cuba after he led an ambush of Oakland police officers, which ended up wounding two officers as well as Cleaver himself and killing 17-year-old Panther Bobby Hutton. From that point, as described in Chapter 37, the Panthers slid into violence so shocking that knowledge of it has been largely suppressed by the left.

Urban Riots. The 1960s also saw a series of more than 100 urban riots that polarized the country, beginning with the six days of rioting in Watts. I am not saying the Watts riot was a *root* cause of polarization. The riot itself had causes. One was the passage of an amendment to the California Constitution re-legalizing the housing discrimination that kept Blacks in ghettos. It was passed soon after the Civil Rights Act by a two-thirds (!) majority of California's voters. Police brutality was another cause, though it was not the triggering incident. Nonetheless, the Watts riots were highly polarizing.

White radicals. Bill Zimmerman, a 1960s radical writing in *The New York Times* in 2017, presents a sympathetic summary of "The Four Stages of the [Vietnam] Antiwar Movement." In the first two stages, according to Zimmerman, the antiwar movement was almost entirely nonviolent and got its point across with "teach-ins" and marches. During this time, it had a huge positive impact on public opinion. Had members of the antiwar movement swallowed their pride and worked for Humphrey, there's a good chance they could have elected him and pressured him into winding down the war—he was already moving that direction by the time of the election.

Zimmerman describes the third stage, which occurred after Nixon was elected, as follows:

> Alienated and enraged, we moved on to the rejection of mainstream lifestyles, violent clashes with police and militant opposition to the government. Our strategy was to force an end to the war by creating instability, chaos, and disruption at home.
>
> Loyalties shifted. Earlier, the dominant slogan had been, "Hey, hey, L.B.J., how many kids did you kill today?" In 1969 [a dominant slogan was] "One side's right, one side's wrong, victory to the Viet Cong." ... Rejecting the social order, many activists called themselves revolutionaries ... often becoming trapped by arcane factional disputes ... Students for a Democratic Society began their bombing campaign.

The Wrecking Crew. After Kennedy's landmark Report on Civil Rights and Johnson's passage of the Civil Rights Act in July 1964, Johnson received over 61% of the popular vote, the largest percentage the Democratic Party had received in its 190-year history. And the momentum continued for a year. But four years later, after Stokely Carmichael's repeated trashing of Martin Luther King Jr., after a string of horrific urban riots, after the rise of the Black power movement and the Black Panthers, after the Weather Underground's bombing war against "Amerika," and after the antiwar movement turned anti-American, the Democrats lost to Richard Nixon.

While it's true that racist Southern Whites switched parties because the Democratic establishment had backed civil rights, the civil rights movement did not increase emotional polarization, and it was essential. The actions of the radical left proved tremendously polarizing and destructive.

Conclusion

Both the civil rights movement and the anti-Vietnam-war movement forcefully and, in the beginning, civilly took on social problems of enormous importance. Both gained huge followings. The power and breadth of these movements attracted radicals who saw themselves as heroic visionaries. As so often happens, these pseudo-revolutionaries pushed these movements to extremes and destroyed them.

The same thing may be happening to the Democrats today.

Civil grass-roots politics, whether in the form of direct action or electoral organizing, is generally effective and minimally polarizing. Incivility polarizes society and strengthens intolerance and anti-democratic forces, even when it wins short-term victories. Most often though, its victories are only against those who, like Martin Luther King Jr., are most effective.

- Offensive radical action and incivility contribute to the enduring culture war that unifies and strengthens Trump's base.

CHAPTER 4

How to Depolarize a Cyclops

Do I not destroy my enemies when I make them my friends?
—Abraham Lincoln

"This guy, sitting in my car, was an Exalted Cyclops." Daryl Davis was explaining on National Public Radio why he talks to the Ku Klux Klan. Davis continued: "He made the statement, which I'd heard before, 'Well, we all know that all Black people have within them a gene that makes them violent.' I turned to him and I'm driving and I said, 'Wait a minute. I'm as Black as anybody you've ever seen. I have never done a carjacking or a drive-by, how do you explain that?' He didn't even pause to think about it. He said, 'Your gene is latent. It hasn't come out yet.'"

Time out. What's an Exalted Cyclops got to do with defeating Trump? As I will argue throughout this book, polarization usually comes from people getting deceived and sucked in. So to become depolarized, a person needs to first realize they've been trapped. But what can we do to get our adversaries, who have been sucked in, to realize their mistake?

The first step is to check our own polarization. When we are *de*polarized, rather than view our "enemy" as evil, we can instead view them as "well-intentioned" but sucked into a trap. That changes everything. We can stop hating them.

> **Many have trouble understanding** that if someone does something awful, they still may not be evil. So remember, FDR put 110,000 innocent Japanese in concentration camps for three years, and LBJ escalated the Vietnam war, killing hundreds of thousands. Both did something awful, but they were not evil. People are easily deceived about what is right, but few are truly evil.

Not feeling hated and condemned, they no longer need the protection of hating us, making it easier for them to depolarize.

This may sound like some abstract theory that could only work under the best of circumstances. To prove otherwise, I need an example of how it can work repeatedly under the worst of circumstances. So how about depolarizing an Exalted Cyclops of the Ku Klux Klan and then repeatedly depolarizing Klan members? That should be proof enough.

Daryl Davis, a Black musician who played piano for Chuck Berry, Jerry Lee Lewis, and B.B. King, has made it his mission to meet Klansmen and then change their minds. Yes, he dramatically reduced the polarization of an Exalted Cyclops, as well as many more Klansmen, by viewing them as "well-intentioned but sucked in" and acting on that basis.

Back to Daryl and the Cyclops. "He's sitting over here all smug and secure, like 'See, you have no response.' And I thought about it for a minute. I said, 'Well, we all know that all White people have a gene within them that makes them serial killers.' He says, 'What do you mean?' And I said, 'Well, name me three Black serial killers.' He thought about it—he could not do it. I said Ted Bundy, Jeffrey Dahmer, Charles Manson, John Wayne Gacy. All Whites. Then I said, 'Son, you are a serial killer.'"

"He says 'Daryl, I've never killed anybody.' I said, 'Your gene is latent. It hasn't come out yet.' He goes, 'Well, that's stupid!' I said, 'Well, duh. Yes, but you know what …' Then he got very, very quiet and changed the subject. Five months later, based on that conversation, he left the Klan. His robe was the first [Klan] robe I ever got." Davis is the subject of a 2016 documentary, *Accidental Courtesy*. He's been collecting Klan robes for 30 years now.

How Davis Depolarizes Klansmen

To depolarize the Klansmen, Daryl Davis first depolarized himself, or perhaps he just never was very polarized on racism. That's the secret to depolarizing others—first, we need to depolarize ourselves. That inevitably changes how we treat our adversaries.

What does it mean that Daryl Davis is depolarized on racial issues? Of course, he still detests racism and works against it far more than most people do. He knows the Klan is ignorant, ridiculous and racist. He knows the Klan's history better than almost anyone and hates what they've done and sometimes still do. He has been afraid for his own safety.

Being depolarized means he sees Klansmen as his "fellow countrymen," and believes that, in a certain light, they are not evil. I will define that carefully and then explain why not being polarized himself lets him do some amazing things—he's probably convinced more than 100, directly or indirectly, to leave the Klan and has more than 24 robes to show for it.

I am not saying anyone else should try collecting KKK hoods and robes. Daryl Davis is extraordinary. But his success proves that being depolarized can open the door to depolarizing others. For an Exalted Cyclops to hand over his hood and robes to a Black man takes an enormous change of mind and heart.

> Pointers and opportunities for actually talking to the other side in a way that depolarizes can be found at howtotalkpolitics.com and from organizations they link to. Also, watch 'The Best of Enemies.'

What Are "Good Intentions"?

Before explaining how to self-depolarize, one paradoxical but crucial concept needs careful review—"good intentions." That term comes in several variations: "good intentions," "well-intentioned" and "well-meaning." In any of these cases, it helps to keep this proverb in mind:

The road to hell is paved with "good intentions."

In that proverb, and as it is typically used, "good intentions" means that the person with the intentions *believes* his or her intentions serve some greater good and are not merely selfish. This is what I will always mean (unless I indicate otherwise). It's unfortunate, of course, that people can be so wrong—but that's why the proverb is so well known and helpful.

For example, studies show that, in accordance with this proverb, most suicide bombers have "good intentions." You don't blow yourself up because you are selfish. Some suicide bombers are convinced they will be rewarded in heaven because they are doing something that's actually good. They are not just selfishly trying to get into heaven by fooling God.

They really do have "good intentions," as that term is commonly used, but those intentions really are "paving the road to hell." That's exactly what the proverb is warning us about.

Some people's intentions, however, really are purely selfish, so they should be called bad, evil or selfish intentions.

This may seem obvious but it can still sound confusing because we use both "good" and "evil" to describe two very different things: "intentions" and "actions." (I include taking political positions as a kind of action.) Here are the four possibilities:

- "Good intentions" can lead to evil actions—or good actions.
- "Evil intentions" can lead to evil actions—or good actions.

That last possibility, evil intentions leading to good actions, is pretty unusual but every once in a while, someone intends to shoot the good guy (so to speak) and hits the bad guy instead. Anything is possible.

The first possibility, "good intentions" leading to evil actions, sounds just as strange, but it's not unusual and the proverb is a helpful reminder of that. To be clear, when I use "good intentions" (in quotes) I will always mean that the person with the intentions believes their *intentions* are good and not selfish—even if the *actions* they lead to are horrible.

Escaping Polarization

Here's a key rule for depolarizing ourselves that uses this concept of "good intentions":

To depolarize: Assume that most people we disagree with have "good intentions" and have just been sucked in by a trap; they are not evil or stupid. They have been deceived.

Making this assumption may sound difficult or illogical, so let me point out why it's a bit easier than it might appear to be. First, this approach only asks you to "assume" they are just sucked in. It's like assuming someone is innocent until proven guilty. It does not mean we can't look for more evidence.

Second, we get to see them as "sucked in," so we can still feel a bit superior. (Perhaps that's not so nice, and we may be wrong ourselves. But there's no use pretending we're angels.)

When we depolarize, we still get to think our opponent is dead wrong. That should be good enough. There's no need to think they are evil or stupid unless we really know that to be true.

Can the Answer Be So Simple?

Polarization comes at us from many directions—racism, sexism, religion, healthcare, welfare, foreign policy and so on. So how can there be one simple answer? Recall the two kinds of polarization from Chapter 1: *issue* polarization and *emotional* polarization. It's the emotional one that is amplified in vicious circles and becomes so dangerous. The escape strategy only works for *emotional* polarization, which always has the same conclusion: they're evil. It does not need to address *issues*. That's why it can be simple.

Conclusion

Emotional polarization is seeing your opponents as evil or genuinely stupid. But if they have been caught by a trap, which is quite likely, then they probably have "good intentions." They may be ignorant or bamboozled, but they're not evil.

- Racism is may still be our worst social ill, and that's why it's important to reclaim past knowledge of how to combat it.

CHAPTER 5

Three Political Traps

You can fool all of the people some of the time.
—Unknown

You wouldn't think Donald Trump and socialist Hugo Chavez would have much in common. But both trapped their bases with charismatic populism. Another, very different trap is the myth that the Clinton-endorsed crime bill of 1994 caused the mass incarceration of Blacks. The crime bill myth still entraps all sorts of people, especially Democrats.

Understanding these traps will help us understand how Trump's base has been trapped and see some of the traps that our side gets caught in. Politics is mostly a game of traps. To understand it, we need a clear idea of what a Political Trap is and a familiarity with the three most common kinds of traps.

What's a Political Trap?

The polarization escape strategy explained in Chapter 4 urges us to assume our opponent has "good intentions" but has been sucked into a Political Trap. The examples of traps that I present here are so different from each other that it might seem that the "trap" concept can't be defined. Yet such traps can be recognized by three simple characteristics of those who have been trapped:

1. Having "good intentions"
2. Being deceived by the trap
3. Regret if they see through the deception

Here's an excellent example of these three characteristics at work. Edgar Maddison Welch read online that Comet Ping Pong, a pizza parlor in Washington, D.C., was holding child sex slaves owned by Hillary Clinton and her campaign manager. Edgar arrived from North Carolina with his assault rifle and revolver to rescue them. Shooting off the lock on a door, he discovered … a computer room. The judge gave him four years in prison.

Welch got caught in a weird Political Trap. But weird as it is, Welch demonstrated the inevitable three characteristics of someone sucked into a Political Trap: "good intentions," being deceived, and regret after recognizing the deception.

Even the judge agreed that Welch had "good intentions" and saw himself as risking his life to save children. Had Welch's intentions been bad, had he just wanted to harass a pizza joint for the heck of it, we would not say he'd been sucked into a trap. A person who's trapped by politics *always* has "good intentions." That's what I mean by trapped.

Clearly, Edgar Welch was deceived. But once he knew the truth, he certainly regretted having been sucked in.

The stories that follow illustrate the three most dangerous Political Traps currently active in U.S. politics and provide an orientation to three major parts of this book:

1. Charisma Traps (See Part 2)
2. Populism Traps (See Part 3)
3. Mythology Traps (See Part 4)

Charisma Traps

Charismatic leaders specialize in winning people's loyalty. If this is done with honesty and charm, they're not sucking anyone in. But often, loyalty is won by telling an audience exactly what they want to hear—regardless of the truth. This is the trick of demagogues. The worst example of this was, of course, Hitler. Fortunately, most demagogues are far more benign.

With radio, TV and now social media, the need for leaders to be charismatic continues to grow. Enter the reality-show host, Donald Trump.

Is Trump Charismatic? If you're progressive, you might not think so. That's because he is only charismatic to his followers. But that's all that matters. Charisma is not just about personality; it is about emotional bonding with followers.

Trump defeated 16 less-charismatic Republican candidates in 2016 as well as his less-charismatic Democrat opponent. Charisma is now one of the strongest Political Traps in American politics. In Trump's case, his followers are so enraptured that they have been sucked into believing many of his most outrageous lies and false promises.

Populism Traps

Populism divides society into the righteous people ("Us") and the corrupt elite ("Them"). It also promises that if "the people" stick together, they can overthrow the corrupt elite and quickly bring about a just society. Left-wing populists won't fall for a right-wing populist trap, but they can easily be sucked in by a left-wing populist. Here's the perfect example.

Venezuela's former president, Hugo Chavez, was a quintessential populist who seemed to have accomplished the impossible by leading a successful left-populist revolution. Naturally, that made Chavez and Venezuela the perfect populism trap for leftists.

Hugo Chavez was elected president and took office in early 1999. Immediately, he did what political scientists say populists always do: He attacked the checks and balances of liberal democracy.

By the end of his first year, Chavez had used a national referendum to replace the constitution with one that increased his powers, threw all national elected officials out of office and replaced all Supreme Court justices. In the years that followed, he shut down much of the media and kept imposing new restrictions on his opposition. In 2005, tens of thousands of people who signed petitions for a recall referendum found they could not get government jobs or contracts, qualify for public assistance programs or receive passports.

To suck in our radical left, he announced a program of cheap oil for poor families in the U.S. Northeast. By the end of 2005, Chavez was delivering free oil to Joseph Kennedy II's Citizens Energy Corporation, and by the end of 2006, Kennedy was running Chavez-friendly commercials paid for by Chavez. The oil program continued through 2014 and delivered about $400 million worth of free or heavily discounted oil to poor Americans in 20-plus states.

Of course, it made no sense for Chavez to take that $400 million away from Venezuela's much-poorer poor—except as a propaganda measure. Among those sucked in by this populist "success story," you will find Bernie Sanders, Jesse Jackson, Sean Penn, Oliver Stone, Danny Glover, Michael Moore, Naomi Klein and millions more. Of these, Sanders is the most interesting example. On February 7, 2006, at a joint press conference with Venezuelan Ambassador Bernardo Alvarez, Sanders announced that he had brokered a long-term oil deal for some of Vermont's poor. He said it should not be viewed as political.

Then in 2011, after the U.K.'s highly-respected Freedom House had declared Venezuela "not an electoral democracy," Sanders wrote an article, still posted on his Senate website in 2019, that drew a surprising conclusion:

> These days, the American dream is more apt to be realized in South America, in places such as Ecuador, Venezuela, and Argentina, where incomes are actually more equal today than they are in the land of Horatio Alger. Who's the banana republic now?

How is that? The U.S. is more of a "banana republic" than Venezuela, where you are more apt to realize the American dream? That was one huge endorsement of Hugo Chavez and his populist, democratic socialism. It didn't occur to Sanders that Venezuela's reduced income inequality was built on an oil-price bubble, and not on a socialist miracle.

On September 14, 2015, someone in the Clinton campaign sent an email to a Huffington Post reporter. It noted the oil deal that Bernie brokered with Venezuela.

Sanders immediately responded: "They ... even tried to link me to *a dead communist dictator.*"

Yes, he was talking about *that* "dead communist dictator," Hugo Chavez, who died in 2013. Some on the radical left went bananas. How could Sanders call their hero a "communist dictator?"

Remember the third characteristic of someone who has been sucked in: "The person would regret being sucked in if they saw through the deception." Sanders finally saw through the Chavez deception, and he was regretting it when he was forced to implicitly admit that he himself had brokered a deal with a "communist dictator" to influence his voters.

This is not surprising. People are most easily sucked in by those who pretend to share their worldview. Populism is indeed a powerful trap for those inclined to support the concerns of ordinary people. Because they feel so strongly about their good intentions, they are the most vulnerable to being sucked in.

The Political Mythology Trap

Political myths about the past are used to support arguments for how things should be done now and who is to blame. Myths of past political heroes and anti-heroes are powerful because they sound true (at least to their target audience), and they claim the authority of reality. They are effective partly because they are hard to check—so most people never check them. Here's an example of a devastatingly wrong political myth that is explored in depth in the next chapter.

Joe Biden announcing the signing of the 1994 Crime Bill

The 1994 crime bill. It is now widely believed that the Clintons caused the mass incarceration of Blacks by passing the 1994 crime bill and that they did so for racist reasons. Those who believe this are justifiably concerned with the terrible toll taken by the overuse of incarceration and by biases in the criminal justice system. So they do have good intentions.

They also meet the second criterion for being caught in a Political Trap. As we will see in the next chapter, they have been deceived. Finally, they are well-meaning people who would regret falsely accusing the Clintons if they understood what really happened back in the 1990s—the bill was strongly backed by the Black community and did not cause the mass incarceration of Blacks.

Conclusion

A Political Trap is something that deceives well-intentioned people about a political issue in a way that they would regret if they saw through the deception. Such traps come in many varieties, but the charisma, populist and mythology traps are common and particularly relevant today.

CHAPTER 6

The Crime Bill Myth

We do believe and emphatically support the bill's goal to save our communities, and most importantly, our children.
— 39 African-American Religious Leaders

Ricky Ray Rector was a brain-damaged killer who barely knew his own identity, let alone the fate that awaited him. At his last meal, he saved his pecan pie to eat the next morning. Just weeks before the critical New Hampshire primary, Bill Clinton proved his toughness on crime by flying back to Arkansas to oversee that execution.

Michelle Alexander used this pithy anecdote to introduce Bill Clinton in her famous 2010 book, *The New Jim Crow*. She used it again in 2016 to condemn both Clintons in her widely distributed article, "Why Hillary Clinton Doesn't Deserve the Black Vote." The radical left has deceived Democrats into believing their party is responsible for mass incarceration. This is a mythology trap, the third and most complex kind of Political Trap.

My hope is that seeing how this particular political mythology trap works and where it came from will free us from its grip and somewhat immunize us against similar deceptions. I also hope that learning that our Democratic leaders are good-hearted and not worse than the Klan (as some portray them) will restore some of the unity we need to fend off Trump.

Back to Ricky Ray Rector. Researching the 1994 crime bill, I'd come across variations of Alexander's damning anecdote a dozen times, and I just could not understand why Clinton did not pardon a man who had no real concept of what he was doing. It sounded completely heartless (as it was intended to). So I looked up the Ricky Ray Rector story. It only took a minute and changed my understanding of the situation forever. The facts also provide a good example of how the radical-left mythology traps are produced.

In 1981, Rector and friends drove to a dance hall. When one of them couldn't pay the $3 cover charge, Rector pulled out a .38-caliber pistol and shot the place up, wounding two and killing another. Three days later, he agreed to surrender, but only to the well-liked Officer Robert Martin, whom he had known since childhood. Rector arrived at his mother's house, greeted Officer Martin, waited until the officer turned his back, and shot him dead. Rector then walked out and shot himself in the head, resulting only in a frontal lobotomy, not in his intended suicide.

Rector himself had chosen death but missed and accidentally condemned himself to a life of terrifying hallucinations.

At that time, almost 80% of the country was in favor of the death penalty for murder. I'd guess that for a double murder that included shooting one of the community's best-liked police officers in the back, the percentage would have been closer to 95%, especially in Arkansas. Had Clinton pardoned Rector, Clinton would have had no chance of being elected president. Instead, he would have cemented the Democrats' undeserved reputation for favoring criminals over the general public.

Considering that Michelle Alexander is a highly acclaimed legal scholar and that this is one of her prized anecdotes, Rector's back story is a lot to leave out.

'The New Jim Crow'

Alexander's book is the best-selling book on the criminal justice system—ever. The paperback version spent at least three years on *The New York Times* paperback bestseller list and was still #3 eight years after the hardback's publication. Her remarkable claim is that the drug laws were designed to produce mass incarceration with the "well-disguised" intent to function "in a manner strikingly similar to Jim Crow," the segregation laws overturned by the civil rights movement.

In a nutshell that's the crime bill myth, and like most myths, it sounds pretty amazing. But is mass incarceration of Blacks and Whites really "strikingly similar to Jim Crow?" Or is it an evil of a very different kind?

The first obvious difference between Jim Crow laws and the crime bill is the attitude of Blacks. None of them favored Jim Crow laws, but when the 1994 crime bill passed, Gallup found that more Blacks (58%) favored it than Whites (49%). Note, too, that two-thirds of the Black Congressional Caucus voted for it. Like the background to the Ricky Ray Rector story, these facts are typically omitted by the myth makers (I've never seen an exception).

Because mass incarceration has nothing to do with segregated lunch counters, schools, buses, or other public places that Jim Crow laws targeted, the only possible "striking similarity" to Jim Crow left is the impact of felony convictions on the right-to-vote. And that's where Alexander rests her case.

But Jim Crow laws prevented almost all Southern Blacks from voting and cost the South nothing to implement, while the drug wars and mass incarceration keep only a fraction of Black people—those with felony convictions—from voting and about that many Whites as well. It costs the country around $100 billion per year. This looks nothing like Jim Crow and makes no sense as an effective way to suppress the Black vote.

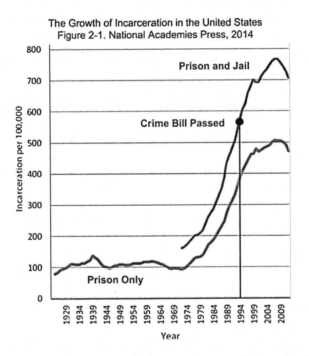

The Growth of Incarceration in the United States
Figure 2-1. National Academies Press, 2014

In short, mass incarceration is in no way parallel to the Jim Crow laws. The very title of her book is a deception. But as the graph above shows, mass incarceration did grow by five times over a 30-year period. So if it wasn't about Jim Crow, what was going on?

What About Crime?

Could the crime bills have been about crime or drugs and not about suppressing Black votes? That's a novel idea. Prohibition was a kind of 13-

year drug war that had nothing to do with racism, but it did criminalize having a beer. Overreaction to drugs and crime is nothing new in America.

You might think that a book about why so many people are incarcerated would include statistics on how many people commit crimes. Most such books are full of them. But not *The New Jim Crow*. It's a bit like telling us that Ricky Ray Rector was mentally impaired and not mentioning how that happened.

Alexander notes that "African Americans are incarcerated at grossly disproportionate rates throughout the United States." This is true. As the NAACP reported in 2018, "African Americans are incarcerated at more than five times the rate of Whites." But Alexander does not mention that on average from 1980 to 2008, the homicide rate for Blacks was 7.6 times higher than for Whites.

I'm not saying the crime-rate difference is the whole story. And I'm certainly not saying there isn't racism in the criminal justice system! But covering up the crime rate is actually a way of covering up (unintentionally in Michelle Alexander's case) the main impact of racism—a tragic mix of unemployment, crime, and broken families in the Black community.

A frightening 30-year crime wave also explains a lot about the popularity of tough-on-crime legislation. As that wave crested between 1985 and 1993, the surge in violence by boys ages 14 through 17 was unprecedented. For Whites, the homicide rate more than doubled in just those eight years, and for Blacks, it more than quadrupled.

This was associated with the crack cocaine epidemic, which Alexander discusses at length without mentioning the violent crime wave or the use of children by drug cartels. All this was headline news at the time.

Impact of the 1994 Crime Bill

A story in the radical-left magazine, *The Nation,* claims the 1994 bill "inaugurated" the "era of mass incarceration." Others just say it caused a spike in it. Let's take a look.

Obviously, the bill was decades too late to have "inaugurated" the era of mass incarceration. *The Nation* just lied about that. It did not cause a spike in incarceration either. But the real question is not about grand totals, it's about what happened to Blacks. In particular, did the 1994 bill target Blacks? The next graph shows the Black imprisonment rate.

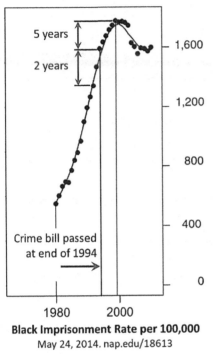

From Figure 2-11, Chapter 2 of "The Growth of Incarceration in the US," National Academies Press

Black Imprisonment Rate per 100,000
May 24, 2014. nap.edu/18613

This graph shows that the state and federal imprisonment rate for Blacks was increasing most rapidly just *before* the 1994 crime bill and that this increase slowed immediately and stopped after five years. Meanwhile, the White incarceration rate continued its upward trend for at least another fifteen years, adding well more than 50% to its 1994 level. And the Black incarceration rate continued down during this same period. The raw data can't prove much, but it cuts strongly against the view that the 1994 crime bill was biased against Blacks.

Note that I am not saying the 1994 crime bill was all positive. Much of it was designed to get the Republican votes needed to pass it. And I've always been opposed to incarceration except when needed for public safety.

What Did Blacks Say About It?

The Nation, in an article obviously influenced by Alexander, tells us, "Representative Ron Dellums, co-founder of the Congressional Black Caucus, voted against it." Like Alexander and the rest of the radical left, *The Nation* just happened to leave out that another 23 members of the Black Caucus, including its chairman, voted for the bill. Only 11 voted against it. This is easy to find out—much easier than the point about Dellums.

Right after saying Dellums voted against the bill, *The Nation* tells us: "So did 34 Senators," as if those Senators had been liberal Democrats who agreed with Ron Dellums. In fact, every one of them was a Republican except for one Alabama Senator who became a Republican three weeks later.

So why did the Black Caucus favor the crime bill? The best answer to this question may be a letter sent to the White House by 39 African-American religious leaders from around the country.

STATEMENT BY AFRICAN-AMERICAN RELIGIOUS LEADERS

We believe there is no more important responsibility of society than to raise its children to become upstanding adults. ... All of society—including government—must pitch in. That is why we support the President's crime bill. While we do not agree with every provision in the crime bill,

- We do believe and emphatically support the bill's goal to save our communities, and most importantly, our children.
- We believe and support the $8 billion in the bill to fund prevention programs such as grants for recreation, employment, and anti-gang and comprehensive programs to steer our young people away from crime.
- We believe in drug treatment to help get federal and state inmates out of the cycle of dependency.
- We believe in programs to fight violence against women.
- We believe in banning assault weapons and preventing these deadly devices from falling into the hands of criminals and drug dealers.
- We believe in putting 100,000 well-trained police officers on the streets of our most violence-plagued communities and urban areas.
- We believe that 9-year-olds like James Darby of New Orleans, who was killed by a stray bullet only days after writing a plea to President Clinton to stop the violence, must have the opportunity to live and learn and grow in safe, decent communities.

For all these reasons, we support the crime bill and we urge others to join us in this crusade.

Although this letter has been widely reported and is easily available, I have never found it reported by the radical-left myth makers.

Another endorsement that is suppressed came near the end of the negotiations over the bill. In July, 10 Black mayors wrote to Black Caucus Chairman Kweisi Mfume saying, "We cannot afford to lose the opportunities this bill provides to the people of our cities." The signatories included the mayors of Detroit, Cleveland, Atlanta, and Denver.

Shortly before the bill was passed, the homicide *victimization rate* for Black males 14 and older was more than eight times higher than it was for White males in the same age range. This is why Black communities were so anxious to have more policing. They were not being foolish and they were not falling for an evil Democratic plot. They were facing a vastly worse crime problem than was the White population.

Republicans: The Most Important Factor

A key fallacy of the crime bill myth is that the Democrats got exactly what they wanted. It's true that Joe Biden was the author, and that he worked on it for years. But no, he did not have a free hand. There were Republicans in Congress, a factor the radical left overlooks entirely.

Passing any high-profile law through the U.S. Congress was almost as contentious in 1994 as it is today. With crime as the nation's #1 concern, there was bound to be a crime bill. It's worth noting that most Republicans did everything they could to block the Democrats' bill. Had they succeeded, there would have been a truly punitive Republican crime bill passed after the Republicans took back both houses of Congress in 1994.

Given the sentiment in the country, Clinton's strategy for passing the Biden bill was to talk tough on crime and give away what mattered least to win the Republican votes that were essential for passage. The Republicans had discovered technicalities that required 60 Senators to secure the bill's passage, and there were only 55 reliable Democrats.

The Democrats had to win over five semi-liberal Republicans. They won over six. In reality, it was Republicans, not Joe Biden, who put the limit on how liberal the bill could be.

So What *Did* Cause Mass Incarceration?

Michelle Alexander's views have become so pervasive that many readers may be surprised at the suggestion that the war on drugs was not intended primarily to suppress African Americans, nor is it the main reason for mass incarceration. Let me turn to an unbiased source with impeccable credentials: David Cole, the ultra-progressive National Legal Director of the American Civil Liberties Union.

As Cole explains, "In her widely read 2010 book, *The New Jim Crow*, Michelle Alexander argued that the war on drugs, pursued for the purpose of subordinating African Americans, is primarily responsible for mass incarceration. These views have become conventional wisdom in liberal circles."

Then he asks, "What if they are wrong?"

Cole answers this sacrilegious question by reviewing two heavily researched books published in 2017. The first is *Locked In: The True Causes of Mass Incarceration and How to Achieve Real Reform,* by John Pfaff. Pfaff points out that although there is discrimination against Blacks regarding imprisonment for drug offenses, drug offenses are not a large part of the incarceration problem. "The racial disparities in prison populations would barely budge if all the people serving time [only] for drug crimes were immediately released," he wrote.

Pfaff then explains the increase in the prison population from 1994 to 2008 as mainly due to the actions of district attorneys. There are 3,000 district attorneys in the country, and they decide who to charge and what to charge them with. This is not controlled by laws on sentencing or by money for prisons or police. Instead, DAs respond to public pressure. This leads to Pfaff's central conclusions:

> The 'New Jim Crow' hypothesis, for example, claims that crime control was used as a way to roll back the gains won by the civil rights movement. ... [However,] as a general rule, public punitiveness has tracked crime, and prison growth, in turn, has tracked punitive attitudes.

The second book Cole reviews is even more surprising. The Pulitzer Prize-winning *Locking Up Our Own: Crime and Punishment in Black America* was written by James Forman Jr., a professor at Yale Law School and the son of a prominent civil rights leader. He knows firsthand what he's talking about, as he served as a public defender in Washington, D.C., for six years, including during the passage of the 1994 crime bill. As Cole tells us in the *New York Review of Books* (June 22, 2017):

> Forman's moving, nuanced, and candid account ... shows that some of the most ardent proponents of tough-on-crime policies in the era that brought us mass incarceration were Black politicians and community leaders who supported these policies, not to subordinate African-Americans, but to protect them from the all-too-real scourges of crime and violence in many inner-city communities.

Conclusion

In the 1990s, increased crime was real, and the public demanded action. The big question was whether a crime bill would be one sponsored by Democrats or by Republicans. Just before losing their leverage in Congress, the Democrats passed the most progressive bill they could, considering their need for five Republican votes in the Senate. All Democratic Senators, even the most progressive approved this, as did a huge majority of House Democrats.

Since then the radical left has developed a myth that they use to attack the Democratic Party. This mythology trap is based on the massive suppression of relevant facts, including most crime statistics, information concerning Black support for the 1994 bill, and recognition of Republican limits on what could be passed.

- Democrats passed the most progressive crime bill they were able to. The only alternative was to let the Republicans do it.
- The 20-year rise of the Black incarceration rate slowed immediately and stopped five years after the bill's passage, while the white rate continued to increase for at least 20 years.
- Most Blacks favored passage of the 1994 crime bill, including two-thirds of the very-progressive Black Congressional Caucus.

Traps and Polarization

Political Traps cause issue polarization, while Moralistic Traps cause emotional polarization—they make one or both sides see the other as immoral or evil, which often leads to hate.

Political Traps	Moralistic Traps
Charisma trap	Racism trap
Populism trap	Purity trap
Mythology trap	

All three common Political Traps tend to lead to simplistic moral views about what's right, and these three traps feed into the purity trap (the mistake of assuming people are evil if they fail some purity test). The racism trap includes all forms of identity prejudice. The racism and purity traps are the two main Moralistic Traps.

Traps are defined by the effects they have on those they trap. All those trapped share three characteristics:

1. Having "good intentions"
2. Being deceived by the trap
3. Regret if they see through the deception

It's common for people to be caught in more than one trap. For example, Trump entraps people with his strongman charisma and with his right-wing (exclusionary) populism.

To *de*polarize the political parties and the country, people need to escape the Moralistic Traps. This only requires that those caught in them find:

The way out: Assume that most people we disagree with have "good intentions" but have just been sucked in by a Political or Moralistic Trap—and they are not evil or stupid.

CHAPTER 7

The Purity Trap

*The progressives act as though anyone who dares disagree
with them is bad. Not wrong, but bad, guilty of some human
failing, some impurity that is a moral evil that justifies their
venom.*

—Maureen Dowd, *The New York Times*, 2019

Dr. Peter Hotez wrote a book about his daughter, *Vaccines Did Not
Cause Rachel's Autism*. An anti-vaxxer concluded: "You have no morals
whatsoever and you know that you are a fucking liar. I hope you rot in
hell" (CNN, 3/21/19). The anti-vaxxer was caught in a purity trap. Two
observations make this clear—first, anti-vaxxers commonly believe that
"we all know vaccines cause autism," and second, this one concluded
that Dr. Peter Hotez has "no morals."

The purity trap is *not* another Political Trap. Rather, it is a kind of
Moralistic Trap. Moralistic Traps cause *emotional* polarization, the kind
of polarization that's ripping us apart by causing hatred. Political Traps
only cause *issue* polarization, which generally only causes disagreement.
So why did I spend so much time on Political Traps when it is the Moralistic Traps—the purity trap and what I will call the racism trap—that create the real dangers?

The answer is straightforward. Political Traps lead us to the simplistic
ideas that are almost always the source of the purity trap—the trap that is
central to almost all radical-left politics.

The Purity Trap: Becoming a Purity Tester

The purity trap is the mistake of assuming people are evil if they fail
some purity test, aka a litmus test, such as "Do you believe vaccines
cause autism?" Like all Moralistic Traps, it convinces us that our opponents are not just mistaken—they're immoral. And that leads to the emotional polarization that's ripping us apart.

Paul Krugman's op-ed "Don't Make Health Care a Purity Test" mentions this purity test: Do you agree that Medicare-for-all is the best healthcare proposal? According to Krugman, some Berniecrats apply that test to politicians they wish to condemn as "corrupt shills for the medical/industrial complex." The Berniecrat applying the test has been caught in the purity trap. Simply put:

Those who believe in a purity test are caught in a purity trap.

Purity traps cause people to hate. Worse, they often cause them to hate their allies. The thinking of someone caught by a purity trap, although it may be subconscious, goes something like this:

1. ***Everyone knows*** that my purity test specifies the only moral position on [a certain issue].
2. Therefore, everyone who disagrees knows they are taking an immoral position so they must be doing it for some evil reason.

The problem here is the assumption that "Everyone knows." That's just about never true. If we don't stop to think, it may seem like they should know. But if we do stop to think, we will realize that even the best and brightest make basic mistakes. And most of us make lots of mistakes. You never know what someone is thinking.

Given how error-prone people are, it is a bit silly to assume that people just couldn't be mistaken. For example, take climate-change deniers. How could they make a mistake about that? Well, don't all Democrats believe that the oil companies have been deceiving people? So then lots of people must be deceived—mistaken. It's always like that. Mistakes are everywhere. You can almost never rule them out.

That means that using a purity test—you disagree with this, so you are immoral—is just ridiculous. There's no way to know that the truth isn't: "You disagree with this, so you made a mistake."

And the truth is even harsher. Most people who are illogical enough to believe in purity testing are quite likely just wrong. They should be saying: "You disagree with this; hmm, maybe I'm wrong." But let's not hope for miracles.

Purity Really Is Dangerous

As an example of how the purity trap causes serious damage to the Democrats, consider a story written by one of *The Atlantic* magazine's most respected (but now retired) national correspondents.

Only one week before the first Democratic primary in 2016, Ta-Nehisi Coates began his discussion of the 1994 crime bill as follows:

> Black voters particularly should never forget that Bill Clinton passed arguably the most **immoral** 'anti-crime' bill in American history and that Hillary Clinton aided its passage through her invocation of the super-predator myth [emphasis throughout the book is my own].

Coates is clearly thinking of this purity test: Do you agree that the 1994 crime bill was extremely immoral? By telling Black voters what they "should never forget" while giving them no evidence, Coates is implicitly suggesting that this is something everyone knows is true.

He then rules out, again without evidence, the possibility that the Clintons were simply wrong. His "anger over the Clintons' actions **isn't simply based on their having been wrong** but on their **craven embrace ... of law and order Republicanism** in the Democratic Party's name."

This is precisely where the purity trap logic takes us once we make the assumption that *everyone knows* we're right about our purity test. Because Coates thinks *everyone knows* the crime bill was immoral, his only logical conclusion is that the Clintons knew it was immoral, they did it anyway, and their actions were craven.

As always, once you buy "everyone knows," you're trapped. The rest is completely logical. The only trouble—as always—is that "everyone knows" is just bullshit.

Bullshit History

As we know from Chapter 6, two-thirds of the Congressional Black Caucus, 10 Black big-city mayors, 39 prominent Black pastors and 58% of all Blacks favored what Coates calls "arguably the most immoral 'anti-crime' bill in American history." Well, it's immorality certainly wasn't obvious to everyone.

If it wasn't obvious to all those well-informed Blacks, who's to say it was obvious to the Clintons? And if it was not obvious to them, then they could have just been wrong and not cravenly immoral, as Coates claims.

As usual, the first step of the purity trap—everyone knows—is wrong, and this time, outrageously wrong.

You may wonder how Coates could miss that much Black history, but it seems plausible given what else he missed. Where he claimed that "Hillary Clinton aided [the 1994 crime bill's] passage through her invocation of the super-predator myth," he put a link in his *Atlantic* article to Hillary Clinton saying "super-predator." If you click it, you'll see that, sure enough ... but wait, what does it say in big characters at the top of every frame of that video? It says "01-28-96" (See clipped frame in Chapter 30). That's a year and a half *after* the passage of the 1994 crime bill. So she did say that to aid the passage of the crime bill. In fact, as I recount later, the word had not even been invented in 1994.

Coates just made up his accusation.

What went wrong? I think Coates may have explained it back in 2012 when he wrote in *The Atlantic*, "I read what I like before I read what's important. That's who I am. It's my version of the 'senior editor' ... I also don't believe it's my job to be right." Amen.

Judging Ta-Nehisi Coates

If I were to fall into the purity trap as Coates has, I would conclude that Coates himself is immoral: Everyone knows the Clintons were on the same side as most Blacks. So when Coates denies this, it must be a deliberate deception, and he must be immoral.

But the purity trap always leads us astray. So how do you get out of it? The only way out is to reject step 1—"Everyone knows." And I do. It is not obvious to everyone that most Blacks backed that bill. It must have not been obvious to Coates. So the whole "everyone knows" argument falls apart.

People make mistakes. And they make a lot of them when they get sucked in. I'm guessing he was sucked in by Michelle Alexander's book, *The New Jim Crow*. That has become a powerful radical-left Political

Trap and many Democrats seem to be caught in it. Political Traps are the most common source of the "It's obvious to everyone" assumption that leads into the purity trap.

Therefore, I conclude that Coates is "well-intentioned" and just deceived by a Political Trap. I still think he's worth reading.

Conclusion

It's important for Democrats to be aware of the purity trap. It has the effect of making those caught in the trap see other Democrats as immoral and as a hated (or disparaged) enemy.

The purity trap is also responsible for making many Democrats hate Republicans and vice versa. The simplest cure for this is to remember that Republicans could be "well-meaning" but sucked into some Political Trap. Taking this approach shouldn't be all that difficult.

Charisma Traps

When combined with a populism trap, a charisma trap may be the most dangerous. Chairman Mao and Hitler are famous examples of deceptive charismatic leaders. Both had personality cults, and both made use of populism. In spite of this, the power of a charisma trap often goes unrecognized. As with any trap, failing to recognize it, or its power, just makes it more dangerous. So it's worth taking a look at the great variety of charisma traps and who they catch.

Seeing who has been fooled, and sometimes made a fool of, can teach us to have sympathy for its victims, and not take for granted our own ability to see through its deceptions. In fact, a major point of Part 2 is to convince you that everyone is vulnerable, and traps play a huge role in both Republican and Democratic politics.

But people do vary greatly as to their susceptibility. The good news is that we can learn to be less susceptible. The bad news? We usually learn the hard way.

This section begins with examples that are amazing but not too close to home. Then it works up to ones that directly concern today's dysfunctional and polarized politics, and finally to Trump. Understanding Trump's charisma will help us defeat him.

> The next 20 chapters have several purposes, one of which is to argue that political delusions are central to politics, and consequently, rational explanations based on economic self-interest are wholly inadequate. However, I am not claiming that economic realities are inconsequential, only that they are filtered through something akin to mass psychosis.
>
> This means theory must be well-check against reality, and it will most often be found wanting.

Synopsis of Part 2

Chapter 8. Smart People Get Sucked In. If you get sucked in and taken for a lot of money, don't be embarrassed. You're part of the smart set—secretaries of state, top investors, and super-rich CEOs.

Chapter 9. Good People Get Sucked In. If you're a kindhearted person not out to make money, be careful. President Obama, millions of regular folks (including me) and even some four-star generals got sucked in by a Mother Teresa wannabe.

Chapter 10. Jonestown: Evil Charisma. First Lady Rosalynn Carter, Vice President Mondale, a governor of California, a mayor of San Francisco, and a Black Panther were all sucked in by a charismatic, "progressive" mass murderer.

Chapter 11. Alex Jones: More Evil Charisma. You may be shocked to learn how many Trump supporters, and even Democrats, bought Jones' conspiracy theories that claimed Hillary Clinton was into "satanic ritual abuse."

Chapter 12. The Charismatic Progressive. In 1948, the charismatic Henry Wallace, who had been Roosevelt's vice president, built the third and final Progressive Party. Unfortunately, as Wallace later admitted, he had been duped by the Communist Party.

Chapter 13. Trump: Charismatic Sociopath. Sociopaths have no conscience and treat life as a game. Trump just wants to win and has strongman charisma that appeals to his base. That tells us how to resist him instead of accidentally helping him bond with his base.

CHAPTER 8

Smart People Get Sucked In

She is on the verge of achieving her vision ... transforming healthcare around the world ... the social implications are vast.

—Secretary of State Henry Kissinger

Henry Kissinger found her striking, somewhat ethereal, iron-willed and fierce, with a combination of single-minded dedication and great charm. Everyone from Fox News to *Scientific American* called her charismatic.

Charismatic leaders tell their faithful followers what they want to hear. It is simply astounding how well this works, which is the point of this chapter. If brilliant and world-wise men can be so easily sucked in and taken for large sums of money, then what chance do the rest of us have?

While this story is not about politics, it shows that the delusions of politics can be chalked up to a general human weakness. So if you see someone who has been trapped, even if they are your political enemy, have some sympathy—even if you're sure it could never happen to you.

Big Names, Smart People and a Blood Hoax

After dropping out of Stanford as a sophomore, Elizabeth Holmes became the world's youngest self-made woman billionaire. In September 2014, at age 30, she made the *Forbes* 400 list of the richest Americans. Her Silicon Valley company, Theranos, had 500 employees and was valued at $9 billion. She owned 50%.

On her board of directors sat former Secretaries of State Henry Kissinger and George Shultz, and Senator Sam Nunn. Her investors included media mogul Rupert Murdoch ($125 million invested), former Senate majority leader Bill Frist, Bechtel Group Inc. chairman Riley Bechtel and Oracle cofounder Larry Ellison, along with savvy Silicon Valley investment bankers.

Trump's first Secretary of Defense, James Mattis, described Holmes as having "one of the most mature and well-honed sense of ethics—personal ethics, managerial ethics, business ethics [and] medical ethics—that I've ever heard articulated." Oh, right.

In April 2015, Kissinger wrote for *Time* magazine, "I told her she had only two prospects: total failure or vast success. She is on the verge of achieving her vision ... dedicated to transforming health care around the world ... the social implications are vast."

The promise of Theranos was that its revolutionary Edison blood-testing machine would quickly perform more than 200 tests on a single drop of blood taken from the tip of your finger.

But in January 2016, federal inspectors found "deficient practices" at a Theranos laboratory that "pose immediate jeopardy to patient health and safety." And on April 18, 2016, Theranos voided tens of thousands of results—all of the results from its Edison machine for 2014 and 2015. As it turned out, the machine could perform only about 15 of the tests, and those unreliably.

A month and a half later, *Forbes* reevaluated Elizabeth Holmes' net worth as zero. Kissinger, Shultz, Frist, Nunn, Murdoch, Bechtel, Ellison and many more had been "sucked in" by an "ethereal, iron-willed" charismatic college dropout.

In March 2018, Holmes was charged by the Securities and Exchange Commission with fraudulently raising $700 million, fined $500,000 and lost control of her company. In June 2018, she and former Theranos president "Sunny" Balwani were charged with nine counts of wire fraud for defrauding investors, doctors, and patients.

Would You Know If It Happened to You?

This book is about politics, but the psychology of being sucked in, bamboozled, conned, deceived, deluded, duped, hornswoggled, hoodwinked, outfoxed or flimflammed pops up in all kinds of situations—not only political ones. My point in this chapter is a general one, and no one has illustrated it better than Elizabeth Holmes.

If so many smart people and their money can be sucked in for so long by a charmer with barely more than a high school education and no real achievements, *surely it could happen to us.*

Well, yes, of course, we knew that. But here's the catch: If it did happen to us, would we know it? The answer is simple, absolute and frightening: *Not a chance.*

The proof? Just try believing these two things at once: (1) I know my new friend has discovered the cure for cancer. (2) I also know my new friend is just conning me. If you believe #1, you've been sucked in. If you believe #2, you know you've been sucked in. But it's impossible to believe both at once, so we can't be sucked in and know it at the same time. When we're sucked in, we never know it. But here's why there's still hope.

Suppose we have great faith in Joe Marvelous. If I ask, "Have we been sucked in by Joe?" we'll likely answer "No." But actually, the only honest answer is: "We're not sure." Because if we were sucked in, we wouldn't know it.

But this doesn't mean we can't have any idea if we've been sucked in or not. We might suspect that we have been, but we wouldn't know for sure. So we should learn to be more skeptical just in case. Unfortunately, we usually forget to be skeptical just when it matters most.

Conclusion

Elizabeth Holmes' investors showed that even being smart and experienced couldn't save them from a charisma trap.

- If we've been sucked in, we may suspect it, but we might not. You just never know.

CHAPTER 9

Good People Get Sucked In

What Greg ... practices more than anyone else I know is the
simple truth that ... by helping [children] learn and grow,
he's shaping the very future of a region and giving hope to
an entire generation.

—Admiral Mike Mullen
Former Chairman, Joint Chiefs of Staff

Greg Mortenson strikes almost everyone as deeply honest. He seems sincere and dedicated to humbly serving others. He builds schools for children, particularly girls, in the remote and desperately poor parts of Pakistan and Afghanistan. Who could doubt such a selfless person?

Mortenson's charismatic appeal is similar to that of a political leader: It's based on doing good and solving social problems. Mortenson told his followers he and he alone knew the solution to pressing social problems. He took advantage of the good intentions of his supporters. It's phenomenal how well this works.

Some politicians play this game almost as well as Mortenson. They know what works. They must appear to be on the side of the commoner, the marginalized and the poor. They must appear to be humble and trustworthy. You and I and the rest of the base they play to want this. Badly. We are sick of phony politicians who serve only themselves and the rich. And that makes us vulnerable to the Mortensons of this world and to the politicians who are frauds.

But what makes this form of a charisma trap so dangerously hard to detect is that the fraudsters often deceive themselves. Greg Mortenson surely believed he was the next Mother Teresa. Some politicians are the same. They are sure they are essential to social progress—which justifies all sorts of deceptions for the sake of their cause.

Almost never do we get a clear view of such games and deceptions, but we are in luck with Mortenson. A fellow mountaineer and board member of Mortenson's foundation decided that he might have been conned and that he should check.

In the Beginning

After 10 years of hard work, fundraising, negotiating with locals, and supervising construction in remote villages, Mortenson got his first big story in *Parade* magazine. Then his Central Asia Institute (CAI) took off. Three years later, in 2006, he published *Three Cups of Tea*, which was on *The New York Times* bestseller list for four years and sold four million copies.

The book raised $70 million in donations for CAI and made Mortenson famous. *Three Cups of Tea* became required reading for U.S. servicemen bound for Afghanistan. NBC reported in late 2009: "Since April, Mortenson has facilitated more than 35 meetings in Afghanistan between local shura, or tribal leaders, and U.S. military commanders, including Generals Stanley McChrystal, the top U.S. commander in Afghanistan, and David Petraeus, the head of U.S. Central Command." In March 2010, President Obama donated $100,000 of his Nobel Peace Prize to Mortenson's CAI.

Then, in April 2011, came the *60 Minutes* expose and writer Jon Krakauer's *Three Cups of Deceit*. Mortenson had made it impossible for his institute to track his finances. But at the request of donors, the American Institute of Philanthropy investigated and found that Mortenson had pocketed all of the proceeds from speaking fees and royalties, a book

CAI was spending heavily to promote. It also turned out that in some years less than half of the CAI's expenditures went toward schools.

Again, we see brilliant, tough-minded people being sucked in. Mortenson told people what they wanted to hear—he had a simple solution to a difficult problem, and they could donate to his CAI and feel good about it. What's amazing is that everyone was blinded to the most glaring sign—that this was far and away too good to be true.

Fact or Fantasy?

Three Cups of Tea is half fantasy. The book opens with the heartwarming story of how Greg lost his way and was saved by the town of Korphe when he was half-dead from exhaustion. He first repaid them with his medical skills—his exploits are described in detail—and then promised he would return to build the town a school. None of that story was true, although he did eventually build a school in Korphe.

He did not lose his way coming back from his attempted climb of K2. He stuck with his three companions, arrived at a respected mountaineering hotel, rested up and then visited the village of Khane (not to be confused with Korphe), where he promised to build a school. He did not keep that promise. He wrote of his promise to Khane in a 1994 article for the American Himalayan Foundation newsletter. The founding story of his own myth is entirely fake.

Winning over the Taliban. The most harrowing story in the book recounts his capture by the Taliban, who held him for eight days in a small cell where he expected to be executed at any moment. At 4 a.m. on the eighth day, he was thrown blindfolded into a pickup truck. It drove off into the night, and then...

> The truck slid to a stop amid the deafening cacophony of dozens of AK-47s firing on full automatic. Khan unwrapped Mortenson's blindfold. "You see," he said. "I told you everything would work out for the best." Over Khan's shoulder, Mortenson saw hundreds of big, bearded Wazir, dancing around bonfires, shooting their weapons in the air. On their firelit faces, Mortenson was amazed to see not bloodlust, but rapture. ...

And so it turned out that Mortenson, in one brief interview while he was held captive, had convinced the Taliban that building schools for girls was just what they needed. To prove their commitment, the revelers were stuffing rupees into his pockets to help him with his projects. Fabulous!

This is some of the "insightful" analysis of the Taliban and local customs that the U.S. military was gaining from Mortenson and his book.

The *60 Minutes* documentary debunks this story by interviewing the non-Taliban tribesmen who Mortenson actually spent a pleasant week with, while his wife Tara was expecting him to fly home because she was due with their first child in a month. Quite a cover story—complete with fantasized hand-wringing about what poor Tara would do after his execution.

The Miracle of Mother Teresa. As a final example of Mortenson's deceit, consider his visit with the deceased Mother Teresa. This story provides a window on Mortenson's fantasy of winning the Nobel Peace prize just as Mother Teresa did. He was nominated for it three times.

Mortenson's Chapter 18, "Shrouded Figure," says that "by the spring of 2000," he began to study other education programs, visiting the Philippines and Bangladesh. On the way back he flew from Dhaka to Calcutta, where he had a "brief layover." There he saw a headline stating that his childhood hero, Mother Teresa, had died.

In great detail, Mortenson describes how he grabbed a "black and yellow Ambassador cab" and asked the driver to take him to see her. They arrive at dusk to find that "hundreds of hushed mourners crowded the gates, holding candles and arranging offerings." Undaunted, the driver "got out and rattled the metal gate loudly" and "shouted in Bengali, "Open up!"

This worked like a charm, and soon Mortenson is with her: "She lay on a simple cot, at the center of a bright room full of flickering devotional candles. Mortenson took a seat against a wall. The nun, backing out the door, left him alone with Mother Teresa."

What makes this such a remarkable story is that Mother Teresa had died *three years earlier*.

Could Mortenson's coauthor, David Relin, just have mistyped the date? Nope. Back in Chapter 15, the book tells us that at the time of her death, Mortenson was in northern Pakistan.

I read both *Three Cups of Tea* and Mortenson's follow-up book, *Stones Into Schools,* before the *60 Minutes* expose. I bought his stories, fantastic as they were. It just seemed impossible to believe that someone who risked life and limb to help poor girls in remote villages would be so heartless as to deliberately make fools of millions of adoring followers. What kind of person could do both?

At least it is comforting to know that I am in the company of millions of other normal, good-hearted people and even of tough-minded people like Generals McChrystal and Petraeus. But it is frightening to remember that during the time I was sucked in, I had no idea that I was.

Lies That Destroy Trust

As Jon Krakauer, author of *Three Cups of Deceit* and Mortenson's best-informed critic, says of Mortenson, "He is not Bernie Madoff. He has done a lot of good. He has become the most effective spokesperson for girls' education in developing countries and he deserves credit for that." But he has also destroyed a lot of trust, and trust is at the heart of the social changes Mortenson and his supporters are working for.

Even worse, he has handed a large box of ammunition to all who oppose his cause. Those who pushed for the use of *Three Cups of Tea* in the military are now taunted with how they believed Mortenson's fantasies of Taliban dancing around bonfires for girls' schools. The good-hearted, liberal *New York Times* columnist Nicholas Kristof is endlessly pilloried for playing Mortenson's fool.

Mortenson did some good, and perhaps, if he's lucky, even more good than harm. Charismatic leaders can be good, evil or a horribly confusing mixture. This is part of what makes them hard to judge. After the *60 Minutes* expose, David Relin, Mortenson's co-author, was accused of lying but claimed he was taken in. He was. But he committed suicide.

Conclusion

Because most charismatic political leaders pretend to be champions of progress or righteousness, well-intentioned folks must be even more cautious than others to avoid being sucked in.

CHAPTER 10

Jonestown: Evil Charisma

If you're born in capitalist America, racist America, fascist America, then you're born in sin. But if you're born in socialism, you're not born in sin.

—Jim Jones, summer, 1973

"How can I demonstrate my Marxism? My thought was, 'Infiltrate the church.' I consciously made a decision to look into that." That's how Jim Jones remembered the origins of his first congregation, which became the populist-sounding People's Temple. Jones was brought up in a Pentecostal church and had been fascinated by religion and death from an early age. But in 1951, at the age of 20, he began attending meetings and rallies of the Communist Party USA.

We now pigeonhole Jones as a crazy-left cult leader who appealed only to the emotionally needy and organized one of the largest mass murder-suicides in recorded history.

But this hides the most important lessons of Jones' appeal. Jim Jones was engaged in mainstream politics, and there, too, his charisma was strong. He successfully appealed to the radical left and a few liberals as well, from famed San Francisco supervisor Harvey Milk, the first openly-gay elected official in California, to First Lady Rosalynn Carter.

Similar to the pattern in the previous two chapters, this does not mean his followers and supporters were anything like Jones, any more than most of their supporters or followers were like Elizabeth Holmes or Greg Mortenson. Instead, Jones pretended to be like them and deceived them. But it does mean that some Democrats (just like some Republicans) are highly susceptible to being sucked in by even the worst sorts of charismatic leaders. This has always been true, and it still is.

So this chapter is a warning. There is no current equivalent to Jim Jones. But if someone as unbalanced and psychopathic as Jones could mesmerize such an extensive left audience, surely a more normal-appearing crackpot could be among us today. And we might not know.

It Started with a Good Cause

In 1960, Jones was appointed to the Indianapolis Human Rights Commission. After taking a strong public stand for integration, he was wildly cheered at a meeting of the NAACP and Urban League when he called out for his audience to be more militant. In Indianapolis, he helped integrate churches, restaurants, the telephone company, the police department, a theater, an amusement park, and the Methodist hospital.

However, by December 1963, Jones had his own congregation and assured them there would be a nuclear war on July 15, 1967. In 1965 he moved the Temple to rural Northern California for "safety reasons." There it grew rapidly, and in 1971, moved to San Francisco. By then, Jones was renouncing Christianity and espousing socialism.

In 1975, Mayor George Moscone appointed Jones chairman of the San Francisco Housing Authority Commission. Jones and Moscone met privately with soon-to-be Vice President Walter Mondale on his campaign plane, leading Mondale to publicly praise the Temple. First Lady Rosalynn Carter corresponded with Jones and spoke with him at the opening of the San Francisco Democratic Party Headquarters, where Jones was loudly applauded.

California Assemblyman Willie Brown (who later became mayor of San Francisco) served as master of ceremonies at a dinner in honor of Jones attended by Governor Jerry Brown and Lieutenant Governor Mervyn Dymally. There, Willie Brown called Jones a combination of Martin Luther King Jr., Black Panther Angela Davis, Albert Einstein … and Chairman Mao. San Francisco City Supervisor Harvey Milk visited the Temple and then wrote,

"Rev Jim, it may take me many a day to come back down from the high that I reached today. I found something dear today. I found a sense of being that makes up for all the hours and energy placed in a fight. *I found what you wanted me to find.* I shall be back. For I can never leave."

Drinking the Kool-Aid

The bubble began to burst in the summer of 1977 when *San Francisco Chronicle* reporter Marshall Kilduff wrote an exposé of the People's Temple. The left-leaning *Chronicle* wouldn't publish it. Later, when Jones learned that it exposed years of his physical, emotional and sexual abuse of Temple members, he promptly moved himself and hundreds of his followers to the People's Temple Agricultural Project, aka Jonestown, which he had established a few years earlier in Guyana, South America.

He declared Jonestown (which he sometimes called The Promised Land) to be a communist community and made it extremely hard for members to leave. Relatives in the States became concerned and contacted the State Department in January 1978.

About that time, Willie Brown spoke out against Jones' enemies at a rally at the People's Temple in San Francisco, which was also attended by Harvey Milk and then-Assemblyman Art Agnos. On February 19, 1978, Milk wrote a letter to President Jimmy Carter defending Jones as "a man of the highest character." Moscone's office issued a press release saying that Jones had broken no laws.

On November 17, 1978, Democratic Congressman Leo Ryan landed in Jonestown on a fact-finding mission to investigate allegations of human rights abuses. That day, Jonestown seemed quite wonderful to Ryan, three reporters, and his two staff members. Near the end of a celebration with singing and dancing, Ryan's remarks were positive, and the crowd erupted with a long and enthusiastic standing ovation. Ryan staffer Jackie Speier remembers, "It was a vibrant community. I would never have imagined that 24 hours later those people would be dead."

Ryan and his group were hoodwinked by Jones' charade. What they did not understand, and what is nearly impossible to understand, is how normal people (Jones' followers in this case) can be blinded to horrible things they see with their own eyes. Pressured by propaganda and by physical and psychological intimidation, they rationalized these away and managed to achieve a state of what George Orwell called double-think, where we know one thing and believe the opposite.

But that evening, the spell cast on Ryan's group was broken when they received two notes from people who wanted to leave. The next morning, a woman walked up to Jackie Speier and said, "I am being held prisoner here." Then, Spier recalled, "All hell broke out." Ryan's group and 13 escapees left for the two waiting planes, intending to return for more people later. But Jones' Red Guards caught up with them as they were boarding, killing Ryan and four others. Spier and one other were shot and left for dead, while the plane-load of escapees flew to Georgetown, Guyana.

Jones had spent months brainwashing his followers for "revolutionary suicide." After the airstrip killings, he argued that Jonestown would be invaded and many of its members tortured. Most residents were poor, and 68% were Black. Almost all were progressive and believed deeply in caring for each other.

Guards with crossbows and guns encircled the brainwashed population. Many, especially children, were simply murdered, and all who committed suicide surely did so out of a delusional fear of the coming invasion. Most members drank the cyanide-laced Kool-Aid. A total of 909 followers died, including 304 children. Jones shot himself, presumably to avoid the misery of cyanide poisoning.

Who Was Sucked In?

For more than three years, Jones was highly respected by the left community. Those complimenting Jones ranged from former Black Panther Angela Davis to First Lady Rosalynn Carter and from gay activist Harvey Milk to Vice President Mondale. This encompassed most of the Democratic establishment in San Francisco, the most progressive city in the country. All were sucked in by Jones' charisma and his charade.

Of course, this progressive gullibility has given right-wingers legitimate talking points for decades and tarred the left with the epithet, "drank the Kool-Aid."

I have read only one excuse for such egregious mistakes by progressives: Jones started out good but eventually turned to drugs and went bad. This line of reasoning holds that had it not been for Jones' drug use, the People's Temple might have turned out very differently and that when he was operating in California, he was actually a good progressive leader.

According to his own webpage, Garrett Lambrev was "the first person to meet Jim Jones and join the People's Temple" when Jones moved to California in 1965. Lambrev describes himself as "a recent dropout from a doctoral program in history at Stanford and a seasoned peace activist."

In 2008, Lambrev told the *Cleveland Plain Dealer* that he had been with the Temple for only about two months when Jones was praising the Soviets, and Lambrev spoke up: "Jim, what about the Gulag? What about the labor camps?" He recalls that Jones "turned red and glared at me, and said, 'Who do you think you are? You're speaking to the Almighty God,' and he pounded his fist. I felt so humiliated. ... But I thought, 'He's God. I'm not.' So I went along with that for years. I questioned myself, rather than him." Jones was evil from the start. (Fortunately for Lambrev, he defected two years before the Jonestown genocide. In 2000 he supported Ralph Nader who cost Al Gore the presidency, and in 2015 he became a staunch Berniecrat.)

It's been widely reported that for George Moscone's 1975 mayoral race, Jones organized coercive and fraudulent voting. There are many accounts of earlier sexual abuse and even torture by Jones. So Jones turned to drugs after the truth began to leak out. The fault lay with Jones, not the drugs.

But what must be kept firmly in mind is that the vast majority of Jones' supporters really were sucked in by him. They were not like him. They were not violent or authoritarian people. In fact, they were sheep, not wolves. They had their weaknesses, and Jones took advantage of them. Almost all, even those who benefited politically, were "well-intentioned."

Conclusion

We are left with a rather upsetting conclusion. A very broad spectrum of the left was susceptible to a dreadful charismatic leader who claimed to be on the side of the poor and minorities. This proves that the left can fall for a charismatic leader no matter how hideous he is in reality.

Such leaders can be skilled deceivers, and the most idealistic progressives seem to have a special weakness for believing in magical or revolutionary shortcuts to the Promised Land. If the left can be sucked in by such an obvious predator, they can certainly be sucked in by more reasonable-seeming demagogues who only need to talk the left talk and promise revolutionary change.

Of course, the right is even more susceptible to their own version of this weakness, as Trump is now proving. The right also may be more susceptible to crackpot media personalities such as Alex Jones, as we will see in the following chapter.

- The idealistic, radical left is highly susceptible to hucksters who self-identify as part of the radical left.
- The vast majority of those who are sucked in are well-intentioned and bear no resemblance to the evil charismatic leaders who dupe them.

CHAPTER 11

Alex Jones: More Evil Charisma

Falsehood flies, and truth comes limping after it. When men come to be undeceived, it is too late.

—Jonathan Swift, 1710

Lenny Pozner was no stranger to conspiracy theories. He had even listened to far-right radio host Alex Jones while commuting. "I was always looking for more information so I could get an edge on the next guy," Pozner said. He found Jones entertaining, someone who was "thinking outside the box."

All that changed one morning. Pozner had driven his son, Noah, to school as usual, but an hour later Noah was dead, his jaw and left hand blown off in the Sandy Hook massacre.

It didn't take Alex Jones long to figure out what to tell his listeners. "Sandy Hook is a complete fake ... with actors—in my view, manufactured," bellowed Jones. And a million followers, sucked in by his evil charisma, thought they had "an edge on the next guy." Some became "truthers," harassing Pozner and others for being part of the government's anti-gun conspiracy.

⌒

Jones is a purveyor of conspiracy theories, just as Trump is, and just as Russia and a host of small-time crypto-fascists are. So the fact that he was able to reach millions with the most outrageous imaginable conspiracy theory right before the 2016 election makes understanding him essential. Perhaps the most disturbing part of this story is how deeply he controlled (and still controls) many of his followers. In 2020, we will face an amplified version of this threat from the Trump internet war room, which is already bragging that it will break all norms.

The 'Fake Massacre' at Sandy Hook

The story questioning the reality of the Sandy Hook massacre is horrifying because it has convinced reasonably normal people that truly terrible behavior is actually righteous. Jones' followers took it upon themselves to harass and threaten parents of the murdered children. One particularly hateful attack was on Lenny Pozner. An unemployed waitress, Lucy Richards, called Pozner at least four times with death threats, ethnic slurs (Pozner is Jewish) and profanities. She was later arrested and pleaded guilty.

Nor was Lucy Richards alone. A man was convicted of stealing memorial signs from a local playground. Another was arrested at the memorial of one of the teachers when he confronted her sister, demanding to know if the teacher had really died. Another is in prison for a deluge of harassing phone calls to the medical examiner who signed the coroner reports for Sandy Hook victims.

The "Sandy Hook truthers," as they called themselves, accused teachers, police, photographers, first responders, neighbors, government officials, and witnesses—all were said to be part of the ever-expanding conspiracy.

Pozner tried to reach out to the hoaxers and found that many were "just kids who get sucked into this world and they feel more confident about themselves, more certain, and they feed off the echo chamber of info, usually from websites." Sadly, Pozner realized that there was no point in arguing with these hoaxers. "They got taken in—hook, line and sinker."

Most of the families were harassed to the point that they have taken themselves off social media and delisted their phone numbers. Some have even moved away.

Pizzagate: Cheese Pizza = Child Porn?

In a move that certainly cost Hillary Clinton votes, Jones promoted the myth of "Pizzagate" on October 30, 2016, shortly before the election. The story was that hidden in the basement of Comet Ping Pong pizza restaurant in Washington, D.C. was a child sex trafficking operation. How did Jones know this? Messages from a hacked account of John Podesta, Clinton's campaign manager, contained coded messages referring to the operation. Jones claimed that **Cheese Pizza** was code for **Child Pornography**.

The story was widely circulated on right-wing news sites—not only Jones' InfoWars but on such sites as Planet Free Will and Vigilant Citizen. Comet Ping Pong received hundreds of threats from true believers, as did other nearby businesses. Jones posted a YouTube video on November 4, 2016, saying,

> When I think about all the children Hillary Clinton has personally murdered and chopped up and raped, I have zero fear standing up against her. Yeah, you heard me right. Hillary Clinton has personally murdered children. I just can't hold back the truth anymore.

Edgar Maddison Welch, whom we met in Chapter 5, a 28-year-old Facebook fan from North Carolina, took it upon himself to save the remaining children. Armed with an assault rifle, he searched the restaurant and fired three shots. Luckily, no one was hurt. Welch was sentenced to serve four years in prison and pay damages to the restaurant. Here's a young man so totally sucked into this outrageous story that he was ready to kill.

In March 2017, under threat of a lawsuit for slander, Jones offered a rare "apology" for comments that "could be construed as negative." *Could* be construed! That's outrageous, but did his rantings have any significant impact besides getting one of his fans locked up?

In mid-December 2016, barely a month after the election and more than a week after Welch proved to the nation that the Pizzagate theory was nonsense, *The Economist* magazine and polling company YouGov asked 1,376 adults about the truth of the following statement:

> Leaked emails from some of Hillary Clinton's campaign staffers contained code words for pedophilia, human trafficking, and satanic ritual abuse—what some people refer to as 'Pizzagate.'

Of those asked, 38% said this was definitely (9%) or probably (29%) true. Because the adult population is well over 200 million, that means that more than 80 million Americans were sucked into this conspiracy theory in less than two months. And Alex Jones probably played the largest role in this process—except for the Russians, who hacked Clinton's emails, making them fodder for lowlifes like Jones.

Perhaps more shockingly, 24% of all Democrats and 17% of those voting for Clinton thought her staffers were probably discussing "pedophilia, human trafficking and satanic ritual abuse." This gap is far larger than was needed to throw the election to Trump. This doesn't prove Pizzagate threw the election, but it indicates the impact was likely significant.

Just in case you're wondering if you're in the minority, the answer is: Yes. Only 29% of Americans were sure that Hillary Clinton was not in any way connected with ritual satanic abuse.

From Brain Force Pills to Trump

Jones has been profiting (he sells "Brain Force" pills and "Super Male Vitality" drops on his show) from mass shootings at least since the 1999 Columbine massacre—"the event had Globalist Operations written all over it." He continued with the Aurora theater shooting ("the shooter is a patsy; he was set up, drugged") and the shooting of U.S. Representative Gabby Giffords ("a staged mind-control operation"). According to Jones, all were government plots to get Congress to take away your guns.

Given the type of audience these falsehoods must appeal to, it is no surprise that Trump endorsed these views by giving a half-hour interview to Jones in December 2015, at the end of which he concluded:

I just want to finish by saying, your reputation is amazing. I will not let you down, you will be very impressed, I hope, and I think we'll be speaking a lot.

Delusion-based Politics

Chip Berlet, who studies conspiracy culture for Political Research Associates, a Boston-based think tank, says that "Jones reaches more people over the internet than any conspiracy crank in U.S. history." Twitter, Facebook, and the internet have shifted politics in the direction of charismatic leaders. And they have accelerated the spread of conspiracy theories immensely.

These are not new phenomena, but this is the first time we have had a foreign government playing a significant role. It is also the first time we have had a president who gained political prominence by spreading a conspiracy theory—the Obama "birther" theory.

What has not changed, and what is most important to recognize, is that politics is highly influenced, if not driven, by masses of people who have been sucked into irrational beliefs—even slavery was supported by such a belief. Both sides view the other as uniquely susceptible to delusions, but the truth is they are similarly susceptible.

Twice as many Republicans as Democrats bought the Pizzagate theory. But with the more neutral conspiracy theory that "The U.S. government helped plan the attacks of 9/11," 26% of Democrats thought that was probably true, while only 21% of Republicans agreed.

And don't get your hopes up that only losers buy into these theories. Of those making over $100,000 a year, 34% bought the satanic-emails myth. Even the craziest delusions can be a major force in politics.

Conclusion

Charismatic leaders use conspiracy theories to suck people into hateful politics. Typically, such politics is designed to polarize the country.

- In less than two months, and likely in a matter of days, over a third of the country became convinced that a completely outrageous conspiracy theory could be true.
- In the 2020 election, Trump will make this look like child's play.

CHAPTER 12

The Charismatic Progressive

*More and more I am convinced that Russian Communism in
its total disregard of truth, in its fanaticism, its intolerance
and its resolute denial of God and religion is something
utterly evil.*

—Henry Wallace, 1952

After Teddy Roosevelt's Progressive Party of 1912 and Robert La Follette's Progressive run in 1924, Henry Wallace formed the third and final Progressive Party in 1948. Wallace collected only 2% of the presidential vote. But four years earlier, in 1944, according to Oliver Stone, he came within a few seconds of capturing FDR's fourth-term vice-presidential nomination. Had he not been cheated out of it, Stone tells us, he would have prevented the Cold War. So there would have been no nuclear arms race or Vietnam War.

Stone wants us to "think in a utopian fashion," and Wallace is his "proof" that this could work. Had he not been cheated at the last second by evil Democratic Party bosses, Wallace would, supposedly, have become the utopian savior we've been dreaming of. Stone is not alone in promoting utopian thinking. The best historian of radicalism, Michael Kazin, who is himself a radical, wrote *American Dreamers* to convince us that utopian thinking (dreaming) has been the main contribution of American radicals, and hence the main driver of progressive change.

Since the excitement of Obama's election, radical utopianism has experienced a resurgence, first with Occupy Wall Street, then with Bernie Sanders, Alexandria Ocasio-Cortez and her Green New Deal and finally Elizabeth Warren. This has happened periodically throughout our history, and utopian thinking is the driving force behind most radical mythology. Because Henry Wallace is such a perfect example of a utopian savior, it's worth looking at his fascinating story.

Wallace was honest and brilliant, and in the end, his honesty saved him. But he was also a mystic and a utopian dreamer. This is what made him charismatic to the radical left. It also made him vulnerable to the ultra-left Communist Party, which led him to his downfall. This is the part of his story that we'll look at here. I'll leave the part about the evil party bosses for Chapter 24, The Myth of the Utopian Savior.

Who Was Wallace?

In 1940, Franklin Roosevelt refused to seek a third term as president unless he could have Henry Wallace as his vice president, so Wallace became FDR's vice president from 1941 to 1945. He became the symbol of the "common man" philosophy of the Democratic Party after his 1942 speech, The Century of the Common Man, was distributed to millions around the world. In 1944, Eleanor Roosevelt, labor leaders and the left demanded Wallace again, but it was not to be. In spite of that loss, by 1947, he was drawing huge audiences as he toured the world. But in 1951, after the fallout from his disastrous campaign for president with the Progressive Party, he was ranked just above the "least approved man in America," the gangster Lucky Luciano.

You can thank the Communist Party USA for that ending.

To tell his story, I have relied primarily on two thoroughly documented books that are sympathetic to Wallace: *American Dreamer: A Life of Henry A. Wallace,* published in 2000 by John C. Culver and John Hyde; and *Henry Wallace's 1948 Presidential Campaign,* published in 2013 by Thomas Devine.

The Best Secretary of Agriculture

Because this chapter focuses on Wallace's tragic side, I want to remind the reader of Wallace's brilliance and honesty, and all the good he accomplished.

By the age of 15, he developed better methods of judging the quality of corn varieties, and in 1926, he founded the Hi-Bred Corn Company, which was sold to the DuPont Corporation in 1999 for about $10 billion. He was one of the fathers of the first green revolution.

As Roosevelt's first secretary of agriculture, Wallace was a brilliant and practical administrator with the ability to foresee future needs. Almost two years before the U.S. entered WWII, Wallace began stockpiling rubber because he figured it would be needed for war, and its supply would be vulnerable to Japan.

Wallace also foresaw that the New Deal's Agricultural Adjustment Act would be struck down by the Supreme Court, which occurred on January 6, 1936. Wallace, however, had put in place a team to devise a replacement bill. Fifty-five days later, Congress passed and Roosevelt signed a new agricultural act, and Wallace's part of the New Deal was back in action.

In 1942, Wallace gave his most famous speech, "Century of the Common Man," in which he talked at length of "people's revolutions." The speech was internationally distributed, and Wallace became a hero to the left throughout the Americas.

The Guru: Nicholas Roerich

Wallace's relationship with Nicholas Roerich provides insight into Wallace's eventual downfall at the hands of the Communist Party. Importantly, it also calls into question whether Wallace, had he become president, would have been any match for Stalin, as Oliver Stone claims.

Wallace's utopian inclinations led him down various mystical paths for a decade, and in 1929, he came under the spell of Nicholas Roerich, a Russian artist, guru and con man who dressed in Tibetan robes. Eight days after becoming Roosevelt's Secretary of Agriculture in 1932, Wallace wrote Roerich one of his famed "Dear Guru" letters:

I have been thinking of you holding the sacred most precious casket. And I have thought of the New Country going forth to meet the seven stars under the sign of the three stars. ... We await the Stone and we welcome you again to this glorious land ...

Roosevelt's suggestion. During his first term, Roosevelt suggested to Wallace that some plants from Central Asia could be useful in the U.S. Knowles Ryerson, a scientist in the Agriculture Department, was delighted, as the Department had been wanting to launch an expedition to the Gobi Desert for years.

Over the protests of the U.S. Agriculture Department, Wallace assigned his guru Roerich to lead an American expedition to Central Asia in June 1934. Ryerson, quite understandably, freaked out, noting that Roerich was not even a U.S. citizen. Wallace wouldn't budge.

Roerich in the Far East. Most unfortunately, Roerich, protected by a posse of eight bodyguards dressed in Cossack outfits, was soon found headed for an area of active confrontation between China and Japan. Even more unfortunately, Wallace defended Roerich and granted him additional funds.

Then he fired Ryerson! Wallace apologized to Roerich for the "insubordination" of Ryerson's team and ordered the scientific half of the expedition to return home.

Wallace wises up. It wasn't until July 1935, after U.S. diplomats in Asia began sending back frantic reports and damning stories of Roerich began to appear in the press, that Wallace ordered Roerich to end his expedition—within six months.

Wallace was never a knowing party to Roerich's scams. He was just sucked in, duped, hornswoggled and flimflammed. As we've seen before, this can happen to anyone. But utopians are unusually susceptible—precisely because they are so idealistic. Wallace simply could not comprehend that someone who seemed to be an idealist like himself might have ulterior motives.

During the period after Roosevelt's death, when Oliver Stone thinks Wallace could and should have been negotiating an end to the Cold War with Stalin, Wallace viewed Stalin as a fellow idealist—just like he viewed his guru Roerich. The consequences of taking such a view of Stalin would have been rather more catastrophic than his mistakes with Roerich. But Stone has once again duped millions of progressives into believing that Wallace, a starry-eyed utopian savior, could have saved the world by reaching a friendly agreement with the well-intentioned, Joseph Stalin.

Communists Built the Progressive Party

Although Wallace had been Roosevelt's third-term vice president, FDR replaced him for his fourth term with Harry Truman and appointed Wallace Secretary of Commerce. Not long after FDR's death, Wallace gave a major speech on foreign policy, which upset the Secretary of State, who was then negotiating with the Soviets. This led Truman to fire Wallace and eventually led to Wallace running on the Progressive Party ticket against Truman in 1948.

Progressive Citizens. The first step toward launching the Progressive Party was to form Progressive Citizens of America (PCA) in December

1946 with C. B. "Beanie" Baldwin in charge. Baldwin had been with Wallace since the 1930s, and by the mid-1940s, Baldwin had become Wallace's most trusted advisor.

Unknown to Wallace, Baldwin had taken the PCA position so he could form a third party and run Wallace against the Democrats. Lillian Traugott, Baldwin's wife, who was active in PCA, later stated, "It took a good deal, believe me, to persuade Wallace that this was the way to go. He didn't like it at first but finally came around."

Concealed Communists. Long before he "came around," however, Wallace heard that the Communist Party was organizing much of the support he was seeing. So Wallace asked Baldwin to investigate accusations of Communist infiltration of the PCA. Baldwin reported that there was nothing to these accusations. What he failed to report was that he and his wife, Lillian, were both concealed Communists (those who denied their membership in the Party to do undercover work).

John Gates, a leading Communist who defected from the Communist Party (CPUSA) in 1958, confirmed that "Beanie Baldwin worked tooth and nail to get Wallace to commit himself" and that Baldwin reported to the chief agent of the General Secretary of the CPUSA.

Numerous other concealed Communists were active in the Progressive Party, including Wallace's speechwriters. Hannah Dorner, who persuaded Wallace to delete anti-Soviet sentences from the speech that cost him his job as Truman's Secretary of Commerce, and Tabitha Petran, head of the Progressive Party's "research group" who provided the content for most of Wallace's speeches, were also concealed Communists.

Eleanor Roosevelt, who had been taken in by such methods 10 years earlier, wrote in her daily news column that "Mr. Wallace should really take a good look at those who controlled his convention, both in his own age group and among the younger ones." The parallels with Bernie Sanders, who is now, in effect, a concealed socialist (see Chapter 23), and his Democratic Socialist of America followers should not be missed.

The Communist Line. The Communists knew Wallace well and knew how to convince him. For example, when Wallace first heard of the Marshall Plan, he was favorably impressed. But Stalin was not. The word was passed down to the Communist Party USA (funded by the Soviets) and then to Wallace, who slowly changed his mind.

In testimony to the House Committee on Foreign Affairs, Wallace warned that the Marshall Plan was concocted by militarists and Wall

Street monopolists "to suppress the democratic movements in Europe." (Didn't happen.) It "would convert western Europe into a vast military camp, with freedom extinguished." (Also didn't happen.) When he finished, he was asked by a liberal Democrat how his views differed from those of the Communists. Wallace replied that he was "not familiar with the Communist approach" since he did not "follow the Communist literature." I believe him. He was, quite literally, duped by the Communists.

Unknown to Wallace, his testimony had been written by two concealed Communists, "Progressives" Victor Perlo and David Ramsey. We learned only in 1995 that Perlo had worked with the Soviet secret police (then the NKVD).

'Where I Was Wrong'

Before Truman finished his one elected term as president, on Sept. 7, 1952, in *This Week Magazine* (nationally distributed in 37 Sunday newspapers) Wallace published "*Where I Was Wrong,*" a much-advertised retraction of the foreign policy positions he had campaigned on as the Progressive candidate.

In this article, he concluded that Russia really did want the Cold War; it was not just Truman and the "Wall Street monopolists."

Russia ... certainly wants such a continuation of the Cold War as it will enable her, through her satellites and internally-planted subversives, to take over the greatest amount of territory possible. ... the question now is whether she will be able to take over all of Asia.

The first of the "circumstances which have caused me to revise my attitude," Wallace wrote, "were the shocking revelations of the activities of Russia's atomic spies." By then he would have known that Dr. Klaus Fuchs had passed both hydrogen- and atomic-bomb secrets from Los Alamos to the Soviets and that the Rosenbergs had done the same with atomic secrets. Wallace continued:

> As I look back over the past 10 years, I now feel that my greatest mistake was in not denouncing the Communist takeover of Czechoslovakia of 1948. ... At that time, I labored under the illusion that the Communists ... had the support of most of the people.

He then says his analysis "failed utterly to take into account the ruthless nature of Russian-trained Communists whose sole objective was to make Czechoslovakia completely subservient to Moscow." He continued, "Today, knowing more about Russia's methods, I am sure it was a serious mistake when we withdrew our troops [before North Korea invaded]."

This is the man who Oliver Stone thinks should have been negotiating with Stalin to end the Cold War. It took Wallace almost until what would have been the end of his presidential term to wake up to the nature of Stalin and the Communists. And Stone along with his historian, Peter Kuznick, either due to shocking ignorance or duplicity, misinformed a few million viewers by omitting Wallace's public refutation of their utopian claims. They are what the Communists refer to as "useful idiots," and for a while, so was Wallace. Finally, Wallace concluded:

> More and more I am convinced that Russian Communism in its total disregard of truth, in its fanaticism, its intolerance and its resolute denial of God and religion is something utterly evil.

Years later, at a Washington dinner party in 1962, Wallace remarked to Truman, "You were right to fire me when you did."

Conclusion

Wallace's mistakes were sometimes tragic, but he was unpretentious, always honest and always working hard for what he believed in. The top level of the Communist Party was also hard-working, but their goal was to split the Democrats, capture the left wing of the Party and weaken the moderates. In other words, they used Wallace to polarize and weaken the Democrats to their advantage.

The Progressives in the base of the Communist Party, and also those outside the Communist Party, like Wallace, were literally Communist dupes. They were sucked in. Like Wallace, they were mainly honest people. They, not conservatives, were the people hurt by the Communists of the radical left.

Wallace was hurt most. His political career was ruined. He was made to look like a fool. He lost most of his New Deal friends. His unwitting association with Communists made him the target of one of the worst red-baiting campaigns ever. He spent years back in Iowa pounding out replies on his typewriter to false accusations that he was a Communist and a traitor.

- Speaking from the heart doesn't mean you're right.
- Idealists are easily taken in by other idealists (like Wallace) and by manipulators (like the Communists).

CHAPTER 13

Trump: Charismatic Sociopath

Revolutions in democracies are generally caused by the
intemperance of demagogues.

—Aristotle, 330 B.C.

"I could stand in the middle of Fifth Avenue and shoot somebody and I wouldn't lose voters." Trump was dead-on regarding the power of his charisma. Comedian Jimmy Kimmel had no trouble finding Trump supporters that loyal. And yes, they even said that if he shot someone on Fifth Avenue, they would absolutely still vote for him. And what if he punched the Pope in the face? "I'm a Catholic. Punch away," said a loyal supporter.

Trump's charisma is powerful. We have misunderstood it and paid the price. According to Andrés Miguel Rondón, a Venezuelan who lived through the rise of Hugo Chávez, the opposition's misunderstanding of the connection between Chávez and his base was what kept him in power. Trump relies on strongman charisma, just as Chávez did. His followers see themselves as unfairly under attack and look up to him as their protector.

Mueller and Maddow

The Russian investigation provides a prime example of a backward left strategy. Night after night for two years, MSNBC and its commentators presented circumstantial evidence that Trump had secretly colluded with Russia. And maybe he had. But Robert Mueller's all-star team couldn't prove it. Now there is nothing immoral about speculating, but what MSNBC commentators did not consider was the relationship between Trump and his base, and how it would strengthen his base when the commentators were proved wrong about Mueller's conclusions.

Just hours before the first summary of the Mueller Report was released, an MSNBC commentator who was a former intelligence officer, predicted that the report could contain findings that would "technically eclipse Benedict Arnold," George Washington's trusted general who defected to the British in 1780—the most notorious traitor in American history. Holy moly, what a scoop!

Given the outcome, nothing could have better confirmed the view of Trump's base that they were under attack by an unhinged enemy who would believe anything about them and their leader. This only reinforced their perception that they needed a strongman like Trump.

In fact, Mueller's report so unhinged Rachel Maddow that she blurted out Trump's main talking point before Trump did: "He [Mueller] decided to take it upon himself to declare definitively, 'Yeah, you know, I looked at all that stuff, and I can tell you there is no crime there, it's fine.'" Mueller did no such thing. That was actually fake news.

In fact, Mueller had declared, "While this report does not conclude that the President committed a crime, it also does not exonerate him." And just for emphasis, he wrote that into the report three times. But Maddow channeled Trump rather than Mueller.

Trump's charisma depends on him and his base being in extreme danger (as in: "our country is being taken from us") and on Trump being his base's protective strongman. This calls for the opposite of MSNBC's strategy. We should look like we are not attacking him and appear to give him the benefit of the doubt. Then—and you can depend on this—it just happens to turn out that he is more duplicitous (as in Ukraine) than we "thought" (or pretended to think). This way, we look fair and responsible while he looks unhinged.

Had we been giving Trump the benefit of the doubt, at least in public, the impact of Muller's report would have been quite different. His conclusions—that Trump could well have obstructed justice, that he didn't cooperate, so we don't know if he committed a crime, and that Russians helped elect him—would have buoyed our spirits and brought discouraging realism to his base. But that never happened because our side did not understand the way Trump's charisma works. The problem is, we say what we want to hear, not what will help us split Trump from his base.

Without months of MSNBC's exaggerated predictions about the Mueller Report, the Ukraine scandal might well have had a far more significant electoral impact.

What Is Charisma?

To understand Trump's charisma, and avoid counterproductive strategies, you must first understand the concept of charisma. So far, I've discussed only charismatic leaders who ranged from problematic to horrible. But charisma *per se* is not a negative trait. It only confers power and, as always, power can be used for good or evil. FDR was highly charismatic, as are Barack and Michelle Obama.

That raises a fundamental question: How can Michelle and the Donald both be charismatic when they have almost nothing in common? Is the concept meaningless? The answer is simple; they do have something huge in common. They both form a tight emotional bond with their supporters. What's charisma to some is repugnance to others. The strength of your charisma is measured both by how many people find you appealing and how appealing they think you are.

Looking up "charisma," we find something like "a personal magic of leadership arousing special popular loyalty or enthusiasm" (*Merriam-Webster*). This misses a key part of the concept—it's not just about the leader's personal magic; the followers' tastes are just as important. Here's a definition that takes that into account:

A leader is charismatic if a large number of followers find the leader attractive in a way that creates a strong emotional attachment to their leader.

As demonstrated by the crowds at his rallies, Trump excites intense loyalty in his base. He is definitely charismatic for a very large audience.

What Makes Trump Charismatic?

Whatever appeals to his base makes Trump charismatic. In general, this is likely to be some combination of four characteristics that people look for in a leader.

- Identification with followers
- Competence
- Self-confidence
- Charm or warmth

While charm may come to mind first, this characteristic of charisma matters more for celebrities than politicians. Trump slides by without charm or warmth, but he does *appear* to have self-confidence. Does he ever! For politicians, the first three traits are most essential. But does Trump really have even those? The trick is that some leaders can and do fake all of these traits. If the followers believe their leader identifies with them, they can easily be deceived about competence and self-confidence.

At first, Trump, the arrogant billionaire, had a hard time convincing his base that he identified with them. He announced his run for office with a speech chock-full of himself but little else. That didn't work, so he shifted to talking about policy positions. Eventually, he found the lines that drew the biggest applause, such as: "I'll build a wall, and Mexico will pay for it." His followers trained him to say whatever they wanted to hear, and he was open to taking any position or attitude they wanted.

He also promised to be their champion—their strongman—and they longed for that. His vulgarity helped prove he was one of them, and not part of the establishment, despite his enormous wealth. And besides, he really does despise the establishment, which shuns him for his crudeness.

As for competence, he argued that a billionaire businessman must be competent: "Nobody knows the system better than me. Which is why I alone can fix it." Again, this works mainly on those who want to believe.

A Charismatic Sociopath?

Sociopaths actually find it easier to be charismatic than "normies," as they call the rest of us. If that sounds unbelievable, just Google the words "sociopath charisma" (without quotes). Without a conscience, sociopaths are great at being insincere and telling people whatever they want to hear. Manipulating people to get their way is what they live for.

There's been some debate over whether Trump is a narcissist or a sociopath. Well, of course he's narcissistic. He vastly overrates himself and sees others as unimportant. But he's also a sociopath; those two character traits are quite complementary. What confuses the left, and sucks in the right, is not his obvious narcissism but his sociopathic behavior, so that's what I'll focus on.

It's often said that Trump is crazy or mentally ill. That's what Trump wants the left to believe—that he's incompetent, a bit crazy and easy to defeat. But he's crazy like a fox, which makes him more dangerous, not less. I'd be the first to tell you that conscience may be the most important human trait. But if all you care about it is "winning"—if you're Donald Trump—you're better off without one. And that's basically the definition of a sociopath.

It's fascinating to read what sociopaths say about themselves on the web. As they explain, it's hard for them to understand typical humans. Our emotions cause us to do a lot of weird things, and we share an unspoken language of facial expressions and body language that reflect these emotions. What for us is instinctual is a mystery for them. However, high-functioning sociopaths can and do learn how to mimic our expressions and emotions. They call this learning to make masks. Google "sociopath mask" (without quotes) and you will get a million page hits.

If you watch him, Trump is downright awful at faking emotions. His charisma depends on his use of a few emotional masks—anger, disdain, and admiration. The first two are often faked, and the third always is.

Understanding sociopaths should be simple, but for us "normies" it's actually extremely difficult. Their way of thinking just doesn't seem possible to us. Because it's so difficult but so important to understand Trump, I'm going to spend a bit of time explaining what I've learned, some of it the hard way.

How a Sociopath Thinks

Perhaps the best way to understand sociopathic thinking is to imagine playing a game—anything from poker to football to Monopoly. Games have strict rules, but they let us leave our conscience behind. If you're playing poker, lying (bluffing) is not only okay, it's expected. You would be considered a fool if you told the truth. In football, teams do their best to mislead the other team with sneaky plays. In Monopoly, we attempt to drive our opponents into bankruptcy by any means necessary. And we feel absolutely fine about all of that. That's one reason we love to play games—they free us from the burden of our conscience.

A sociopath sees life as a game. End of story. Without a conscience, they just play to win, any way they can. And they feel absolutely fine about it—no matter what it takes. It's fine to lie and it's fine to break the law. Just don't get caught. If you can get away with it, you're stupid not to.

About 1%, or three million Americans, really do think like this most of the time. I've seen three cases of this up close. Two had good careers and led useful lives while causing a lot of unnecessary hurt. The third chose an extremely different strategy and ended up with a 15-year-minimum prison sentence, although he had appeared normal enough to a friend of mine that she rented her basement apartment to him.

That demonstrates a key point. Just like normies (us), sociopaths choose many different careers, from caregivers to criminals to political leaders, so they can be very hard to spot. But one of the easiest clues to spot is this: Do they lie and not seem to care at all when they get caught as long as they suffer no consequences? Trump passes that test every day.

Trump Tries to Destroy the West?

The media still doesn't get it—that Trump really is a sociopath. To prove to myself once again that they don't, I googled "Trump" on *The New York Times* website. I didn't want to fight a straw man, so I picked our most sophisticated source of journalism. I scanned down Google's list until I found an op-ed discussing what Trump was up to. It happened to be by David Leonhardt, one of my favorite columnists and an associate editor. Sure enough, there was the mistake I'm talking about. So I'm not cherry-picking. This misunderstanding of Trump really is ubiquitous, although more people seem to be catching on.

Four sentences into the op-ed, I found: "President Trump is trying to destroy that alliance [with Western Europe]. Is that how he thinks about it? Who knows? It's impossible to get inside his head and divine his strategic goals, if he even has long-term goals." So Leonhardt asked himself exactly the right question—what is Trump thinking?—but finds he has no answer. Trump has been telling us his whole life that he has only one strategic goal, the same as any sociopath: to win and win as big as possible. Western Europe? What the hell has that got to do with it?

Trump's strategic goal is to win reelection by the largest possible margin, then to go down in history as America's greatest president. That's precisely what's in his head. That's his long-term goal—yes, Leonhardt, he has a long-term goal! Every sensible analysis of Trump's political tactics must start from this point—but few do.

"He is threatening the Atlantic alliance over a lie [about Canadian tariffs]." Leonhardt was referring to evidence that Trump is pursuing a long-term goal to "destroy the West." Finally, he guesses, "Maybe it's ideological ..." Trump, ideological? Get serious! He has taken every side of every issue at one time or another. He takes whatever position seems to him at that moment to best serve his goal of winning big.

But Leonhardt misses that point. He writes nothing about Trump's focus on his own personal victory in 2020. Nonetheless, Leonhardt's op-ed is brilliant. It alerts us to the dire consequences of the path Trump is on now. But because Leonhardt and others keep forgetting what Trump is after, they are not thinking very clearly about what might change his mind—and sometimes that really matters. Instead, they suggest useless logical arguments against his position; that assumes he's thinking about U.S. policy. European trade ministers brought binders of data to the G7 trade negotiations to convince Trump not to start a trade war.

Idiots. What were they thinking?!

Trump the sociopath is taking his positions on trade because he thinks it plays well with his base and helps his chance to win big. But he'd happily change positions if he thought it would help him even more bigly in 2020.

Conclusion

The only thing that will stop Trump from doing something horrible is to convince him it will hurt his chances of winning in 2020. This puts our focus back on his base and especially on swing voters, right where it should be. We should speak to them. That is how to win some of them over, and also how push Trump towards less dangerous positions.

Attacking Trump personally is mostly counterproductive. Such attacks just make his base more defensive and energized. Always remember, he's clever and focused on his goal.

PART 3

Populism Traps

These are populist times, but make no mistake, populism is a danger to a liberal democracy—a representative democracy with checks and balances. In fact, we have our checks and balances because the founding fathers saw populist demagogues as the greatest danger.

Populism, the "ism" of the people, is a partial worldview that can be grafted onto many other perspectives. So there are left-wing populisms and right-wing populisms. What they have in common is the view that "the people" are virtuous and the "elite" are corrupt. Consequently, "the will of the people should prevail."

Of course, there is no single "will of the people," so this can mean direct (not representative) democracy with one-person/one-vote. Or it can mean that a populist leader, claiming to represent the people, decides. Either way, minorities are not well protected. For example, a populist movement passed California Proposition 14 in a 65-percent landslide to amend the state constitution and deliberately reinstate housing discrimination in 1964.

In an undemocratic society, populism is likely to be a step in the right direction. But in a liberal democracy such as ours, it will damage democracy and will likely reduce minority rights and lead to authoritarian leadership. Surprisingly, this is generally true of left-wing populists as well as right-wing populists. Often, populist leaders are not actually populists but just play the part to gain authoritarian powers.

Synopsis of Part 3

Chapter 14. What is Populism and Why Should We Care? Populism is a polarized "us versus them" worldview. It pits the "virtuous" people against the "corrupt" elite. It can be left-wing or right-wing, but neither offers the protections of pluralism.

Chapter 15. Trump: A Fake Jacksonian Populist. Trump is no Andrew Jackson, but he found that if he mimics Jackson's populism, he can appeal to America's populist Jacksonians, long a powerful force.

Chapter 16. 'Our Revolution' Meets the Jacksonians. Failing to understand populism, Robert Reich and pro-Sanders PACs imagine a political revolution that will join Tea Partiers with progressives.

Chapter 17. Economics vs. the Culture War. Trumpish populism is not mainly caused by poor economic conditions. Rather, it's motivated by the culture wars.

Chapter 18. Sanders' Populist Strategy. Sanders is at least playing the role of a populist leader. His immediate goal is to take over the Democratic Party.

Chapter 19. Good Populism: The Kingfish. Huey Long was a populist in a one-party democracy. He was no purist but rather a crafty dealmaker who didn't care where his money came from. He got stuff done.

Chapter 20. Utopian Populism. When it comes to plans for reducing inequality, Huey Long outdid Sanders and Warren 85 years ago. But popular as he was, he could not have pulled it off.

Chapter 21. Don't Be the Enemy They Need. Trump needs enemies on the left. They prove to his base of supporters that they are in danger and give them all the more reason to protect their strongman.

CHAPTER 14

What is Populism and Why Should We Care?

In Republics, the great danger is that the majority may not sufficiently respect the rights of the Minority.

—James Madison, December 1829
Father of our Constitution and Bill of Rights

Unlike in the Johnny Cash song, Norman Williams never "shot a man in Reno just to watch him die." But in 1982, Williams did burglarize a California apartment being fumigated. On the way out he himself was robbed at gunpoint. Even though he helped the police recover the stolen property, his burglary was strike one. A decade later, he stole some hand tools from an art studio, but when confronted by the homeowner, he dropped them and took off running. Strike two.

Then in 1997, he stole a floor jack from a tow truck. Strike three. Twelve years later, he was still literally "stuck in Folsom Prison" serving a life sentence under the harshest three-strikes law in the country. This *populist* three-strikes initiative had been passed by an overwhelming 72% of California's voters.

Populism vs. the Founding Fathers

There was a time when citizens could not pass laws directly. That was before the Populist Party, organized in 1892, adopted the first party platform favoring state initiatives. But now most states allow initiatives— that's direct democracy or what the Founding Fathers called "pure democracy." The populist "will of the people" makes the rules.

Our Founding Fathers studied democratic institutions, starting with Greece, and decisively rejected this approach precisely because they knew it would lead to injustices like California's three-strikes law. They did not mince words:

It has been observed that a pure democracy if it were practicable would be the most perfect government. Experience has proved that no position is more false than this. **The ancient democracies in which the people themselves deliberated never possessed one good feature of government.** Their very character was tyranny.

—Alexander Hamilton

James Madison, known as the father of the Constitution and the Bill of Rights, analyzed the situation at length before concluding:

In all cases where a majority are united by a common interest or passion, the rights of the minority are in danger.

Instead of imitating an ancient populist style of democracy, Madison advocated "a republic, by which I mean a government in which the scheme of representation takes place." When it comes to passing laws, this is in direct opposition to the populist principle of one person, one vote. Only representatives can vote. (Of course, it is not in opposition to one person, one vote for electing representatives.) Madison also advocated the system of "checks and balances" between branches of government, which he viewed as a curb on the tyranny of populist majorities.

Norman Williams was saved by one of those anti-populist checks and balances when he was freed by a judge in April 2009, thanks to the efforts of Steve Cooley, a Republican district attorney from Los Angeles, and Michael Romano, founder of the Three Strikes and Justice Advocacy Project at Stanford Law School.

Populist Discrimination

Following the 1963 Rumford Fair Housing Act, which banned the racial discrimination in housing that kept Blacks in ghettos, the California Real Estate Association (CREA) immediately launched a populist repeal campaign. In November 1964, Californians voted two to one for an initiative (Proposition 14) that overturned the Fair Housing Act.

It wasn't long before the California Supreme Court ruled Proposition 14 unconstitutional, and the U.S. Supreme Court agreed. That's what checks and balances are for—reigning in populism.

Besides protecting racial minorities, checks and balances also protect political minorities. For example, in 2018, the Pennsylvania Supreme Court redrew Pennsylvania's highly gerrymandered Congressional Districts that had strongly favored Republicans.

But the danger of populism is greater than it would seem from these examples. Its greatest danger is discussed by Alexander Hamilton in the first of the 85 Federalist Papers (October 1787):

> Of those men who have overturned the liberties of republics, the greatest number have begun their career by paying an obsequious court to the people; commencing demagogues, and ending tyrants.

By December 2019, it had become clear that Trump is attempting the type of populist takeover that the Founding Fathers most feared. The greatest danger is from charismatic demagogues who court "the people." This populist process is now threatening and compromising many democracies around the world. Although Hamilton's observation gets to the heart of the problem, in practice, the variety of charismatic leaders can be confusing. Modern political science provides some clarity

How Can Populisms Look So Different?

Can Bernie Sanders and Donald Trump both be populists? One is a socialist, and the other, a capitalist of the first order.

It's kind of like asking how a golf cart and a Tesla Model S can both be electric vehicles. They don't have much in common, just an electric motor and wheels. It's the same with populism. Populism is the "ism" of the people. So all populisms prioritize "the will of the people." But that's not all they have in common.

To see their commonalities, contrast populism with "liberal democracy"—one that protects the rights of minorities with representative government and checks and balances. Populism sees no need for such complexities because it imagines there is a single "will of the people" that should prevail. In other words, those who disagree with "the people" are simply wrong and don't need the protections of checks and balances.

The result of this view is that, around the world, wherever populism is gaining strength, it is eating away at the protections provided by liberal democracies. Of course, we are seeing that right here at home, but it is worth noting how widespread this backsliding has become. So let's take a quick look at the global populist wave that recently crashed on America's shores.

The International Populist Wave

Populists took control in Italy in 1994; Venezuela in 1999; Turkey in 2003; Bolivia in 2006; Hungary in 2010; India in 2014; Greece and Poland in 2015; the United States in 2017; Italy (again) in 2018; and Brazil and England in 2019. There is no shortage of other populist parties on the move in Europe, so it appears that the populist wave does have real momentum.

The strange thing about this wave is the chaotic diversity of its leaders. In chronological order from 1994 to 2019, they are: a billionaire capitalist; a military socialist; an Islamist; a indigenous South-American socialist; an authoritarian nationalist; a Hindu supremacist; a radical leftist; a devout Catholic nationalist; a billionaire capitalist; a duo consisting of a left comedian and a right-wing nationalist; an authoritarian social conservative; and an Oxford-educated journalist. Despite the differences among these leaders, they all have something in common. That something is populism.

The Simplest Populism

Most societies have ended up with a few people being rich and powerful and the rest having little power or income. It's not surprising then to find regular folks thinking the elite are corrupt, unfair, or in some way morally defective—especially because that view generally has quite a bit of truth to it.

Given these observations, the *simplest imaginable* view of the current unfair state of society from the perspective of ordinary people is:

1. Society has two parts: the virtuous people (Us) and the corrupt elite (Them).
2. The people want what's right, and the "will of the people" should prevail.

That view is populism—in theory. But in the real world, what we call populism is always this view (call it basic populism) plus something more. This solves our original puzzle—how can Trump and Sanders both be populists? Sanders' populism is roughly basic populism plus "socialism," while Trump's populism is akin to basic populism plus White nationalism.

I owe this definition of basic populism to Cas Mudde, a Dutch political scientist and a professor at the University of Georgia. He calls it "the thin ideology of populism," but his concept is the same as what I call "basic populism." The point is that by combining basic populism with various other "isms," ideologies or worldviews—call them what you like—populist leaders can invent very different real-world forms of populism. And that is exactly what happens.

There can be socialist populism, progressive populism, racist populism, Muslim populism, green populism, libertarian populism and so on *ad nauseam*. The reason Mudde calls populism a thin ideology is because there's not much to it. About all that populisms are guaranteed to have in common is a belief in Us as virtuous, Them as corrupt and that the will of the people should prevail. But these beliefs have important consequences.

Exclusionary Populism

As you may have already guessed, different types of populism define "the people" differently. Not understanding this is a major reason that left populists, who have a broad view of "the people," get confused about Trump's base.

Trump's base excludes minorities and progressives from "the people," and Trump signals that by calling his base "the real people." Bernie Sanders includes everyone but the 1-percent richest and "establishment" politicians and calls this version of "the people" either "the 99%" or "the American people." When political scientists want to talk about populism, they often talk about "the virtuous people," but don't take this too literally.

Unfortunately, the above definition of "basic populism" doesn't cover Trump's populism or most other right-wing populisms because it omits the possibility of excluded groups, such as immigrants. Such groups are neither part of "the people" nor part of "the elite." So Trump's type of populism—exclusionary populism—divides society into three groups, not two. The definition is easily fixed as follows:

New definition: Basic populism holds the following views:

1. Society has two or three parts, the virtuous people (Us), the corrupt elite (Them) and possibly an out-group (also Them).
2. The people want what's right, and the "will of the people" should prevail.

Typically, in exclusionary (right-wing) populism, the people see the elite as being in cahoots with the out-group. For example, Trump's populist movement sees the urban progressive elite as in cahoots with immigrants and Blacks—so they all are part of Them.

Frame taken the instant Trump became President
WhiteHouse.gov

Pluralism Isn't Populism

These days, every politician claims to be on the side of "the people." Does that mean that every political ideology is some kind of populism? That would make the concept useless. But no, we have had only two truly populist presidents: Trump and Andrew Jackson. So there must be alternatives to populism. What are they?

Robber barons—members of the elite by any definition—are not often populists. They don't tend to think the common people are virtuous or that they themselves are corrupt. Most likely they would think almost the opposite. So they tend to be elitists. **Elitism** is the most obvious alternative to populism.

Another non-populist worldview is more subtle. We may believe the elite are corrupt and the common people are virtuous, but we might not believe there is any such thing as "the will of the people." Then we're not populists. If instead, we believe that "the people" are composed of different groups with different views on what is right and just, then we likely believe that a central purpose of democracy is to find the best compromise among these groups. This is **pluralism**, not populism. And that is, of course, why we have a Republic with checks and balances.

If you look at the hodgepodge of identity groups recognized by the Democratic Party, it's hard to believe there is a single "will of the people." The Democrats and Republicans are, by nature, both pluralist parties.

This is a problem for populist leaders. But differences can be papered over by whipping up hatred of some outside group—bankers, billionaires, Muslims, Blacks or Mexicans—which is what populist leaders do. Still, pluralism is the most realistic view of the world. And it's the safest because it rejects the polarizing Us-Them perspective.

Conclusion

Pluralism is the sensible alternative to populism. That is exactly the view that the Founding Fathers designed our Constitution to encourage and support. That design is now called liberal democracy because it protects a diversity of ideas and interests against the tyranny of some majority.

They knew their design was not perfect and, in fact, there were important things that many of them wanted changed even before the Constitution was ratified. One of these was an end to slavery. But they knew they could not get everything they wanted and that new problems would arise. So they built in flexibility.

The Constitution has since evolved towards a more populist structure, for example much broader voting rights and the direct election of senators. These changes have been for the better. But it would be a serious mistake to ignore the Founding Fathers' warnings about the dangers of what we now call populism.

- Populism is an "Us versus Them" worldview.
- There is no "will of the people."
- America was designed to prevent populism. We have "a republic, if we can keep it," according to Ben Franklin.

Chapter 15

Trump: A Fake Jacksonian Populist

Fear not, the people may be deluded for a moment but cannot be corrupted.

—*Andrew* Jackson

"They were immigrants seeking sanctuary from a devastated homeland, refugees who generally arrived without the encouragement or direction of officials, and often against their wishes." That's not a bad description of the immigrants crossing our southern border.

"They delight in their present low, lazy, sluttish, heathenish, hellish life." That sounds a bit familiar—but way too articulate to be Trump. Rather, both of these quotes are the words of a minister from the Deep South concerning immigrants in 1768, several years before the Revolutionary War.

Just who were these immigrants? They were none other than the Scots-Irish ancestors of Trump's Jacksonian base. Understanding this and the Jacksonian folk culture is essential to understanding his base. And that understanding is the key to seeing them as human and reducing polarization. Both quotes are from Colin Woodard's eye-opening book, *American Nations*.

There is more truth than you might think to what the Southern minister said. Walter Russell Mead, a historian of what he calls the Jacksonian "folk-ideology," describes the Scots-Irish as having

> ... a culture and outlook formed by centuries of bitter warfare before they came to the United States ... The Revolutionary [War] struggle and generations of savage frontier conflict in the United States reproduced these conditions; the Civil War ... renewed the cultural heritage of war."

Before the Revolutionary War, many Scots-Irish were organized as clans, which were famous for engaging in blood feuds (think Hatfields and McCoys). Many who were not in clans essentially "went Native," abandoning farming and husbandry for hunting and fishing, and wearing furs like the Native Americans.

But that was 250 years ago! How could this history be relevant today? Well, that's why Woodard wrote his book. Let me mention a little evidence that cultures and cultural attitudes persist. The country music you hear today derives from those Scots-Irish immigrants, as does the Bible Belt with its Trump-voting evangelicals. Notice that the Bible Belt is neither Catholic nor Episcopalian. Why? Because the Scots-Irish fought the British Catholics and Anglicans for hundreds of years. Cultures, politics, and religions mutate rather slowly.

Cultural durability also accounts for the endurance of prejudice in Germany. Nico Voigtländer and Hans-Joachim Voth noted that attacks on Jews in the 1920s were six times more likely to occur in towns and cities where Black Death-era [anti-Jewish] pogroms had also occurred. This effect could still be detected after 600 years.

Jacksonian Doesn't Mean Deep South

The Jacksonian tradition comes from the Scots-Irish, who left the lowlands of Scotland for Northern Ireland in about 1600. Life was as rough in Ireland as it had been in Scotland, so in the 1700s, before the American Revolution, about a quarter-million Scots-Irish headed to Pennsylvania, and then down the backbone of the Appalachians.

They were Scottish Presbyterians—not the Irish Catholics who arrived much later. Neither were they related to the Deep South's slave society, which in fact was English by way of Barbados—the center of the African slave trade. In *American Nations,* Woodard describes the "Deep South nation" as

> ... a near-carbon copy of the West Indian slave state these Barbadians had left behind, a place notorious even then for its inhumanity [but] enormously profitable to those who controlled it ... [Its] culture was based [on] ... a tiny elite commanding total obedience and enforcing it with state-sponsored terror.

The Scots-Irish, in contrast, were as near as you'll find to anarchists, and at a crucial juncture, they allied with the Yankees to tip the balance toward democracy as our nation was forming. They were fighters. Jim Webb, a Democratic Virginia Senator, called his 2004 book about his Scots-Irish heritage *Born Fighting.* So, as George Washington was camped out for that terrible winter at Valley Forge, it should not surprise us to find that half his men were Yankees and the other half were Scots-Irish—or as some now disdainfully call them: hillbillies, rednecks or White trash.

Both Appalachian and Deep South cultures were violent, but the slaving culture was self-consciously aristocratic while the Jacksonians were self-consciously anti-elitist. The bottom line here is that it is completely unfair to tar the Jacksonians as part of the Southern slave culture even though some, like Andrew Jackson, did own slaves.

Is Trump a Jacksonian?

Trump is not a Jacksonian populist. He just *plays* one on TV—and in the White House. As terrible as he is at impersonating Jackson, he's fooled many. Many of those who hate Trump now trash Jackson, thinking that will discredit Trump. It does not. It simply reinforces the view of Trump's base that Trump is like Jackson, who they love as a courageous war hero and an authentic (albeit right-wing) populist.

Despite superficially similar personal characteristics, the differences between their psychologies are enormous. A sociopathic president only champions his country to further his own interests, while an ultra-patriot like Jackson would give his life for his country.

Don't get me wrong. I'm not ignoring Jackson's fiery temper or excusing his misdeeds. But Jackson joined the American Revolution when he was 13, while Trump relied on fake medical reports arranged by his father to gain five draft deferments. Jackson's father died before he was born; his two brothers and mother died serving in the Revolutionary War when he was 14. Thirty years later, Jackson got his revenge in the Battle of New Orleans. There, while commanding a force of irregulars, he defeated the British, who attacked him with twice as many well-trained troops. "Defeated" is a bit of an understatement. The British suffered more than 20 times the number of casualties as the Americans.

Jackson's parents emigrated from Northern Ireland but were of Scottish origin. They were Scots-Irish and part of a culture of honor. Unlike Jackson, Trump subscribes to no honor code—he would never feel bound to make any sacrifice for his beliefs, his clan or his nation.

Honor cultures are generally violent, but those who subscribe to them consider themselves honorable, and their sense of duty to their family, clan or nation requires a strong conscience—not the absence of one.

Trump Is a Leader of Jacksonians

As we saw in Part 2, charismatic leaders are often not who their follow-ers think they are. College dropout Elizabeth Holmes conned secretaries of state and fancy investment bankers. Greg Mortenson conned four-star generals and a president. Jim Jones conned Democrats all the way up to Rosalynn Carter, who could not have been more different from Jones.

So it's not surprising to find that Trump has conned his Jacksonian base. It doesn't mean they're bad or stupid. What's surprising is that there is still a large and important Jacksonian base for Trump to lead.

Mead claims that "Jacksonian culture, values and self-identification have spread beyond their original ethnic limits" and that "Northern im-migrants gradually assimilated the values of Jacksonian individualism. Each generation of new Americans was less 'social' and more individu-alistic than the preceding one."

Although the Scots-Irish are the source of Jacksonian populism, it now has a life of its own, to put it mildly. Jacksonian folk-ideology has spread widely. And although Trump is not a Jacksonian himself, he can still be an effective Jacksonian leader by faking it. That makes Trump's leadership not only powerful but also extremely dangerous.

Left- vs. Right-Wing Populism

But is the Jacksonian folk-ideology populist? Trump is "not a populist," says the left-wing *New Republic*. "Not in the original sense," adds *In These Times*. "Not a real populist," explains CNN.

There's a reason Democrats are blind to Jacksonian populism. The first party to call itself populist, but officially known as "The People's Party," was formed in 1892, and it was left-wing. As a result, the radical left, which likes populism, also likes to believe all forms of populism must be left-wing. But as I explained in the previous chapter, political scientists define populism more broadly, and Andrew Jackson fits their definition. He was anti-aristocratic and saw "the people" as good and the elite as corrupt. His campaign slogan was "Let the people rule." But in reality, his populism was right-wing exclusionary populism, the kind of populism that has out-groups (in this case, Native Americans and Blacks) who are neither part of the real people nor part of the elite.

We are now up against a powerful right-wing populism with deep roots in American history and a powerful charismatic leader. So far, Democrats have very little understanding of this phenomenon, and understanding our opponent is crucial. As Sun Tzu, the oft-quoted author of *The Art of War*, pointed out 2,500 years ago, understanding your opponent is essential for achieving victory and avoiding defeat.

How Did Trump Come to Be a Populist Leader?

When Trump threw his hat in the ring in June 2015, he mentioned himself more than 200 times in his announcement speech and referred to "the people" just once. But in his Inaugural address, he referred to himself only four times and had become the perfect (fake) populist.

In that speech, he often spoke of "the people," saying, "We are transferring power from Washington, D.C., and giving it back to you, the people" ... "the people have borne the cost" ... "the people did not share in its wealth" ... "controlled by the people" ... and finally saying that his inauguration was "the day the people became the rulers." That speech was written by Stephen Miller, his chief policy adviser, and strategist Steve Bannon, who astutely modeled Trump's address on the populism of Andrew Jackson. By the way, it's no accident that Jackson's portrait now hangs in the Oval Office.

Trump once explained that, at first, he talked about himself, but that bored his audience. Later he shifted to discussing policies, with no better luck. Finally, he started speaking as a populist and connected.

He tells his followers that the elite are corrupt, but that they, the "real people," are great—and they believe him. They believe him because they want to. They trust him because he does not act like the elite but like one of them when he crassly tweets insults at private citizens, praises the likes of Alex Jones, and stoops to name-calling with Kim Jong-un.

He's not bad at playing the role, but many of his actions, especially on healthcare and taxes, contradict his populist claims. Exposing these kinds of discrepancies would weaken him. We need to keep that in mind.

Jacksonian Populism Matches Trumpismo

Andrew Jackson was running for President as a populist, and the Whigs (who later morphed into Republicans) found this so hilarious that they called him Jackass Jackson. So Jackson put a donkey on his campaign poster to remind the millions of White men without property (who had just been given the right to vote) what the Whigs thought of them. He won in a minor landslide, and the donkey became the symbol of Jackson's new Democratic Party.

The Democratic Party remained based in the South of the former Confederate States and the Appalachia of the Scots-Irish for decades. But much of the Jacksonian element turned Republican under Nixon. With Trump's election, they now form his base.

But does Trump really reflect Jacksonian folk ideology, or is Trumpismo just some reality show that Trump has cooked up? Is it just random demagoguery? To find out, let's look at his talking points.

1. Build a wall to keep out Mexicans and ban Muslim immigrants.
2. Support the Second Amendment and gun rights.
3. Attack the elite—the two establishment political parties and Wall Street.
4. Attack trade deals that help foreigners (e.g., Mexico and China) and hurt Americans.
5. Attack "politically correct" rhetoric in favor of offensive discourse.

How can we tell whether this list really represents Jacksonian populism and not just some ad-hoc Trumpismo? To make a fair determination, I reviewed a description of Jacksonian thought written before Trump was in the race. If Trump's talking points line up with that, then he is indeed mimicking his Jacksonian base rather than his base just accepting his demagoguery.

In an article he wrote in 1999 during the George W. Bush administration, historian Mead cites the following as key characteristics of Jacksonian ideology:

1. "[The] Jacksonian community ... automatically and absolutely excluded: Indians, Mexicans, Asians, African Americans, obvious sexual deviants and recent immigrants of non-Protestant heritage."
2. "Jacksonians see the Second Amendment, the right to bear arms, as the citadel of liberty."
3. "Jacksonians are profoundly suspicious of elites."
4. "[Jacksonians worry that] the politicians turned the government against the people. [Are they] ... giving all our industrial markets to the Japanese?"
5. "The Jacksonian hero dares to say what the people feel and defies the entrenched elites."

Compare those two lists point by point. The alignment between Trump's talking points and Mead's description of Jacksonians seems nearly perfect if you just substitute Muslims for "recent immigrants of non-Protestant heritage" and the Chinese for "the Japanese." So Trump learned his talking points from a genuinely Jacksonian source—his base.

Mead's 1999 article also noted that "historically, the law has been helpless to protect" the excluded groups from discrimination and "mob violence, including widespread lynchings." He also observed that twentieth-century Jacksonians are "skeptical about ... welfare at home, foreign aid abroad" and are most upset by "stories about welfare abusers in limousines." Their "profoundly populist worldview" contributes to their view that "while problems are complicated, solutions are simple." The Jacksonian tradition is strongest among ordinary people, is more "entrenched in the heartland" than on the coasts, and has been "associated with White Protestant males of the lower and middle class."

In a 1999 remark that proved prescient, Mead wrote, "Jacksonian America has produced—and looks set to continue to produce—one movement after another." And so it has.

Conclusion

- Right-wing populism has at least as deep a tradition in America as left-wing populism.
- Trump's power comes from his ability to appeal to the populist Jacksonian folk-ideology.
- His talking points are mere imitations of Jacksonian beliefs that he uses to connect with his base of true believers.

CHAPTER 16

'Our Revolution' Meets the Jacksonians

The People's Party [won] the U.S. presidency and a
majority of both houses of Congress in 2020.
—Robert Reich, March 25, 2016

There's a theory going around that Tea Partiers are Berniecrats—they just don't know it yet. Seriously. Sanders doesn't say that; he leaves it to his surrogates, like his PACs and Professor Robert Reich. But the idea comes from Sanders' socialist background.

Socialism assumes the working class is unified by an economic ideology but that workers sometimes get confused by establishment propaganda. So the Berniecrat "Brand New Congress" PAC, set up by one of his presidential campaign staffers in 2016, set out to run 400 Congressional campaigns in 2018. The idea was to elect a majority of Democrats *and* Republicans who would pledge allegiance to Sanders' agenda and carry out his "revolution."

If this theory is right, we should help his two PACs, "Justice Democrats" and "Brand New Congress," and his super PAC, "Our Revolution," take over the Democratic Party. If it's not true, attacking all the "establishment" Democrats from inside the Party could be a disaster.

Well, this theory has been tested, and the results are in. The message for the 2020 election is absolutely clear—and shocking. So we will first take a brief look at this revolutionary plan and then examine the outcome of the 2018 midterms. Finally, we'll look into the misunderstanding of Trump's base, which is even more dangerous than these revolutionary fantasies.

Robert Reich Explains Bernie's Revolution

"Millions who called themselves conservatives and Tea Partiers joined with millions who called themselves liberals and progressives." Yes, in a fantastical March 2016 op-ed, Professor Robert Reich predicted that he would someday look back on Bernie Sanders' Revolution which happened when the Tea Party went socialist. He continued, "The People's Party [won] the U.S. presidency and a majority of both houses of Congress in 2020."

Reich was contending there was still time to rip out the base of both major parties and join them at the hip to form the "People's Party" for a socialist/populist takeover in 2020. Bernie would be president. There would be peace and prosperity in the Promised Land. Reich, who served under Presidents Ford and Carter, and as Bill Clinton's Secretary of Labor, is Sanders' most distinguished interpreter.

It seems he's been beguiled by both the promise of the revolution, which he's waited a lifetime for, and confused by a misunderstanding of Trump's base.

Brand New Congress. A month after Reich's 2016 op-ed, 20 volunteers from Bernie Sanders' campaign, led by top campaign staffer Zack Exley, formed "Brand New Congress." As the *Huffington Post* explained at the time, they were "looking ahead to the 2018 midterm elections to replace Congress all at once" with lawmakers who agree with Sanders.

As Exley explained, "We want a supermajority in Congress ... and I think we get it by running Dems in blue areas, Republicans in deep-red areas, and by running independents wherever we didn't defeat incumbents." The first step would be to recruit 400 Congressional candidates by July 2017.

Just after finally endorsing Hillary Clinton in July 2016, Sanders announced his plan to form his super PAC, "Our Revolution." In early August, he began raising money for it and on August 24 he held a launch party.

In January 2017, Exley joined Saikat Chakrabarti, another top staffer from Sanders' campaign, to form "Justice Democrats." They recruited Alexandria Ocasio-Cortez, and two years later she was in Congress with Chakrabarti as her chief of staff.

Sanders' PACs Tackle the 2018 Midterms

In November 2016, the Democrats lost the presidency and both houses of Congress, and in 2018, the House was their only real chance to retake some power. There were 82 "battleground" House races (as identified by Ballotpedia) that could flip a seat from red to blue or blue to red, and fortunately 73 of these started out Republican.

As we now know, a blue wave flipped 43 seats from red to blue while we lost only three blue seats. Democratic turnout was massive.

Sanders' three PACs were, of course, busy "helping out." They fielded many candidates and eventually, between the three of them, made 117 endorsements. Only 38 of these were for battleground seats. Surprisingly, the three PACs agreed on only two of these candidates. (Radical factionalism is legendary.)

So how many of their endorsed candidates were part of the 43 who flipped blue seats to red and gave us back the House? The shocking answer is none, as in zero. So much for taking a supermajority of Congress all at once. Bernie's minions could not take back even a single seat from the Republicans.

And did they back any of the six Democrats who held onto their battleground seats? No. But they did back 10 Democrats who won. Who were they? The main thing to know is that every winning candidate they could find to endorse, whether their own candidate or an incumbent, was in a district where Clinton beat Trump by at least 30% (as in 65% to 35%). Apparently, with their politics, it's unlikely a candidate can win if the district isn't deep blue.

The most they could hope for, had they stopped their infighting, would have been to flip 40% of the Democratic seats from very progressive to Berniecrat progressive. That would just polarize the party and make it harder to get anything done.

Taking a look at the 10 winners they backed, we find that five were incumbents from deep-blue states that didn't need their help. Another was Jesus Garcia, who scored 44% against Rahm Emanuel when he ran for Chicago Mayor in 2015. He didn't need their help either.

The Big Win—Alexandria Ocasio-Cortez

The Bernie PACs' final four victories are known as "the Squad," so-called because they began posting "Squad pics" after the November election. They are Congresswomen Alexandria Ocasio-Cortez, Rashida Tlaib, Ilhan Omar, and Ayanna Pressley.

Ayanna Pressley primaried (to use a Tea-Party term that's been picked up by some Berniecrats) Mike Capuano, a 10-term incumbent, and a member of the Congressional Progressive Caucus who supports Medicare-for-all. Pressley won 59 to 41%. She didn't need the Bernie PACs. Nothing wrong with this, but nothing much accomplished.

Alexandria Ocasio-Cortez (AOC) primaried Joseph Crowley, a 10-term incumbent backed by the very-progressive Working Families Party. She won her primary by 4,018 votes with 7.2% of registered Democrats voting for her while Crowley got only 5.5%.

Her largest margins of support came from neighborhoods in western Queens with lower Latino populations and higher White populations. She did poorly in the Black neighborhoods.

Chakrabarti, president of Justice Democrats, recruited AOC early and put together a coalition made up largely of people who had organized for Bernie Sanders' presidential campaign. They were joined by "Brand New Congress" and "Democratic Socialists of America," but not by Sanders or his own super PAC, "Our Revolution." Of course, it helped that Ocasio-Cortez performed her part brilliantly.

Ilhan Omar won her primary with 48.2% of the vote—not quite a landslide—and Rashida Tlaib won hers with only 31.2%.

Who Won the 2018 Midterms?

The entire "Squad" comes from dark-blue districts where Clinton decisively beat Trump by from 55% to 71%. (Yes, a 71% margin means 85% for Clinton and 14% for Trump!) Squad members and their supporters are on the left edge of those districts. They are in no way indicative of where the party or the country is or is headed.

The three Berniecrat PACs with their 117 endorsements didn't manage to back a single candidate who came within a mile of making a difference. In contrast, the moderate "New Dem" PAC endorsed 77 candidates and 42 won, including 33 who flipped red seats to blue. The "New Dem" PAC is tied to the New Democratic Caucus in the House.

The most important takeaway from this analysis is that every non-Berniecrat Democrat is focused on fighting Trump, and they're doing a damn good job of it. But Sanders and his PACs are focused on fighting only Democrats. In the crucial 2018 midterms, Berniecrats didn't help at all.

They predicted they could take a super-majority of Congress, and all they could do is win four seats in deep-blue districts. That tells you exactly how much their super-optimistic predictions are worth.

Left Populism vs. Jacksonian Populism

Sanders' "our revolution" theory misses the difference between right and left populism. That difference is what dooms his efforts.

Left populism focuses on economic issues—which is completely sensible. But the populism of Trump's base is Jacksonian, and it focuses on the issues raised by George Wallace (Ch. 2) and by Trump. Those are mainly cultural issues—race, immigrants, guns, sexual minorities, religion, abortion, climate change, and political correctness.

Left populism presents a simple populist dichotomy. The elite consists of the richest 1% and their political enablers, and the rest are "the people."

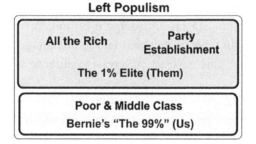

According to the left-populist view, pretty much everyone is part of Us, so Trump's base is naturally in there with us. This makes Reich's view of "Our Revolution" and the dream of "Brand New Congress" seem like a real possibility.

To find out if Trump's base is really with us (but "they just don't know it yet"), we should take a look at the Jacksonian view of the world. That's shown in the diagram below.

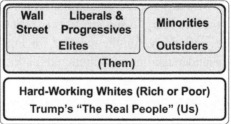

Notice there are still two main groups—Them and Us. But Jacksonians, like most right-wing populists, split Them into the Elite and the Outsiders. These are the minorities, Blacks, immigrants, and sexual minorities. The outsiders are excluded from "the real people" and are clearly not part of the elite. In this way, Jacksonians exclude about half the Democratic Party from "the real people." But that's not all.

A second surprise is the most shocking. Jacksonians see White liberals and progressives as part of the elite! In right-wing populism, the elite are usually seen as being in cahoots with the excluded group. Democrats are obvious champions of the poor and minorities—that's what Democratic identity politics is all about. In the Jacksonian view, Democrats are in cahoots with the "outsiders."

The third surprise is their sympathy for the "hard-working" rich. Jacksonians will tell you "they worked hard for their money." Sometimes they sort of have a point. Consider Steve Jobs and LeBron James. The result is that Trump's base classifies most billionaires as part of "the real people." Even Trump, a presumed multi-billionaire born with a silver spoon in his mouth who brags about taking advantage of tax loopholes, gets a pass. Again, this makes a progressive alliance with the Tea Party hard to imagine.

Jacksonian Trumpsters see it working like this: Democrats arrange help for minorities from the federal government, and in return, these "outsiders" vote for us. Of course, they are right about this. The problem is that they exclude, as outsiders, the groups that Democrats most care about. Socialism tries to overcome this divide between progressives and Trump's base by focusing on economic disadvantage. But that's not what the Jacksonians focus on.

Conclusion

It's important to understand the complaints of Trump's base, and it's helpful to try to win some over to our side. All this is depolarizing. But Reich and "Brand New Congress" go completely overboard when they try to recruit half the Tea Party to support Bernie's platform. It makes no sense to trash our own party for the sake of an imaginary revolution based on a total misunderstanding of Trump and his Jacksonian base.

- Bernie's Revolution will not materialize.
- Attempting a revolution will only polarize Democrats and the country. And that helps Trump.

CHAPTER 17

Economics vs. the Culture War

*Imagine if Christians took a year off from the culture wars
... No, you can't escape the culture wars, even if you
wanted to.*

—Daniel Darling, V.P.,
Southern Baptist Communications

Better wages, more good jobs, less inequality! That's what we need, and
it's all good. Surely that would solve our political problems. According
to Bernie Sanders, those economics are exactly what we had before
1973. He's right. The trouble is that before 1973 is exactly when our present political problems exploded. Something is very wrong with this pic-
ture.

Worse yet, we're in a culture war, and
Fox News and its former political commentator Bill O'Reilly understand this
war far better than we do. And they know
how to exploit it politically. O'Reilly
does that in his 2006 book, *Culture Warrior*, where he argues that "secular progressives" (read "Berniecrats and their
ilk") are hostile to Christianity and tradi-
tional American values. In private, according to the *New York Times*, "[Trump]
and his top aides freely admit that he is
engaged in a culture war on behalf of his
white, working-class base."

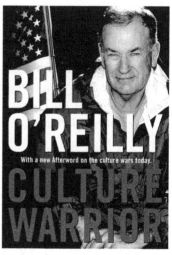

The 'Socialist' View

Having started his political life as a socialist, Bernie Sanders is no culture warrior. Like every socialist, he analyzes politics in economic

terms—the working class, the middle class, and the billionaires. So he explains the Democrats' loss of the White working class by pointing to the loss of good manufacturing jobs and flatlined wages while the rich get richer.

That seems logical enough. Since 1973, hourly wages have gone nowhere fast, manufacturing jobs have been disappearing and inequality has been growing. All those changes impact the White working class.

But political scientists tend to disagree with Bernie's assessment. Sure, they know about wages, job loss, and inequality. Everyone does. But they don't think economics is why Trump's base hates liberals and progressives, or why so many voters in the White working-class went Republican.

Look at it this way: Is Trump's base complaining that the Democrats aren't socialistic enough? That question would send his base into paroxysms of hysterical laughter. No. They're saying: Build that wall, keep our guns, stop abortion, spend more on the military, eff your political correctness.

So which view is right? Is Trump's base upset with Democrats for economic reasons—the Democrats' lack of socialism? Or is it because his base is on the other side of a culture war? This matters because Sanders' "democratic socialists" are attacking the Democratic Party, partly so that they can win over Trump's base with their "socialist" policies.

If they've diagnosed the problem correctly, they may have a point. If they are politically out to lunch (and I explained in the previous chapter just how out to lunch they are), their destructiveness should be resisted. Parties, like almost anything, are far easier to destroy than to rebuild. The big question is: *Can Trump's base be lured back to the Democratic Party with socialistic policies?*

To avoid confusion:

Let me be absolutely clear. I am ***not*** criticizing the goal of a dramatically more egalitarian society, which is the central goal of socialism. I'm strongly in favor of that goal. But socialism has been tried many times and in many places. It's never worked, and sometimes its failures have led to horrendous catastrophes.

Later I will show that most of Sanders' "democratic socialists" are just advocates for FDR liberalism, which leaves capitalism in place. Denmark has some form of that, and we should too.

Testing the Theories of Trump's Base

I've strongly suggested that Trump's base did not switch parties because the Democrats lack socialism, but is there any actual proof of this? We can't read minds, but here's some awfully strong evidence.

Sanders tells us that after 1973 good manufacturing jobs went away, wages stopped going up and income inequality rose. He's right. That's why, according to Sanders, the White working-class left the Democrats. Hang on. Where did that come from? Remember that after the 1972 election, McGovern said: "I opened up the Democratic Party and 20 million people walked out." That was the White middle class and working class doing the walking. They left roughly between 1964 and 1972, all years when Sanders says the economy was good—before it started going bad in 1973. Perhaps we should nail this down.

The 20 million. Relative to LBJ's support in the 1964 election, McGovern lost 38% of Democratic voters. That's a *net* loss—leavers minus joiners—that occurred even though since the 1960s Blacks were rapidly joining the Democratic Party. That loss of 20 million voters is astounding compared to anything we've seen since.

The economy. During the 10 years from 1963 to 1973, according to a graph linked by Sanders' website, hourly compensation of a typical worker (adjusted for inflation) rose 23%. Over the next 40 years, it went up only 9%—10 times slower.

In the 10 years immediately before the 1972 election, the number of manufacturing jobs increased by 16%, and since then they've decreased by 30%. In 1972, according to the Sanders website graph, income inequality was just a hair from the lowest it had been in the previous 120 years. Also note that in 1972 the marginal income tax rate on the rich was 70%; today it's closer to 40%.

Backward. Sanders has the economic story right. Before 1973, all three of his economic indicators for the middle and working classes—manufacturing jobs, hourly wages, and income inequality—were doing great. Yet it was during the best years—before 1973—when 20 million of the White middle and working-class fled the Democratic Party.

Why did the working class leave the Party when the manufacturing economy was booming, and partly come back during the years when economic conditions say they should have left? These facts are completely backward from the vantage point of the economic-anxiety theory of the "socialist" camp.

Culture war. George Wallace and Richard Nixon are the experts on the culture war. They led those 20 million Whites out of the Democratic Party. Did Wallace and Nixon know something Sanders doesn't get?

Just listen to their slogans. Wallace: "Segregation now, segregation tomorrow, segregation forever!" Nixon: "Stand Up for America," "Law and Order." McGovern was ridiculed as the candidate of "Acid, Amnesty and Abortion." This was an attack on the hippie counterculture, the draft dodgers in Canada and the women's movement. Nixon implicitly blamed the largely Black urban riots on the civil rights movement. None of which has to do with Sanders' economic arguments. Those are all culture-war issues. Wallace and Nixon knew exactly what they were doing.

The bottom line is that Trump's base did ***not*** leave the Democratic Party between 1964 and 1972 due to stagnant wages, vanishing jobs or economic inequality. None of that was happening. Instead, their exit was driven by culture-war issues.

That Was Then; Is It Different Now?

By November 2016, the unemployment rate was down to 3% in North Dakota and 2.9% in South Dakota. For many years, neither state has had a shortage of good, hard-hat oil and gas jobs. Yet what happened? Trump won by 36% in North Dakota and 30% in South Dakota.

This is just what we saw in the late 1960s all over again. Although conditions were perfect for winning back Trump's base—according to the socialist theory—Trump still won overwhelmingly. Once again, the answer is not the economy; it's the culture war.

Meanwhile, Blacks, with roughly 10% unemployment (compared to the national average of under 5%) voted heavily for Clinton (76%). So exactly where the socialist theory would predict a group should abandon the Democrats, they overwhelmingly voted for them. Once again, it's obvious that cultural concerns are the reason.

In all these cases, the socialist theory points to the opposite of what happened. The culture-war view gives the obviously correct answer.

But we know that besides its serious cultural-war concerns, Trump's base is interested in more jobs and better pay. Doesn't that prove there's some truth to the socialist theory? Actually no. The problem is that while they do want good jobs, they don't want to get them through "socialist" policies. To check this out, I turned to a sociologist who is well known for getting to know Trump's base.

A Sociologist Gets to Know Trump's Base

Arlie Hochschild, the author of *Strangers in Their Own Land*, is a sociology professor at U.C. Berkeley and a Bernie Sanders supporter. She spent five years interviewing Tea Party and Trump supporters in Lake Charles, Louisiana, where she concluded that Trump supporters were mainly upset with "people of color, women, immigrants, refugees, public sector workers," and with environmental causes. They viewed all of these as, in effect, "cutting in line" in front of them. Shown this assessment, they agreed it was right on target.

When I asked her, at a book talk, how they would feel about taxing the rich to fund a huge infrastructure program to provide jobs, she regretfully answered that Trumpers would oppose it. In other words, their primary concerns were all cultural. To the extent that they are concerned about jobs, they blame their problems on discrimination against them by progressive programs, and they reject the Democrats' main proposal for creating more good working-class jobs.

Despite the fact that many in Trump's base are concerned about jobs, they voted for Trump because they don't like the Democrats' approach to job creation—big government spending on infrastructure. They far prefer Trump's approach: build a wall and wage trade wars with China and Mexico. To cap it all off, Trump's base sees Democratic regulations and the taxing of business as job killers.

By the way, all of this matches Jacksonian populism.

Who Is the System Rigged Against?

The system is rigged, and it is rigged most against the poorest. That's the socialist-populist view, and although it omits race, it is pretty accurate. Trump's base agrees that the system is rigged. But does that mean they are aligned with Democrats?

In August 2017, Public Policy Polling asked voters, "Which of the following groups do you think face the most discrimination in America today?" Of Trump voters, 45% said "White people," while only 5% of Democratic voters said the same.

Trump's base sees Democrats as part of the elite and in cahoots with poor minorities. They see the system as rigged against them by progressives. This is why Trump's base is fighting a culture war, not a war against the elite 1%.

Does Economic Security Prevent Trumpism?

Pippa Norris is a political scientist at Harvard University who studies international populist movements. She points to the surprisingly Trump-like populism in Sweden and Denmark. Both have exactly the strong safety-net features that should (according to Sanders) win the support of the working class. The right-wing Danish People's Party sounds a lot like Trump. It has the second-largest representation in Parliament. The Party's stated goals are to protect the Monarchy and the Evangelical Lutheran Church of Denmark; to enforce a strict rule of law; and to limit immigration to prevent Denmark from becoming a multicultural society. This is cultural backlash pure and simple. In Denmark, the problem can't be either economic insecurity or inequality.

So what's going on? Norris summarizes the effect saying, "A lot of data suggests that countries with more robust welfare states tend to have stronger far-right movements. Providing White voters with higher levels of economic security does not tamp down their anxieties about race and immigration." She conjectures that when people actually have economic security, they focus more on polarizing cultural issues.

Conclusion

The populist view that the system favors the rich is certainly true. Democrats agree that we need to undo that bias. The socialist theory that economic "class analysis" explains politics has some truth to it. But only some. It does not explain much about Trump's base and the political polarization that's ripping us apart.

That's not an argument against a higher minimum wage or national health insurance. But it is an argument for not putting all our eggs in the "socialism" basket. We need to put an end to our vicious downward political spiral into polarization, and that requires that Democrats face up to and understand the culture wars.

- Trumpish populism has increased in times and places with good working-class economies.
- Trump's base is mainly motivated by the culture wars.

CHAPTER 18

Sanders' Populist Strategy

*President Kennedy was elected while I was a grad student
at the University of Chicago. I remember being physically
nauseated by his speech, and that doesn't happen very often.*
—Bernard Sanders, 1987

We've had two right-wing populist presidents, Jackson and Trump, but never one from the left. These are populist times, and in 2016, Bernie Sanders came surprisingly close to filling that gap. He looks unlikely to do any better in 2020, but the populist moment has not passed.

Elizabeth Warren is running quite a populist campaign but she is running as a Democrat and shows little sign of trying to overthrow the Democratic Party. Alexandria Ocasio-Cortez, however, would likely follow Sanders' path if she gets the chance. And there's no telling what other surprises lie in wait.

With this in mind, let's take a look at Sanders' 2016 campaign to see what we can learn about a *left-populist takeover*. Of course, populism, as explained earlier, takes many forms, so examining Sanders' strategy cannot provide a definitive diagnosis. But a look at his strategy may still teach us some valuable lessons about left populism in America. Because Bernie Sanders says he speaks for the people—the 99%—surely it's not possible that he would hide a one-percenter in his back office to work on campaign strategy. Well, yes, actually he would. Let me tell you about Tad Devine.

Tad Devine: The One-Percenter Strategist

Devine often makes more than a million dollars a year, double what it takes to be a one-percenter. And Sanders paid him $5 million to be his chief strategist for his one-year primary campaign in 2015–16.

So who is this guy? He's worked for some establishment Democrats you may have heard of: Jimmy Carter, Walter Mondale, Michael Dukakis, Al Gore, and John Kerry. Sanders started working with him in the 1990s.

Then in 2006, Devine landed a new kind of client—Viktor Fedorovych Yanukovych. But of course! He's the Ukrainian candidate who messed with their 2004 election and triggered the "Orange Revolution." That forced a rerun, which was fair, and Yanukovych lost. Enter Paul Manafort, who hired Devine to flip the next election to Yanukovych.

Manafort?! Wasn't he Trump's campaign chairman from June to August 2016, the man who Donald Trump dumped for having sleazy Ukrainian connections? That's him. He was convicted of tax and bank fraud in 2018, and as of July 2019, he was set to be released from prison at the end of 2024. And Yanukovych? He's now in exile in Russia and wanted by Ukraine for high treason.

Back to Tad Devine: He repackaged Yanukovych and helped reelect him in 2010 by recommending an advertising campaign comprised of 75-percent attack ads—his specialty. Devine quit in 2012 after Yanukovych jailed a former rival for the presidency and built a $100-million mansion complete with a zoo and replica galleon on an artificial lake.

But four months after "quitting," Devine wrote a strategy memo for Manafort saying, "The number of people who admit they are having difficulty feeding their family throughout Ukraine today is stunning." His strategy memo urged Yanukovych to "signal" his concern. How touching.

The progressive magazine *Mother Jones* reported in 2014 that Devine's consulting firm won a national political-consultant prize for creating "one of the most brutal attack ads you'll ever see." So here's my question:

> Why did Bernie Sanders hire as his chief strategist a one-percenter and attack-ad specialist who made millions working to install a dictator?

Populism: The Will of 'the People'?

In his book, *Our Revolution*, Sanders twice refers to himself as a populist. Nearly everyone agrees because he divides the world into Us, "the American people," aka the 99%, and Them, the Wall Street billionaires and their lackeys, the Democratic establishment.

Sanders also adopted another defining aspect of populism, which goes a long way towards explaining his use of Tad Devine. To be a true populist, you must believe that the people have a single, incorruptible "will" that should prevail over the immoral elite.

But "the people" never do have a single "will." Instead, they have a lot of disagreements. So a populist movement remains chaotic until it adopts a charismatic leader who defines "the will of the people." Pippa Norris, a leading expert on populism, explained the need for such a leader:

> Even though [populism] is about *popular sovereignty* ... in practice, what happens is the *power is seen to reside in the individual leader*, the charismatic leader who represents the voice of the ordinary people.

Bernie Sanders was the left's charismatic leader in 2016, and "popular sovereignty" was seen by his followers to reside in him. Because he alone "represented the voice of the ordinary people," he had a license to do whatever it took to make sure their will prevailed. That included appointing Tad Devine as chief strategist for his campaign.

Sanders running for V.P. in 1904 with his lifelong hero, Eugene V. Debs

Sanders' Plan

In our two-party system, it's almost impossible for a third party to succeed. A million spectators cheered Teddy Roosevelt as he led 150 of his Rough Riders up Broadway after his two terms as president and a year-long African safari. Yet three years later, he gained only 27% of the popular vote running as a third-party, Bull Moose progressive populist. That was in 1912, and no one has come close to that since.

The only way for a socialist or radical populist to win the presidency is by taking over one of the major political parties, as Trump has. So that's Sanders' plan. He is not going to become a Democrat; he intends to turn the Democrats into a party of socialist populism. Here's the evidence.

Not a Democrat. "Of course I am a Democrat and running for the Democratic nomination," claimed Sanders in February 2016. He needed to seem to be a Democrat so the Party would let him run, but he needed his base to know he really was not. In March, at an MSNBC town-hall event in Ohio, when asked why he decided to run as a Democrat, he had two answers: (1) "media coverage," and (2) "I'm not a billionaire" (he wanted to get his hands on that filthy Democratic money). The easy answer should have been, "Because I am now really a Democrat." But he wasn't. His website and his literature continued to list him as an independent.

On the first day of his "Unity Tour" in June 2017 with Democratic Party Chairman Tom Perez, Sanders' supporters booed Perez. During the tour, Chris Hayes of MSNBC asked Sanders, "Do you consider yourself a Democrat?" Sanders said, "No, I am an independent."

How could such a "let me be very honest" truth-teller justify saying he was a Democrat so he could run as one when he wasn't? The answer is populism. He really believes he is the only true voice of the virtuous 99%, and it would be immoral for him not to make his best effort to take over the Democratic Party and implement the will of the people. This is all an integral part of a populist strategy.

Discrediting the Party. Sanders complained endlessly during the primaries about how the Democratic superdelegates were rigged against him, and how he could win the majority of elected delegates and the superdelegates would still take away his victory.

His purpose was both to delegitimize the party in the eyes of his followers and potential followers and thereby weaken it and to engineer rule changes (some of which happened) that would make the party more vulnerable to a hostile takeover. The point of superdelegates is to protect against both hostile and incompetent takeovers. It's not a bad system because superdelegates just vote in line with the majority of elected delegates unless the party is in danger of choosing a candidate who's too likely to lose the election.

To see that Sanders' complaints were insincere, consider what happened next. On June 8, 2016, Clinton secured the majority of elected delegates (not counting superdelegates), and there was no longer even a slim hope for Sanders. And what did Sanders do then?

Unbelievably, Sanders spent more than a month asking the superdelegates to do for him exactly what he had previously accused them, without a shred of evidence, of plotting to do for Clinton. He asked them to overturn the will of the voters and rig the outcome for him.

Again, this was the result of a populist mindset. Populist leaders believe they speak for "the virtuous people," so anything is justified.

Trying to defeat Trump? Sanders finally endorsed Clinton on July 12 and declared, "I intend to do everything I can to make certain she will be the next president." It was a promise he made more than once.

By the time he made the promise, his mind was elsewhere. Two days later, he announced he was about to write the book, *Our Revolution*— during the crucial final months before the election. The day after that, he discussed his new super PAC, also called "Our Revolution," with *USA Today* and immediately began raising money for it. Sanders did not make a single campaign appearance for Clinton until he spoke to a small group of students in New Hampshire in early September.

He was in a rush with the book because he expected Clinton to win, and he wanted to start discrediting her as soon as possible. Launching his new super PAC before the election had the same purpose.

Finally, in mid-September, he appeared on MSNBC's *Morning Joe* and made a strong case that Clinton's policies were far better than Trump's. But when asked about Green Party candidate Jill Stein and whether he trusted "that [Clinton] will honor [the Democratic platform]," he dodged both questions. Because his principal surrogate Cornel West was vociferously backing the Green Party candidate against Clinton, these were the two most pressing questions for his followers. He never addressed either one.

By weaseling out of those questions, he gave a pass to voting for Stein, who more than tripled her vote over the previous presidential election when there was no Trump emergency. Had Sanders kept his promise about supporting Clinton at that opportune moment, he would have done more to defeat Trump than he did in all his (minor) appearances after the Democratic convention. But he knew the only way he'd have another shot at the presidency was to weaken President Clinton (hence the rush to publish his anti-Clinton book) or to let her lose.

Our Revolution. In June 2017, a leading progressive magazine, *The Nation*, asked Nina Turner, president of "Our Revolution," Sanders' 501(c)(4) dark-money super PAC: "How will Our Revolution relate to the DNC, the DCCC and the DSCC?" She replied, "I don't think it is our job nor our obligation to fit in. It's their job to fit in with us."

Then the *Nation* asked: "And what about the Democratic Party at large? Do you see Our Revolution working to bring some unity to factions in the party?" Turner's reply: "No, not really." Obviously, Our Revolution is in takeover mode, and just as obviously, that's what Sanders wants.

Conclusion

"So why don't you join the Democratic Party, get funding and then come out as a socialist once you're in office?" asked Catherine Hill, a young Marxist graduate student. It was 1987 and Sanders, with 14% of the vote, had just lost his race against the feminist Democratic Governor of Vermont, Madeleine Kunin. Sanders replied:

> That's the temptation, but it's a fool's temptation. ... You don't come out with any integrity. ... The assumption is that you're going to sucker the system—people who always vote Democratic will vote for you ... The position of integrity is to declare who you are and not fool people. ... You don't change the system from within the Democratic Party.

But Sanders kept thinking and finally came up with a compromise that he must feel keeps his integrity. He's sticking with *not* joining the Democratic Party. But he's jiggered his integrity rule—now he feels it's okay to "sucker the system" into thinking he's a Democrat in order to get their "media coverage" (in debates) and their money. But he stays honest with his supporters about not being a Democrat. However, Chapter 23, will show that he's misleading them about socialism.

This works well because the Democrats are either trusting or afraid of the far-left outrage culture. If they wanted, they could easily call Sanders' bluff by requiring Democratic candidates to affirm that they are not independents—Sanders could not swallow that.

In short, a real populist leader will only join a party they control. And they will not feel compelled to be honest because their loyalty is to a higher cause—socialism, channeling "the will of the people," or in Trump's case, loyalty to himself.

CHAPTER 19

Good Populism: The Kingfish

We're all here to pull a lot of pot-bellied politicians off a little woman's neck.

—U.S. Senator Huey Long

Huey Long was the corrupt machine politician they say he was. To be perfectly honest, he built the biggest political machine Louisiana had ever seen and completely took over the Louisiana political establishment. He was a flashy dresser with no taste. He loved to hear himself talk. Political correctness never crossed his mind. And he probably failed every left purity test you can think of.

I have argued that adopting right-wing populism would be disastrous, and left-wing populism would be a dangerous step backward from our pluralist democracy with its checks and balances. But left populism has pluses as well as minuses, and if I were to ignore the pluses, you would be right to consider me biased. In this chapter, let me introduce you to one of my favorite politicians: the quintessential progressive populist, Louisiana Governor and Senator, The "Kingfish," Huey P. Long.

I wouldn't vote for him today, but in 1920s Louisiana, with only one party, controlled by "the interests" and backed by the Klan when necessary, even left populism was a step forward. Unfortunately, most present-day progressives who've even heard of him still view him as "the Big Sleazy." There is some truth to this view, but there is also the reality of 1920s Louisiana to consider.

The list of negatives is *not* why I'm one of Long's fans, but they account for half of the reasons why the Kingfish could teach our current Democratic Party leaders so much. He spent his whole life fighting privilege on behalf of the poor. And he fought harder and smarter than anyone else. While on the Supreme Court, President Taft called Long "one of the best legal minds" he had ever encountered.

The lesson for us today is the contradiction between Long's corrupt machine politics and his spending a lifetime "pulling the poor parts of Louisiana out of the mud" (literally in the case of his road-building projects). As you read this, ask yourself how it is possible to break all our new-new-left dogmas and purity tests while advancing economic and social equality. No, I'm not advocating sleazy machine politics, I'm just saying our purity tests with their moralistic conclusions don't hold water.

Reality in 1920s Louisiana

U.S. Senator Tom Connally, who chaired an investigation into Louisiana politics in the 1930s, concluded, "I advise anyone who thinks he knows something about politics to go down in Louisiana and take a postgraduate course." And that was mainly a comment on Long's opponents. Before Huey, not only was politics in every city and town in Louisiana run by a political "ring," typically under the control of the sheriff, but the threat of political violence was ever-present.

Usually, this violence amounted to nothing more than a fistfight. But soon after being elected governor in 1928, Huey hired a bodyguard, fearing he would be shot. Indeed, five rifle shots were fired into his home. In early 1935, the Square Deal Association was formed and threatened to assassinate Long. With the help of an infiltrator, Long tricked about 100 of them into arming themselves and assembling at the airport, where he had the National Guard confiscate their guns. At one point he told a U.S. Senate colleague, "If there were just a few people plotting it [his assassination], I think I might live through it." But in late 1935, he was assassinated by a lone gunman opposed to his politics.

After reading T. Harry Williams' authoritative biography, it is hard to imagine that Huey could have accomplished much of what he did without engaging in a great deal of sleazy politics. I will leave it to you to decide if what he accomplished was worth it.

An Early Start

Huey was born a politician. After finishing sixth grade, he simply walked into the eighth-grade classroom and convinced the teacher to accept him. In his senior year, he won a debating contest. Afterward, while staying with the state superintendent of education, he promised, "Mrs. Harris, you have been mighty good to us, and when I get to be Governor, United

States Senator, and President of the United States, I am going to do something for you."

His parents had a decent house and enough land to grow most of their own food. The family read books together, often the *Bible,* and the children were expected to get some college education. Before he was 15, he had read a multivolume *History of the World, Les Miserables,* some Shakespeare, Dickens, Poe, and Balzac.

By the election of 1908, the Democrats called on him to debate a couple of local Socialists. He rejected socialism and argued instead for a populist program placing restraints on big business. Huey was still not quite 15.

Change from the Top Down

After a few years as a traveling salesman, Huey spent a year studying for the bar and passed the exam at age 21. He began getting worker-injury compensation cases and observed the stinginess of the compensation. In 1916, he provided his local State Senator, S. J. Harper, with some amendments to increase the benefits allowed by the compensation laws, and Harper presented them to the legislative committee. Huey tried to speak to them but was silenced and ridiculed. As the committee adjourned, Huey stood and spoke.

> For 20 years has the Louisiana Legislature been dominated by the henchmen and attorneys of the interests. Those seeking reforms have from necessity bowed their heads in regret and shame when witnessing the victories of these corrupting influences at this capitol.

Through the press, his dramatic speech reached his intended audience and activated latent popular support for his reforms. The Harper Amendments were passed.

Note that Huey was not being propelled by a mass movement. Far from it, he was acting solely on his own initiative. This change did not come from the bottom up. This was true for every one of his progressive reforms. He envisioned both what was needed and what was possible. Of course, his vision reflected the needs of the people, but the change came from the top down in every case, although he needed and won popular support. Huey was a real leader, not a demagogue. But he was a populist leader who did not persuade from his bully pulpit, but rather was in touch with "the people" and used dealmaking and backroom politics to do what they wanted.

Huey: The Godfather of Occupy Wall Street

In 1918, 93 years before Occupy Wall Street, Huey wrote to major newspapers explaining that 2% of the people owned 70% of the wealth. Its most unfortunate effect, he said, was that the ordinary man could no longer provide an education for his children. Then, after a vigorous campaign through the backwoods towns of northern Louisiana, Huey was elected to the Public Service Commission. There he pushed through a reduction in phone rates that made him a statewide hero.

Huey ran for governor in 1924 on a platform that included badly needed road construction and free textbooks and took on the "bloated plutocracy" and the Klan. He campaigned in the small towns saying, "I come from the common people, and I am a friend of labor." Without a real organization, he came in third but easily won in rural Louisiana. Basically, he lost to the machines in New Orleans and Baton Rouge. He immediately began campaigning for the 1928 gubernatorial election.

A Strategic Pragmatist

Huey's first move in the next governor's race was to back Ed Broussard for the U.S. Senate in 1926. Huey would rally northern Louisiana voters to vote for Broussard, and Broussard would rally southwestern, French-speaking voters to vote for Huey in 1928. This is like Bernie Sanders vigorously backing a moderate Republican so the Republican would later back him. Huey was the ultimate pragmatist and dealmaker.

While he ran for Senate in 1926, Broussard, speaking French, introduced Huey to his constituents. Huey displayed his usual humor and earthiness and the crowds went wild for him. He held out the hope of a better life and, said a leader of the French parish of Lafourche, "He taught them to think." Huey carried the French parishes more strongly in 1928 than Broussard had in 1926. He became governor in May 1928, just in time for the Great Depression.

The Most Effective Progressive Populist

Louisiana had about 300 miles of paved roads in 1928, to which Huey added 2,300 miles by the end of his four-year term, and the program was still in full swing. Many poor families could not afford textbooks, and without them, children were not allowed to attend school. One consequence was that Louisiana had the lowest literacy rate in the country. Huey passed a free-schoolbook law (which was opposed because it would benefit Blacks), which was ultimately upheld by the U.S. Supreme Court.

When Huey proposed a tax of five cents a barrel on oil refining, he was impeached and nearly convicted by the conservatives in the legislature. But Huey knew his agenda was popular, especially after the Wall Street crash in 1929, so he decided to take his case to the people of Louisiana by running for the U.S. Senate in September 1930.

Huey ran against Joseph E. Ransdell, a tough establishment politician who had previously won his U.S. Senate seat in a minor landslide. Huey beat him 57% to 43%. In the process, he more than doubled his vote in the Orleans parish where the strongest political machine, the "Old Regulars," had previously held sway. In the labor wards of New Orleans, the ward leaders had not been able to keep their followers in line in the face of Huey's popularity.

The strategy of running for the Senate to strengthen his position as governor proved effective. Huey's stunning statewide victory frightened the legislature into backing essentially all of his policies, and his victory against the "Old Regulars" cracked the powerful New Orleans machine. Within two years, he had smashed it and put in place his own *statewide* machine.

By the end of 1930, Huey had embarked on a massive expansion of Louisiana State University, and by 1936, enrollment had more than tripled to 6,000 students. During his tenure as governor, he more than doubled the capacity of the state's Charity Hospital, reduced its mortality rate and humanized services at mental institutions (including instituting dental care). He inaugurated the first prisoner rehabilitation program in Louisiana history, set prisoners to growing their own food and provided literacy classes.

Huey and the Louisiana Banks

One Friday night, Huey learned that a Lafayette bank would face a run the next morning. Arriving at the bank at 7 a.m., he occupied the president's office. When the bank opened, the first customer, who was attempting to withdraw $18,000, was sent to see Huey. Huey showed him his own check for $265,000 to withdraw state funds and pointed out that he got there first—and that if the customer persisted, Huey would withdraw all of the bank's available funds. The run was averted.

Huey also applied systematic pressure for banks to support each other. Through 1932, Louisiana had only seven bank failures, mostly small ones, while the rest of the country had 4,800.

Huey and Hattie

Huey is often criticized for his machine politics, and that criticism includes an implicit suggestion that he was not so popular or was popular only due to patronage. But one test case conclusively proves the opposite.

When Arkansas Senator Thaddeus Caraway died in November 1931, his wife, Hattie, was in effect appointed to finish out his term. Surprisingly, she announced her run for a full term in May 1932, saying, "The time has passed when a woman should be placed in a position and kept there only while someone else is being groomed for the job." No one in Arkansas thought she had a chance. But Huey had noticed that Hattie almost always voted with the progressives.

Before dawn on August 1, Huey left Louisiana for Arkansas in a car followed by two sound trucks with rooftop speaking platforms and five trucks for technical support and campaign literature. The election was on August 9, and Hattie still had no significant backing.

According to Huey's biographer, T. Harry Williams, "When Huey rose to speak, he held a *Bible* in his hands and began by proclaiming, 'We're all here to pull a lot of potbellied politicians off a little woman's neck.'" Huey spoke five or six times a day for eight days before the election, and Hattie's speaking abilities improved rapidly as they traveled together. Her popular vote equaled the vote total of her six opponents combined. She was the first woman ever elected to the United States Senate.

Huey had *no machine or organization* of any kind in Arkansas. Yet Huey and Hattie won by a landslide with only an eight-day campaign. They won because the people of Arkansas liked their message. The same was true for Huey in Louisiana.

The sad ending to this story is that because Huey out-machined the corporate conservative politicians of Louisiana, he's been blacklisted by contemporary progressive populists, including Bernie Sanders. Most will not even mention his name while they heap praise on his deserving but oh-so-establishment rival, Franklin Delano Roosevelt.

Conclusion

Huey was neither politically correct nor dogmatic. He relied on machine politics as much as he could. That may well have been the right strategy in 1920s Louisiana, but even then, it resulted in terribly corrupt politics soon after his death. In a more advanced democracy, this strategy would be plainly counterproductive.

The left can learn a lot from Huey with regard to dealmaking, taking money and working strategically with the opposition. Probably the best thing about his populism was that although he still used the Us-versus-Them classification, he applied it without prejudice: He knew that some elites were part of "the people" and that some in the lower classes were on the wrong side.

- Huey Long considered dealmaking essential and didn't care who he made deals with.
- He also didn't care where his money came from—he knew it would not corrupt him.

CHAPTER 20

Utopian Populism

When you have a country where one man owns more than
100,000 people own, you know what the trouble is.
—Huey Long, "Share Our Wealth"
radio address, February 23, 1934

Bernie Sanders wants to tax multimillionaire inheritances. That would not bother Facebook's Mark Zuckerberg with his $57 billion—he didn't inherit that. And it wouldn't bother Jeff Bezos or Bill Gates. Sanders also plans to tax Wall Street speculators. That wouldn't bother them either.

Elizabeth Warren wants to tax the wealth of billionaires at 3% a year. That would bother them a little. But how fast does their wealth increase? It must increase by a lot more than 3% a year because if Zuckerberg started at $1 million in college and that increased 3% a year, he wouldn't even be worth $2 million now. But he's worth 30,000 times that much. To get to $57 billion from $1 million (or less) in the 15 years since he launched Facebook, his wealth must have grown at more than 103% a year. Knocking off 3% wouldn't do much harm to his wealth.

There's a vague sort of myth going around that says Sanders and Warren are giving us radical new ideas, and that no one's ever realized that inequality was such a problem. But now, having been woke by these charismatic, incorruptible leaders, and armed with these new ideas, we're almost home free. If we just stand up and wage a political revolution, that will be that.

Is this all so new?

In 1935, Huey Long organized 27,000 "Share Our Wealth" Clubs, and they were not talking about any measly 3%. Huey was proposing that no family needed nor should have more than 100 times the national average wealth or income. And no family should have less than one-third of the average wealth or income. That's easy to grasp and sounds pretty reasonable. What does that work out to in dollars?

The average family wealth (and remember, averages come in high due to the super-wealthy) is somewhere around $700,000. So 100 times that is $70 million, which is $0.07 billion—less than one-tenth of $1 billion. That's Huey's limit. So if Trump were worth $10 billion, as he's fond of claiming, Huey would take away more than 99% of his wealth. That leaves Bernie and Elizabeth in the dust.

It's actually pretty easy to come up with these radical ideas. I'm sure you could come up with three of four of them in the time it takes you to read this chapter. But Huey did much more. He thought through the details—not just of the percentages but of the political tactics he would use as president, the type of rebellion he might face and how he would outsmart it. He published these ideas in a short novel. He was a spellbinding speaker, ahead of the curve on technology (radio at the time) and a great organizer. And in his own way, he was incorruptible.

Also, he had street cred. Reread his list of Louisiana accomplishments, then compare Sanders, who gained fame for fixing potholes in the town of Burlington, to Huey micromanaging the paving of basically every road in Louisiana. Warren has written some good books and reports, but none can come close to matching what Huey Long accomplished in his four years as governor.

Long had one more enormous advantage. The country was five years into the Great Depression, and unemployment was around 20% in spite of Roosevelt's programs. There was no food stamp program, no Social Security, no Medicare. And real incomes, even for the employed, were less than half what they are today. Revolution was in the air.

Share Our Wealth

After one national radio broadcast, Huey received more than half a million letters (yes, written-on-paper letters with envelopes and stamps). By 1935, former Louisiana Governor and now U.S. Senator Huey Long was by far the most famous populist in the country and the most progressive Senator to boot. In early 1934, he launched the Share Our Wealth movement, and by the following year, his Share Our Wealth clubs had over 7.5 million members.

President Franklin D. Roosevelt, fearing Huey would play the spoiler in the 1936 election, called him one of the two most dangerous men in America (for the record, the other was General Douglas MacArthur).

Roosevelt took Long's federal patronage jobs away and gave them to Long's opponents in Louisiana. Roosevelt too could play machine politics, and he was out to knock Huey Long off his pedestal of popularity.

One of Roosevelt's programs, the Federal Theater Project (FTP), opened a fictionalized and highly propagandistic play in 17 cities exactly one week before the 1936 election. The play, *It Can't Happen Here*, by Sinclair Lewis, which theater critics then and now contend vilifies Huey Long, was the FTP's most ambitious production.

In the play, demagogue Berzelius "Buzz" Windrip defeats Roosevelt; implements Huey's income and wealth limits; outlaws dissent; incarcerates political enemies in concentration camps and trains and arms a paramilitary force that attacks demonstrators with bayonets. Long advocated none of Sinclair Lewis' imagined repressive measures. Ironically, it was Roosevelt who imprisoned tens of thousands of innocent Japanese-Americans in concentration camps.

Long was assassinated in 1935, prior to the play's production—as well as the election. But here, in a summary of his posthumously published book, is how Huey imagined his reforms would play out after beating Roosevelt in the 1936 presidential election:

'My First Days in the White House'

Huey P. Long

I. Wherein a New President Takes Office

Huey describes his imagined 1936 election campaign as a "great campaign which was destined to save America from Communism and Fascism." He appoints Franklin Roosevelt as Secretary of the Navy and Herbert Hoover as Secretary of Commerce. His other appointments are more populist.

In his first legislative message to the Congress, he recommends the creation of "a giant national organization for a survey of all wealth and poverty" as the first step towards his Share Our Wealth program.

II. Wherein We Arrange To Overhaul And Revive The Nation

Huey proposes a plan that was actually drafted when General Lytle Brown was Chief of Army Engineers. Huey planned to appoint Brown as his new Interior Secretary and put him in charge of a "vast program for the elimination of dust storms, the reclamation of wastelands, the control of floods, and the development of navigation and water power through-out the entire country."

(Basically, this was like a Green New Deal targeting the devastation of the great Dust Bowl drought.)

III. Wherein We Care For The Soul And Body Of A Great Nation

Soon President Long issues a proclamation stating, "This Government shall extend aid, financial and idealistic, to the several states, so that every worthy boy and girl, every worthy man and woman, may secure an education to the limit of their mental capacity."

(This is not free tuition for the rich and the poor. It is a guarantee that lack of income will not stop anyone from getting the education that is right for them.)

After noting that "One in every three of our teachers was receiving less than $750 a year," he recommends that teachers in all schools bene-fiting from federal funds receive at least $2,000 a year.

Huey also asserts that those who commit a crime to furnish food for their children should not be punished.

Calling upon the Mayo brothers (of the Mayo Clinic), he asks them to prescribe "preventive measures and curative, medicinal treatments for all 130 million Americans" and to help "stamp out a number of diseases that take a terrific toll of human life." Huey assigns the federal government to "provide the needed facilities and equipment." (This, of course, is his version of universal health care.)

IV. Wherein The New President Encounters The Masters Of Finance And Destiny

After a week in office, he receives a letter from the powerful banker J. P. Morgan, stating that he would "utilize every protection of the courts and

Constitution to protect our properties against the seizures contemplated in your Share Our Wealth program."

At the same time, he also receives a very different letter from John D. Rockefeller:

> I have lived a full and rich life, and soon shall be gathered to my ancestors ... I am therefore disposing in orderly process my possessions in excess of five million dollars ... The residue I have instructed my attorneys to turn over to the United States Treasury as a gift to the federal government.

After this lucky break, Huey convenes a National Share Our Wealth Committee of bankers and industrialists, chaired by Rockefeller, to help design the wealth cap.

(Notice how pro-capitalist Huey is. He believes that capitalists can best draw up a plan that "shares the wealth," but he also leaves them in charge of their corporations so they will be well-run.)

V. Wherein The Masters Of Finance Are Ours

In two weeks, the committee reports back with a plan for a Federal Share Our Wealth Corporation. The committee explains that surplus wealth above $5 million per family would be invested in the corporation, and poor families with less than one-third the average wealth would receive stock in this corporation.

"The next afternoon's newspapers in screaming headlines carried the news to a waiting populace that the barons of Wall Street were content at last to accept democracy in America."

VI. Wherein Rebellion Brews And Fades

Congress quickly passes the Share Our Wealth legislation. But soon Huey receives a message that "The Governor of the New England State of X has announced today that his state would resist by force." J. P. Morgan is behind this revolt.

Huey immediately flies to the state capitol. The next morning at breakfast in the governor's mansion, Huey asked, "How is your rebellion?" "All right," the governor answers, "but you have all the rebels. Fortunately, I did not leave the Mansion last night."

They agree that Huey would announce to the crowd that the governor and state would raise the issue of the Share Our Wealth legislation with the U.S. Supreme Court to quickly get the law tested. The Supreme

Court soon accepts it as Constitutional, and political revolution transforms America into the Promised Land.

Conclusions

Huey's plans for fixing America looked completely different than his successes in Louisiana. In Louisiana, he was just helping residents catch up with the rest of America. But his proposals for America proposed leaping more than a century into the future. (Eighty-five years later, we are still nowhere near his complete vision.)

It took Huey 10 years to gain power and master Louisiana. Had he not been shot but won the presidency, his eight years in office (never mind his two-month prognosis) would have looked nothing like his novel's plot. His revolution was just fantasy.

But Huey certainly deserves credit for bringing important progressive ideas into public focus and putting some pressure on Roosevelt. Many others have put forward similar ideas, but few have been so convincing.

CHAPTER 21

Don't Be the Enemy They Need

Radicals must be resilient and sensitive enough to the process of action and reaction to avoid being trapped by their own tactics.

—Saul Alinsky, 1971
Pioneer of community organizing

"Be spittingly angry ... angry enough to curse, scream and name-call" rages Jessica Valenti in *The Guardian*. "Spare me the calls for civility," because expecting me "to speak with civility is absurd." She is defending Robert De Niro's "Fuck Trump!" shout-out at the Tony Awards and comedian Samantha Bee's "feckless cunt" slur against Ivanka Trump.

Valenti is arguing against Frank Bruni. She's found him "yammering" against De Niro and Bee's vulgarity in his *New York Times* op-ed. There he also points out, "Anger isn't a strategy. Sometimes it's a trap." In fact, he's pointing to a central part of the populism traps we've been discussing here in Part 3. Bruni's anger trap is a special case of the trap that famed community organizer Saul Alinsky warned against nearly 50 years ago—"being trapped by our own tactics."

I'll call it the "useful-enemy trap" because populist leaders *need* enemies. The more outrageous, rude and unreasonable an enemy appears, the more useful they are. Valenti and De Niro are most useful ... to Trump. This trap is particularly dangerous because those caught in it aggressively spread their misconceptions and entrap others. Their "righteousness" makes them effective proselytizers.

Two days after Valenti's op-ed in *The Guardian* went viral, comedian Kathy Griffin made headlines by tweeting, with sparkling humor, "Fuck you, Melania. ... you feckless complicit piece of shit." Surely that won over many in Trump's base, don't you think?

(Yes, Griffin was outrageously harassed and threatened by Trumpsters expressing fake outrage over her well-ketchuped, severed, mock

Trump head, and I wouldn't mind her getting even. My objection is to this additional gift she unwittingly bestowed on Trump.)

Why Enemies Are So Useful

George W. Bush's approval rating jumped from 51% to 86% in one week after the 9/11 attacks. It was not simply the attacks that did it. His speeches were good and well-received. But it is no coincidence that his most effective speeches occurred in that particular week. The country was unified by the attacks, and he was clearly on our side and intent on defending us.

The idea that an external enemy is helpful to leaders is anything but new. It is so well known that leaders often invent threats when none present themselves, for example, the threat of weapons of mass destruction in Iraq. So it is hardly surprising that Trump would know that enemies are useful. What *is* surprising is that the far left does not seem to get this.

So Trump plays the left with his outrageous attacks, knowing his base is so aware of the game that they mockingly refer to the far-left counterattacks as "Trump derangement syndrome" (yes, this is a real term; just look up "TDS" in the online Urban Dictionary). And even though they know Trump is deliberately pushing the left's buttons, the counterattacks still prove to them that the "deranged left" is a real danger. Their view is this: "Just imagine if such angry and easily-manipulated people gained power." Perhaps they have a point.

Why Populist Leaders Especially Need Enemies

Populists focus most intently on the corrupt elite, but just being the leader of a mass movement makes a person elite compared to being part of the ordinary people. This is especially true if they happen to be billionaires.

In other words, the first job of a populist leader is to prove he, or she, is an outsider—not part of the elite—despite their power, status and often their wealth. And the best way to prove that is to be attacked by the elite. The next best way is to pretend you're being attacked by the elite.

Trump gets this. That's why he provokes the elite. As I explained in Chapter 15, liberals and progressives are part of the elite as seen by Jacksonian populists. So Trump attacks the liberal media and Democrats, and constantly claims they are attacking him even if they just point out accurate, well-known facts. But his attacks, which are deliberately outrageous, often do provoke the vigorous counterattacks he needs.

There's also a less obvious benefit for an authoritarian populist playing this game. Such attacks and counterattacks polarize the country, which polarizes the government. When the government is polarized, democracy appears weak and ineffective, which causes both sides to break old democratic traditions that our democracy depends upon. The result: Trump wins and democracy loses, which is exactly what he wants and needs.

Anger Is Not a Strategy

Frank Bruni's *New York Times* op-ed—the one attacked by Valenti— begins, "I get that you're angry. I'm angry, too. But anger isn't a strategy. Sometimes it's a trap." But Valenti strongly implies that Bruni opposes being angry about Trump's offenses and that he calls instead for "putting up with injustice" while being "cheerful throughout."

Obviously, Bruni expected this counterattack, which is why he began his op-ed with "I'm angry too." But it's no use because the Valentis of this world can see no difference between being angry and screaming. That, of course, is exactly how very young children think. When angry, all they know how to do is throw a temper tantrum. So for them, anger equals a tantrum. And for Valenti, no tantrum means Bruni must not be angry.

But as adults, we learn to channel our anger in many other ways— even, for example, pretending not to be angry and then proceeding to stab our attacker in the back. Sociopaths like Trump become experts at finding sneaky ways to get even. As Bruni says, "Anger isn't a strategy." But temper tantrums are a strategy, and organizing to beat Republican candidates is another strategy. Both can be fueled by anger. The first is a counterproductive strategy; the second is effective.

Valenti makes no logical argument for her temper-tantrum strategy. Instead, she simply lists terribly offensive things Trump has done. Because these are true, she gets credit with her audience for speaking the (completely obvious) truth. Then she jumps to the conclusion that since he's really horribly offensive, we should be offensive too. What?! We should follow Trump's lead? Mimic his behavior? Some have even taken to saying, "When he goes low, we go lower."

Going lower is a strategy. Cursing is a strategy. Name-calling is another. But anger is just fuel for the strategy we choose. We should use that fuel wisely and choose a strategy that works.

Temper Tantrums vs. the Civil Rights Movement

As the *Jackson Free Press* reported, John Salter, a professor at Tougaloo College, was sitting with his three Black students—Anne Moody, Pearlena Lewis, and Memphis Norman—at the "Whites Only" lunch counter in Woolworth's. Nobody would serve them. This was 1963.

> "The police officers were watching just a few feet away while these thugs were kicking this young Black guy. Kicking him in the face. Finally, they broke it up [and] arrested Norman and someone else. Anne was pulled from her seat, as was Pearlena, but they fought their way back to the counter. John Salter was struck down by a punch, leaving Anne [and] Pearlena, at the counter. They were smeared with ketchup, mustard, sugar, anything that was on the counter. They sat and faced the front."

They did not take Jessica Valenti's advice to "curse, scream, and name-call." They were extraordinarily civil, and their actions were unbelievably powerful. No one will have heard of Valenti's cursing fifty years from now.

At the time of this incident, slavery had ended 100 years earlier, but the Klan was still active and Congress was still unwilling to pass an anti-lynching law. Then-Vice President Lyndon Johnson had himself once argued against such a law.

Certainly, Blacks were angry, and they had every right to be. But they had years of experience and amazing leaders. And so their anger was channeled into effective action, and they ended legal segregation and won the right to vote. No, that didn't end racism, but given what they were up against, no one should belittle what they accomplished. Cursing, screaming and name-calling would have turned the activists into the enemies the segregationists needed.

The civil rights movement followed Michelle Obama's maxim: When they go low, we go high."

The Vulgarity Virus

Valenti does not only attack Frank Bruni but all "those on the left" who call for civility. Dangerously, she warns us to be "extremely wary of every person" who is not outraged enough to curse and scream. She's calling for those on the left to suspect each other's morals—suggesting the most bitter kind of divisiveness, the first step in the new "cancel culture."

This is a powerful way to impose conformity in a group, which is why it is so important that people like Bruni speak against it. But the rest of us also need to point out, when appropriate, that winning matters more than the fleeting personal satisfaction of cathartic cursing. And that such self-indulgent behavior only helps Trump.

Conclusion

True or not, Trump's base feels under attack and views him as their protector. If he is also seen to be under attack by the "liberal elite," that "proves" to his base that he must be on their side. It makes them want to protect him. That unifies and energizes his base. Because an attack on him is seen as an attack on them. When he punches back, his base sees him as defending them.

This is why noisy, toothless enemies are so useful to him. So the best strategy is to let your anger fuel a devastating attack that looks as little like an attack as possible. The lunch counter sit-in was a powerful attack on segregation that just looked like some college kids trying to order a sandwich. According to her daughter, Nancy Pelosi "will cut your head off and you won't even know you're bleeding." That's masterful.

The worst scenario for Trump is to suffer setbacks and defeats without any apparent attack. Not only does that make him look weak; it also doesn't provide his base with a reason to rally around him.

- Trump needs noisy enemies to fire up his base for him.
- The trick is to help Trump destroy himself while no one notices what you're doing.

PART 4

Mythology Traps

People love their myths. For example, "If Teddy Roosevelt were alive today, do you know what he would say? He'd say break 'em up." That's from Bernie Sanders' "Break Up the Big Banks" speech in July 2015. We love it. After all, the big banks and their financial cousins had crashed our economy just seven years ago, and we still had not completely recovered. So we love the idea of the swashbuckling Teddy Roosevelt riding into town and breaking them up. Serves 'em right.

That sort of feeling is what powers myths with their charismatic heroes and villains. But because myths aren't true, they need some protection from reality. Like many political myths, this one makes a claim about what would happen if, in this case, Teddy were alive today. Because he isn't alive, it's hard to refute the claim. That sort of uncertainty protects our beloved myths from reality.

So how can we tell if the Teddy-and-the-banks myth is true? Here's how. It happens that Roosevelt did face a banking crisis that involved big banks failing. And we know what he did. He went straight to J. P. Morgan, the biggest banker bar none, and asked him to help save the big banks! Morgan said he didn't have enough money, so Teddy had the U.S. Treasury help him out. And Morgan saved the failing big banks with no talk of breaking them up.

Most of our myths can be debunked this way, but why bother? They make us feel good, and that's a plus. Unfortunately, they often mislead us into making serious mistakes. Often this happens because they promote ideologies (isms), which are like political religions. So to understand some of the myths, we need basic knowledge about a few isms, such as socialism, capitalism and a few others. I'll start there and then debunk some of the myths.

Synopsis of Part 4

Chapter 22. Socialism, Liberalism and All That. Socialism is good in theory, and Communism is too good to even try. Democratic Socialism is not what they say it is, and it really isn't capitalism.

Chapter 23. Sanders' Socialism Myth. In agreement with the extreme right, Sanders says FDR's liberal policies were socialism.

Chapter 24. The Myth of the Utopian Savior. Nothing is more appealing than a president who will fix the country and bring world peace. Oliver Stone says Henry Wallace came so, so close.

Chapter 25. The Establishment Myth. Some people love to hate the establishment. But their heroes turn out to be the most establishment Democrats of all time.

Chapter 26. The Myth of the Bully Pulpit. To make real change, should a president be a preacher? That's not how Teddy did it.

Chapter 27. The Myth of the Overton Window. To shift public opinion in your direction fast, radicals tell us: Just advocate the unthinkable. That's the force behind polarization.

CHAPTER 22

Socialism, Liberalism and All That

Don't tell me words don't matter.
—President Barack Obama, 2008

Teddy Roosevelt's policies were called socialist, as were Franklin Roosevelt's and Lyndon Johnson's. Barack Obama was constantly called a socialist. All of them rejected this label.

Some may think, *Well, they might not have been socialist, but they were probably "democratic socialists."* But that's not it. For more than a hundred years, "socialist" has been short for "democratic socialist."

To avoid being smeared as a socialist, Elizabeth Warren recently declared herself "capitalist to my bones." So what is socialism, and why have all Democrats gone out of their way to deny they are socialists?

Tweet from Democratic Socialists of America

There's been a lot of talk over the last four years about socialism, communism, democratic socialism, progressivism, liberalism, and capitalism, but little of it makes sense because the definitions have been jumbled. Worse yet, Sanders, who knows better, has been playing games with these terms to confuse his base. So this chapter will aim to clear up the old definitions that are still in use by those who have something more sensible to say than "communism is good."

Every four years, the Gallup Poll asks Americans, "If your party nominated a generally well-qualified person for president who happened to be _____, would you vote for that person?" In 2015 and 2019, they asked about candidates who were Black, Catholic, Hispanic, a woman, Jewish, an evangelical Christian, gay or lesbian, Muslim, an atheist, and a socialist. Americans grew more tolerant of 9 out of those 10 categories. The one category that didn't budge was "socialist."

Four years of Sanders pushing socialism had no noticeable effect. The acceptability of a socialist president remained at 47%. Atheists, who are always second-to-last, rose to 60%. It really is a little bit crazy for Democrats to call themselves the most unpopular term in politics without knowing what it means, and a lot of them are doing that right now.

Socialism: A Good Idea with Bad Results

After capitalism got going, a lot of people noticed that capitalists were wealthy and got paid mainly for being wealthy and investing their wealth in businesses.

People also noticed that workers had to work for their money, and most of them made so little they could barely survive. The poor produced all the goods—they created the wealth—and the rich were paid for being wealthy. That didn't seem fair. The fair thing would be—

Socialism: Everyone gets paid for working. And that's it. No getting paid for being rich.

Of course, there's a little more to it, but that's the core moral principle behind socialism. I, for one, think it's a good one with regard to fairness. And quite a few people see paying people for being rich as totally unfair.

Bad results. The trouble with socialism is that no one has yet been able to make it work. It's simple in theory, but in practice, real-world complexities get in the way. Socialists have proposed two ways to get rid of the capitalists: (1) every business is owned and controlled by its employees, and (2) the government owns all the businesses or at least the big ones. Corporations can, and sometimes do, try the first approach, so we don't need a socialist president for that. But in 150 years this approach has not taken off due to all sorts of problems, such as who votes for whose pay level.

The government-ownership approach to socialism is the one that has caused all the trouble—in other countries. The problem seems to be that well-meaning socialist politicians come to power by promising economic miracles, but their socialist economies don't do well. In a strong democracy, the socialists can be voted back out of power, and sometimes that's happened.

Horrific results. A major reason socialism is hated is that it duped many good Americans into supporting the USSR (the Union of Soviet *Socialist* Republics) and later Mao's China. In both cases, genuinely socialist agricultural policies led to mass starvation and millions died. (You can find this in any decent history of Russia or China. Or you can Google "Soviet famine of 1932–33" and "great Chinese famine.")

It gets worse. When the economy fails after promises of miracles, the ruling socialist party never blames socialism. Instead, they start executing scapegoats or sending them to prison camps, with truly horrific results.

Beyond the USSR and China, we have the North Korean economy, the Cuban economy (which can only be partly blamed on the U.S. boycott) and the recent catastrophic failure of Hugo Chavez's democratic socialism in Venezuela.

Communism Hasn't Been Tried

To understand "democratic socialism," we must get a whiff of communism—undemocratic socialism. What's confusing is that that "communism" has two meanings: the first meaning is something like Communist Party-ism and the second is Marx's theoretical communism.

Theoretical communism would be terrific if it worked as advertised. The moral core of communism, according to Karl Marx (1875), is "from each according to his abilities and to each according to his needs." That only works when people become angels. So the tweet shown above was loved by 1,500+ Democratic Socialists of America who want to lead the country by proclaiming that heaven on earth is a good idea. Brilliant.

The Communist Party USA, which turned 100 in 2019, calls itself communist, but like the USSR, its members never seem to talk about theoretical communism. Marx's idea was first to build socialism under the "dictatorship of the proletariat"—a dictatorship by workers—and then build theoretical communism. They're still stuck on the kind of dictatorship-style socialism that the USSR and China adopted. So "communists" are really just undemocratic socialists.

Democratic Socialism

The Socialist Party of America was formed in 1901 and ran Eugene V. Debs—Bernie Sanders' lifelong hero—for president in 1904. By 1912, the party's platform was calling for the abolition of the U.S. Senate.

The idea was that only the House is based on the principle of one person, one vote. (Your vote for Senator counts a lot more if you live in Wyoming rather than California.) Note that today, Sanders is still saying democratic socialism means "one person, one vote." And he might still be in favor of abolishing the Senate just like his hero, Eugene V. Debs.

Ever since Debs, American socialists have been running in elections and advocating a combination of democratic politics and socialist economics. That's democratic socialism. Since 1904 or earlier, socialism has almost always meant some kind of democratic socialism, and democratic socialism has meant socialism. They're the same. Hugo Chavez was a socialist/democratic socialist who Bernie Sanders endorsed until he called him a "dead communist dictator" (see Chapter 5).

Progressivism

Progressivism, unlike Marxism, socialism/democratic socialism and communism, has American roots. It is most associated with Teddy Roosevelt but started earlier. The laissez-faire (unregulated) capitalism of the 1800s led to the age of robber barons, extreme inequality and dire conditions for much of the working class. Progressivism's first success was the Sherman Antitrust Act of 1890. That same year, Jacob Riis published *How the Other Half Lives*, which inspired working-class housing reforms and opened the door to 20 years of "muckraking," which, in turn, led to many more reforms.

Recently, the term progressive has been revived and has changed meaning. After the New Left smeared liberals in the 1960s and the Reagan smeared the L-word in the 1980s, Democrats largely gave up on FDR's "liberal" label and started calling themselves progressives. But it was just a name change, not a change in political outlook. More recently, the radical left has claimed only they are "progressives," but they still mean "FDR liberals" and just don't know it (that's in the next chapter).

To avoid bucking either new trend, I will continue to use "progressive" to mean all Democrats except the most conservative.

The original progressive movement ended when FDR became President in 1933. Progressives wanted to reduce income and wealth inequality and provide good education and decent jobs for everyone. Generally, they wanted to do this by making Capitalism fairer—busting up the monopolies and trusts of the robber barons; allowing labor unions; and limiting the workday, the workweek, and child labor. They won women the right to vote and the progressive income tax. They also brought us Prohibition.

All this brought about a radical change in thinking—the repudiation of individualism and laissez-faire capitalism. But it did not include government spending for the general welfare. That's where FDR's liberalism comes in. FDR liberalism was the next step after progressivism.

Liberalism

So far I have basically defined liberalism as the views of Democrats who are not part of the radical left. But it will now become useful to define it a bit more specifically. So I will now shift to this definition:

Liberalism favors the types of policies FDR favored plus all forms of civil rights.

As a reminder, I will often call this FDR liberalism. This covers both FDR's New Deal policies and this Second Bill of [economic] Rights, which he proposed in his fourth inaugural address, in 1944. But it should also be understood to cover something like FDR's political philosophy as well. And FDR favored compromising whenever that moved his agenda forward. He also hated socialism. Most socialists contend correctly, I think, that part of his agenda was to save capitalism from socialism.

Before Roosevelt, the term liberalism was used by both Democrats and Republicans to mean something more like "libertarian." In his "Rugged Individualism" speech of 1928, Hoover included a short but forceful section advocating liberalism.

Roosevelt knew his New Deal would be attacked as socialistic, so to protect it he called it liberalism—in essence, camouflaging it as part of the conservative tradition. Of course, this upset Hoover and the conservatives, but FDR won that fight, captured the term for the Democrats and redefined it to mean a philosophy of government responsibility for social welfare.

The result was that liberalism came to mean things like unemployment insurance, Social Security and the like. At the time, this was a radical concept because it went well beyond progressivism.

Since Roosevelt made his Second Bill of Rights speech, there has been much progress towards a more complete safety net, including many improvements to Social Security and the addition of food stamps, welfare payments, a minimum wage, Medicare, Medicaid, Obamacare, and various housing programs.

Of course, there's still a long way to go, but FDR liberalism made a decisive change, and we are still on that track. However, it is a path that leaves capitalism in place as the economic engine. It's just a path to humanizing capitalism.

Capitalism

If you compare laissez-faire, robber baron capitalism in 1900 to capitalism today, the difference is truly revolutionary, despite some backsliding under Reagan. No longer do we have 60-hour (or more) workweeks and child labor, with no old-age security and no safety net. And capitalism can be made much better—just take a look at Denmark.

But what is capitalism? It's actually quite simple. Denmark and the U.S. are capitalist because almost all goods and services are produced by for-profit companies owned by capitalists. Democratic Socialists of America want to eliminate the profit motive: "The economy should be run democratically ... *not to make profits*." If you eliminate profits, you will eliminate capitalists and capitalism.

The only noticeable reduction in capitalism proposed by Sanders and Warren is to put the health insurance companies out of business. That would make the economy about 1% less capitalistic at most. (All health insurance companies combined are only worth one-fifth as much as Apple.) So ending capitalism is not currently on the table.

Conclusion

American politics has proceeded down two lanes: progressivism followed by liberalism, which I'll just call the liberal lane, and the socialist lane. The liberal lane comes from the Enlightenment and has been central to our political and economic development since 1890, with some parts of it, much older—for example, writing the Constitution and the anti-slavery and feminist movements. The other lane—socialism, communism, and neo-Marxism (explained in Part 5)—comes to us from Marx and other foreign sources and has always been a fringe phenomenon in the U.S.

- "Socialism" has meant democratic socialism for more than 100 years here in America. And democratic socialism has always been a kind of socialism.
- Progressivism and FDR liberalism have transformed capitalism from laissez-faire, robber-baron capitalism into basic welfare capitalism. This is still a work in progress.
- FDR viewed his liberalism as saving the U.S. from socialism.

CHAPTER 23

Sanders' Socialism Myths

I am against private socialism of concentrated private power as thoroughly as I am against governmental socialism. The one is equally as dangerous as the other.
—Franklin Delano Roosevelt, March 12, 1935

FDR would surely be the Democrats' patron saint if we had one. In his day, he was known for saving American capitalism from socialism by humanizing capitalism. Socialists have long hated him for that. So why has Sanders, a lifelong socialist, now adopted FDR as *his* patron saint?

What's Sanders Up To?

Since 2015, Sanders has been faking a lane change, politically speaking. As late as 2009, he posted on his Senate website: "I doubt that there are any other socialists in all of the Congress." And he used to publicly back nationalization of all utilities, the oil industry, banks and what have you.

There's no way he can explicitly back away from this now. Socialism is highly unpopular with the broad electorate, and the socialist tradition he's part of has had an uninterrupted string of failures since its beginning. To win the Democratic primary he needs a new identity. So he has started pretending he is FDR's successor. This has had a huge and divisive impact on the Democratic Party, so it's worth looking into.

How Sanders Fakes a Lane Change

There are two major lanes on the liberal side of politics: the socialism-not-capitalism lane and the capitalism-not-socialism lane. I'll call them the socialist lane and the FDR-liberal lane.

Essentially everyone has been clear on the difference until now, except for the far right, which has pretty much called every Democrat, and even Teddy Roosevelt, a socialist, communist or pinko-commie.

All of the Democrats' heroes—the two Roosevelts, LBJ, and Obama—strongly oppose(d) socialism. And all the socialist heroes— Eugene V. Debs, Norman Thomas, Michael Harrington and Bernie Sanders—oppose(d) capitalism.

To remind you of the forgettable socialists, Sanders' lifelong hero, Eugene V. Debs, ran for president six times and scored a record-breaking 6% in 1912. Like Bernie, he was a bit over-optimistic, saying in 1904: "Capitalism is dying, and its extremities are already decomposing."

Reality

Socialist Lane	FDR-Liberal Lane
Socialism (not capitalism) aka **Democratic Socialism**	**Regulated Capitalism** (not socialism) FDR's **2nd Bill of Rights**
Eugene V. Debs Norman Thomas M. Harrington (DSA) Bernie Sanders	Teddy Roosevelt Franklin Roosevelt Lyndon Johnson Barack Obama

Debs' successor, Norman Thomas, famously quipped when asked by a reporter whether Franklin D. Roosevelt was actually carrying out his socialist program: "Yes, he is carrying it out in a coffin." Michael Harrington is considered the founder of the Democratic Socialists of America (DSA), an organization that rejects an economy based on profits—i.e., based on capitalism.

The first figure accurately depicts the two lanes, with Sanders in the socialist lane. Democratic socialism shows up as just another name for socialism, as explained in the previous chapter. None of the socialists were Democrats, and none of the Democrats approved (or currently approve) of socialism. However, in one respect the two lanes are not so different. Both want

Sanders' Socialism Myth

Socialist Lane	FDR Lane
Sanders pretends the socialist lane **never existed.** So he was never in it.	**Democratic Socialism** **Bernie Sanders' Bill of Rights** Teddy Roosevelt Franklin Roosevelt Lyndon Johnson Bernie Sanders DSA

full employment and far less inequality.

The second figure shows Sanders' attempted solution to his identity crisis. Sanders pretends the socialist lane simply does not exist by never mentioning any of it except for democratic socialism which he incorrectly moves into FDR's lane. In fact, he no longer openly advocates any socialist ideas, but instead claims FDR's ideas are democratic socialism. Finally, he removes the word "liberal" from FDR's lane, even though FDR spent his entire presidency establishing that as his brand. So far, Sanders has been amazingly successful with this con game.

If you read his two democratic socialism speeches (November 2015 and June 2019), you will notice that he does not mention any socialists, not even his hero Debs, whom he made a documentary about. He figures (correctly) that if people forget the lane existed, they will forget he was in it. He's counting on his followers being low-information voters.

He also rebrands all the Democrats' heroes as democratic socialists, except for Obama, who is still alive and would deny it the way the president of Denmark did when Sanders called him a socialist. And of course, Sanders inserts himself in place of Obama and claims he is the true successor to the line of Democratic heroes. He also moves DSA into FDR's liberal lane, even though it is an explicitly socialist organization. As a result, its membership ballooned from about 7,000 to about 50,000.

You must admit that's a brilliant strategy. It depends on four myths, but as I've said, people are human, and we fall for such deceptions quite easily.

Sanders' Four Socialism Myths

Embedded in Sanders' redefinition of the FDR Liberalism lane are four specific myths, which Sanders has been selling successfully and which are having a powerful effect on the Democratic Party.

Sanders' Socialism Myths

1. Sanders is a "democratic socialist," *not an actual socialist.*
2. "Democratic socialism" means all the best programs and proposals of the Democratic heroes.
3. FDR and LBJ were democratic socialists.
4. Bernie has Democratic roots, not socialist roots.

Myth 1: *Sanders is not an actual socialist.* Just as a Bartlett pear is a pear, a democratic socialist is a socialist. But his followers don't get that. Politicfact.com was receiving enough criticism for assuming the two were the same that it published and debunked one of the complaints:

Would you kindly clarify your statements that Bernie Sanders self-identifies as a socialist? He says 'democratic socialist.' There is a whopping difference, and your misstatement plays into the Republican candidates' demeaning statements too perfectly.

Obviously, the poor Berniecrat knew that socialism really was a bad idea but thought that Bernie was a good "democratic socialist." In the book Sanders published right after the 2016 election, he called himself a plain old "socialist" four times, and he's been calling himself that for fifty years. Sanders is not confused. He just confuses his followers because a lot of them would be quite upset to learn that he was a real socialist.

Myth 2: *Democratic socialism means FDR's policies, such as Social Security.* "When Trump screams socialism, Americans will know that he is attacking Social Security," says Sanders. In this way, he convinces his followers that Social Security is socialism—because Trump calls it that. Is Trump the authority on socialism?

If FDR's policies were democratic socialism, wouldn't some other socialist have noticed this? But Sanders never cites a real socialist. Instead, he cites the most unbelievable sources—Donald Trump, Ronald Reagan, Newt Gingrich, Herbert Hoover and so on.

Every single source who he cites to prove something is socialist is a conservative who hates socialism! They call everything they don't like socialism. He wouldn't trust these people to tell him the time of day. So why does he think we will believe them? Because we're blooming idiots? Actually, that might be it. Sanders does not have a high regard for the political intelligence of others, especially it seems, his own followers.

All real socialists knew FDR's policies were not socialist policies, and that's why Sanders only cites right-wingers. No socialist agrees with him.

Myth 3: *FDR and LBJ were socialists.* As this chapter's lead quote shows, FDR hated socialism. And LBJ waged the Vietnam War to prevent the spread of socialism.

Myth 4: *Sanders has Democratic roots.* No, he has shown nothing but contempt for Democrats. Writing in *The New York Times*, he discussed the "ideology of greed and vulgarity perpetuated by the Democrats and Republicans." He said such things frequently up until 1990 when he won his House seat with Democratic money. Socialists have always despised the Democrats and wanted to take over the party or replace it with a socialist party. And Sanders has joined three different socialist parties, but never the Democratic Party — until he tried to take it over in 2016. And when that failed, he immediately admitted he really was not a Democrat at all.

In 1963, Sanders volunteered for a socialist kibbutz in Israel. In 1971, he ran for the Vermont Senate as a socialist candidate. In 1974, he said, "All necessities of life must be provided free for people." Food? Housing? Clothes? Cars? You figure it out.

In 1979, he made a documentary of his lifetime hero, Eugene V. Debs. In 1981, he was a functionary in the Socialist Workers Party. In 1985, he visited Nicaragua and praised socialist leader Daniel Ortega, who later became a dictator. In 2006, he brokered a deal with socialist Hugo Chavez. Recently, he has refused to call Chavez's successor, Maduro, a dictator.

There is no way Sanders will be able to back away from his socialism during the general election. But in the primary, where Democrats now treat socialists as part of their team (while socialists knife them in the back), being accepted as a Democrat requires only chutzpah.

The Most Cunning Feature

Sanders has convinced millions of Democrats that FDR was a democratic socialist and that his policies are democratic socialism. But all Democratic candidates (including Sanders) and millions of well-informed Democrats know this is false and that socialism is highly unpopular. This polarizes the Democrats between two factions:

1. **"Socialist" Berniecrats:** Those who praise democratic socialism and support FDR's Second Bill of Rights.
2. **FDR-liberal Democrats:** Those who reject (democratic) socialism and support FDR's Second Bill of Rights.

Notice that both factions support FDR's Second Bill of Rights. As I mentioned, FDR is basically the Democrat's patron saint and they have been implementing parts of his Second Bill of Rights whenever they got the chance, right down to Obamacare in 2010. And Sanders has claimed that bill of rights as his own in both of his "democratic socialism" speeches. So there's no practical reason for either faction to hate the other.

However, those who join the Berniecrats see that Democrats reject socialism/democratic socialism and conclude (falsely) that they are rejecting FDR's Second Bill of Rights. Then they conclude non-socialist Democrats are shills for Wall Street or throwbacks to "neoliberalism" by which they mean Hoover's libertarian view of liberalism!

If you remain an FDR-liberal Democrat, you are not so polarized. You know that Sanders' Berniecrats have just been duped by Sanders, but they are still actually good FDR liberals and not socialists at all (except for a very few).

The polarization of his followers is good, even lifesaving, for Sanders. Otherwise, everyone would see that he's in the socialist lane that's never gone anywhere. But it is devastating for the Democratic Party, which, of course, means it's good for Trump.

Sanders knows how bad this is for Democrats and says, "I and other progressives will face massive attacks from those who attempt to use the word 'socialism' as a slur." They won't just "attempt to," they *will* use it as a slur. And they will be right about Sanders. But you know, and Sanders knows, that the whole Democratic Party will be hurt by these attacks.

None of this would happen if Sanders would honestly admit that he is a socialist and FDR was a capitalist who found socialism of any variety to be dangerous. Even better, he could become the candidate that most of his followers think he is—a true FDR liberal and no longer a socialist, democratic or otherwise. But Sanders wants to destroy the Democratic Party, so we must admit, his strategy is brilliant.

What an Obama Democrat Taught Sanders

Sanders' message is that he alone is the true heir to FDR's liberalism, and today's Democrats are establishment shills who have betrayed FDR. Ironically, Sanders learned to appreciate FDR's liberalism from a moderate Democrat, someone he views as an establishment shill. That certainly gives the lie to his message that Democrats have abandoned FDR's liberalism. Here's the story.

Sanders bases his definition of democratic socialism on FDR's Second Bill of Rights, which in 2015 he called "my vision today." Before he started hiding his true socialism, he never said anything like that. So where did this vision come from?

Take a look at the cover of Cas Sunstein's book, published in 2004. Sunstein was Obama's regulatory "czar." He is all for a "revolution" to finish implementing FDR's Bill of Rights, just like Bernie. Coincidence?

FDR's Second Bill of Rights drew international attention for a couple of years after he proposed it in 1944. Then it dropped out of sight for the next 60 years until Sunstein wrote his book, which was reviewed in *The New York Times* and *The Washington Post*. In 2006, the book was reviewed by Thom Hartmann, a prominent left-wing talk-radio host. That review contained a prophetic prediction.

> If a Democratic candidate for the presidency in 2008 were to take up Sunstein's modern update of Roosevelt's Second Bill of Rights, he or she would certainly win the election.

Hartmann was hinting to Sanders that he should run for president on what he called "Sunstein's modern update of Roosevelt's Second Bill of Rights." Sanders' June 2019 socialism speech, as posted on his website, is entitled, "Sanders calls for 21st Century Bill of Rights."

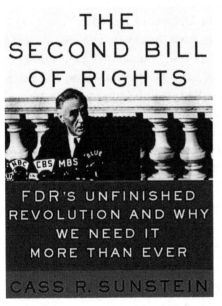

There can be no doubt Sanders got this idea from Hartmann. Starting two years before Hartmann's prescient review, and continuing for a decade, Hartmann hosted Sanders for an hour each week on Hartmann's Friday morning "Brunch with Bernie" national radio show. It's impossible that Hartmann did not tell Bernie about both the book he was so excited about and his idea for a radical winning the presidency.

Sanders spoke with Sunstein just before Sunstein's confirmation hearing in the Senate and decided he was such an establishment shill that he refused to vote for his confirmation.

But Sunstein (via Hartmann) opened Sanders' eyes to the notion that he could win the presidency by pretending to jump on FDR's Democratic-liberalism bandwagon. And if an establishment shill like Sunstein could call for a revolution right on the cover of his book, and still get appointed by Obama, why couldn't Sanders be just as daring?

Conclusion

Sanders' strategy is brilliant. It's helped him cover his socialist past by pretending that a democratic socialist is just someone aligned with FDR. In this way he paints himself as just a good FDR democratic socialist, even though there's no such thing.

Because all knowledgeable Democrats—including all the candidates he's running against—know that socialism has a bloody track record internationally and has been a persistent failure domestically, they reject democratic socialism. And because Sanders has convinced his followers that rejecting democratic socialism means rejecting FDR liberalism, they mistakenly view all knowledgeable Democrats as hostile to FDR liberalism. In fact, FDR is still our hero.

This mistake, fostered by Sanders, is why Berniecrats hate the Democratic Party, just as Sanders always has.

This polarizes the Democratic Party, weakens it internally and makes it vulnerable to Republican attacks. That's okay with Sanders. He's always hated the Democrats. His only goal is socialism, although for now, he is keeping his truly socialist ideas to himself.

- FDR was no democratic socialist.
- Bernie Sanders has always been a socialist, and he still is.

CHAPTER 24

The Myth of the Utopian Savior

*Had Pepper made it five more feet and nominated Wallace
before the bosses forced adjournment against the will of the
delegates ... there might have been no atomic bombings, no
nuclear arms race, and no Cold War.*

—Oliver Stone & Peter Kuznick, 2012
The Untold History of the United States

"There would not have been this Cold War ... Vietnam wouldn't have
happened" claims radical-left filmmaker Oliver Stone. "If only Wallace
[not Truman] had won Roosevelt's vice-presidential nomination in
1946."

All this and more would have been achieved if only Pepper [a Florida
Senator] "had made it five more feet and nominated Wallace before the
party bosses forced adjournment [on that fateful night of the 1944 Democratic convention]."

"Five more feet" and there would have been no 40-year-long Cold
War with the Soviet Union, no nuclear arms race, and no Vietnam War
with 60,000 Americans dead or missing and a million or more Vietnam-
ese dead.

Really? Does anyone even believe such poppycock? It has been the
most-discussed assertion in Oliver Stone's popular 2012 book and 10-
segment TV series, *The Untold History of the United States.*

I have heard the Wallace story presented as evidence that Bernie
Sanders, like Wallace, could transform the country. And when Tulsi
Gabbard, the Congresswoman from Hawaii, was asked by *The New York
Times,* after the second 2019 Democratic debate, what podcasts she lis-
tens to, she only recommended watching Stone's *Untold History.*

As I will show in Chapter 36, Stone's type of utopian thinking has been the core of radical mythologies since Zarathustra. It seems to be built into human nature, and it is likely the most dangerous of myths. It arises during troubled times. It's what powers Trump's political revolution, and it's why we have two potential utopian saviors—Bernie Sanders and Elizabeth Warren—among the top presidential candidates.

The Savior Myth: Pessimistic Optimism

The utopian savior myth varies with the circumstances and the savior, but its essence is present pessimism coupled with future optimism and characterized by these assumptions:

1. These are terrible times, and things are getting worse.
2. There have been many who have come close to saving us, but the establishment keeps blocking them.
3. At last, we have found our savior.

Assumption #1: Things are going from bad to worse. This is the pessimism. It can be absolutely true or mostly invented. Either way, it can power the search for a savior.

This dark side of the utopian myth is best illustrated by an assertion Bernie Sanders made in the carefully crafted announcement of his candidacy for the presidency in May 2015:

> This country faces more serious problems today than at any time since the Great Depression.

He claimed this was true even without counting climate change as one of the problems. And of course, he did not include Trump, who was not even on the horizon. At the time, unemployment was about 5.5% and heading steadily down, and healthcare coverage was at an all-time high. So what was Sanders thinking?

Did Sanders forget what was happening when Obama took office at the start of the Great Recession? The stock market was crashing, people were losing their homes and jobs right and left, the auto industry was diving toward bankruptcy, our troops were still stuck in Iraq and no one knew if we could avoid a second Great Depression. So when Sanders says the country was "facing more serious problems" in 2015, he's saying that Obama started with an economic catastrophe and he just kept making it worse. Really?!

Did Sanders forget about Ronald Reagan? In December 1982, unemployment hit 11%, and Reagan was just starting to bust the unions and ramp up the Cold War. Were we worse off under Obama in 2015 than under Reagan in 1982?

In 1967–68, more than 100 cities exploded in urban riots over racial discrimination, Bobby Kennedy and MLK were assassinated, the Vietnam war was ramping up and Nixon was about to take the White House. Was this period better than America in 2015?

Has Sanders heard of World War II? In 1944, the economy had doubled, leaving the Depression behind. But you couldn't buy a car, and gasoline and many foods were rationed. That year, WWII killed Americans at the rate of six mass shootings, as lethal as the worst we've had, every day of the year. And the rest of the world was suffering casualties at more than 100 times that rate, while the Holocaust was operating at maximum horror.

So Obama in 2015 was worse than WWII?!

Sanders has been a politician his whole life and obviously is well aware of all this history. So this was no mistake. He knew it wasn't true, but he knew his base would believe it and that they needed to believe it if they were going to buy the utopian savior myth. And that's the myth he's selling.

Assumption #2: *Many have come close to saving us.* This is reflected in an interview with Stone that historian Peter Kuznick posted on *TheDailyBeast.com*:

> We also show how close the United States has come repeatedly in its history to pursuing a different course that would further humanity rather than threatening it. We tell the story of Henry Wallace ... Eisenhower the progressive general ... and the remarkable transformation John F. Kennedy underwent in the last year of his life ... he would have pulled U.S. troops out of Vietnam and ended the Cold War.

This assertion—that we've repeatedly come close—matters because no savior has ever saved us. So the only way to maintain optimism for such a miracle is to argue that we keep coming oh-so-close. So it really could happen. Really!

Assumption #3: *At last, we have found our savior.* Here is the optimism, a promise that our terrible troubles will be put behind us and we will be transported to the promised land. Just read the plans of Sanders or Warren, or better yet, the Green New Deal.

Nothing like this has ever been achieved before, though many have made such promises. More amazing still, we will reach this utopian state, not from a high plateau but from a point where our problems are, for example, the most serious in 80 years.

Saviors need to make such grand claims because the socialist lane has no track record of success. Socialists and populists have no Teddy Roosevelt, FDR, LBJ or Obama. So they need to promise the moon. You might not think that would work, but we can see that it does. And even crazier promises must work or companies would not spend good money on ads such as "Learn French in 25 Minutes" (yes, a real ad). Some people will believe anything.

Who Can Do What's Never Been Done?

The root problem here is clearly utopian thinking, and this is no accident. Michael Kazen, a radical and a historian, wrote *American Dreamers* in order to promote such thinking—"Dreamers" is short for radical utopian dreamers. Stone expressed the same view to *The New York Times* when his TV series was released:

> We want to give people the ability to
> ***think in a utopian fashion*** again.

Stone's wish has been granted. America is now thinking in a utopian fashion. Trump won by promising to Make America Great Again, imagining the return of a previous American golden age, and selling himself with the boast, "Nobody knows the system better than me. *I alone can fix it.*" That's the very definition of a savior.

Elizabeth Warren led off her comments in the second 2019 debate by critiquing all of her non-utopian competitors with, "We're not going to solve the urgent problems that we face with small ideas and spinelessness. ... I know what's broken in this country, *I know how to fix it.*" She too seems to believe she's the only one who knows how.

John Delaney, another candidate in the debate, later taunted the two would-be utopian saviors, Warren and Sanders, by saying: "I think Democrats win when we run on real solutions, not impossible promises ... not fairy-tale economics."

Immediately, Warren uncorked a comeback line she'd been wanting to use for a while: "You know, I don't understand why anybody goes to all the trouble of running for president of the United States just to talk about what we really can't do and shouldn't fight for. I don't get it."

Of course, Delaney had just pointed out that she was talking about things we really can't do. He rightly called them "impossible promises ... fairy-tale economics." Rather than providing some evidence that her heroic plans were doable, she chose to call Delaney and the others spineless. Utopians never feel a need to back up their claims. They may toss around a few numbers, but their thinking is this: My plan is right, everyone will come to see that, and if they don't it's their fault, not mine.

That may sound too weird to be true, but Kazin backs that up and cites Max Weber, a founder of sociology (Ch. 38). This is nothing new.

The last time so many Democrats felt as politically disillusioned as we do today, Bob Dylan warned us in "It's All Right, Ma ('m Only Bleeding)" with these words:

Advertising signs that con you
Into thinking you're the one
That can do what's never been done
That can win what's never been won
Meantime life outside goes on
All around you

Utopian politics is all advertising with no substance.

Oliver Stone's Fable of Henry Wallace

So where do such myths come from? I'm sure there are psychological explanations, but all I can do is check the facts behind Oliver Stone's version of the Wallace myth and show you that it is based on what really deserves to be called fake history. It's so wrong and so easily checked that it seems impossible to believe that even a bad history professor could get things this wrong.

To me, this seems like an important lesson about radical claims—don't believe a one of them until you've checked it.

According to Stone: (1) Wallace would have been the perfect utopian savior and (2) came within a hair's breadth of the presidency but (3) was blocked at the last second by the evil party bosses. Those points all support the crucial Assumption #2 of the utopian-savior myth—there have been many utopians who could have saved us if only they had not been blocked.

First, would Wallace have been a utopian savior? Stone claims he would have made a nice deal with Stalin instead of being irrationally anti-communist.

Wallace himself believed this for nearly 10 years. But then he found out he'd been duped by Stalin and by the Communist Party USA, and he became a staunch anti-communist. He admits that while he was duped, he was taking disastrously wrong positions. He would have sold us down the river.

How could Stone's historian not know this? Wallace himself said all this in a long article, *"Where I Was Wrong,"* published in *This Week Magazine*. And that article is mentioned in the most popular biography of Wallace, which was available well before Stone's book and TV series came out (see Chapter 12).

It really looks like deliberate fakery, but as I've said, people can deceive themselves, and some seem to be especially good at it.

Combining the second and third points, did Wallace come within a hair's breadth of the presidency only to be blocked by the evil party bosses? Not at all. Kuznick claims that the Party bosses overwhelmed a dying Roosevelt, who wanted Wallace. But it was Franklin Roosevelt himself who ordered the Democratic bosses to stop Wallace.

Three days before the fateful night when Wallace missed getting the nomination, Roosevelt's four top Party bosses called him on his train, somewhere near El Paso, to ask for his final decision. Roosevelt said, "Go all out for Truman."

In fact, after one of his last discussions with Roosevelt, Wallace had confided to his diary that the president "wanted to ditch me as noiselessly as possible." So why didn't Kuznick pick up a Roosevelt biography at his local bookstore and read about this? Again, it seems impossible that a historian would get such accessible history wrong. But … I'll let you decide.

In truth, the reason a utopian savior has never gained power is not that they've all been blocked by the evil establishment. It's because utopian saviors, like unicorns, don't exist.

Conclusion

When you see a politician exaggerating our problems and promising some kind of revolution that will fix them all, beware. If they claim "only I can fix it," you can be sure they are a huckster from a very old tradition.

Unfortunately, the utopian savior myth never comes true. But sometimes it does succeed in handing power to a pretend savior, and this is when its full danger is realized. Consider Trump, a right-wing "utopian savior." As you can see by looking at the effects of his presidency, the utopian savior myth can result in serious damage.

- The savior myth damages the chances of those who could make progress.
- The "savior" disparages and degrades present institutions and undermines democracy.

CHAPTER 25

The Establishment Myth

*He [Herbert Hoover] is certainly a wonder, and I wish we
could make him President of the United States. There could
not be a better one.*

—Franklin Delano Roosevelt, 1920

"In every single state that we contested, we took on virtually the entire
political establishment—U.S. senators, members of Congress, governors,
mayors, state legislators, and local party leaders." From these words, you
might think that Bernie Sanders had something against everyone, from
top to bottom, in the political establishment but especially those at the
top.

Far from it. He absolutely worships the two most establishment Democrats of all time, Lyndon Johnson and Franklin Delano Roosevelt. Or at
least he pretends he does.

The reason for his contradictory positions is that Sanders' political
agenda overrides everything else. He praises the two most establishment
Democrats to the skies because that helps him shift from the unpopular
socialist lane to the ever-popular FDR lane, as explained in Chapter 23.
And he vilifies all current and far-less-establishment Democrats because
that helps his hostile takeover of the Democratic Party.

Does Sanders Worship Roosevelt?

In his 2015 Georgetown University speech, Sanders pinned his "democratic socialist" vision on FDR's 1944 State of the Union speech, which
he called "one of the most important speeches ever made by a president."
He quoted FDR's view on economic security, and told us, "That was
Roosevelt's vision seventy years ago. It is my vision today."

Astoundingly, Sanders is attributing the heart and soul of his lifelong
socialist ideology to FDR, a man who said "government socialism" is as
dangerous as "socialism of concentrated private power," meaning corpo-

rate control of government for the benefit of the rich, the arrangement Sanders (and most of us) hate the most.

In April 2016, Sanders visited Roosevelt's grave, praising FDR as "one of the great, great presidents in the history of our country." Four days later, Sanders released a TV/YouTube ad showing him and FDR side by side, telling us that Roosevelt found "a way to break up big banks, create millions of jobs and rebuild America. Some say it can't be done again. But another native son of New York is ready: Bernie." Clearly, he wants to be seen as the next Franklin Delano Roosevelt. He couldn't get in any deeper than that.

For the 2020 primaries, Sanders has already begun retracing these same steps, this time basing his "21st Century Bill of Rights" almost point for point on FDR's Second Bill of Rights.

How 'Establishment' was FDR?

Roosevelt was born on a 600-acre estate in Hyde Park, New York, which he eventually inherited. With a trust fund and support from his mother, he never actually needed to work. As a child, he visited the White House and vacationed in Europe every summer. At his wedding, President Teddy Roosevelt gave away his bride, Eleanor. For a wedding present, his mother built them a double townhouse in New York City. She lived in half, and in the other half, Eleanor and Franklin raised five children with the help of seven servants. His "Little White House" in Warm Springs, Georgia, was segregated, and he required his Black and White servants to eat in different locations. Eleanor's trust fund paid out slightly more than Franklin's.

That places him far up into the top 1% in terms of wealth and income. But how was he positioned in the political establishment?

The Democrats decided to run Franklin for the New York State Senate in 1910 because of his name and his ability to finance his own campaign. He didn't ask for any $27 contributions like Sanders does because, like Trump, he didn't need any contributions at all. He served for six years and then was appointed Assistant Secretary of the Navy. Next, he was elected Governor of New York, and in 1932, he won the presidency with a campaign that was about one-quarter financed by Wall Street bankers and stockbrokers. He was elected president three more times. You can't get any deeper into the "political establishment" than that.

More Progressive than Today's Democrats?

Because Roosevelt was at the pinnacle of the Party establishment and far up into the 1%, what excuse could Sanders have for not condemning him to political hell? Perhaps Sanders makes an exception for Roosevelt because he was more progressive than today's evil, "neoliberal" Democratic establishment?

I don't think so.

Let me describe Roosevelt's actions and policies projected forward onto the Obama administration so you can see how they would look in a familiar setting. In other words, suppose a Great Depression had started in 2005 and Obama and had done what Roosevelt did. Here's what that might look like:

A couple of years into the Great Depression of 2005, Obama decided to run for president on a platform promising "a federal budget annually balanced." And he personally promised that when he took office he would implement "an immediate and drastic reduction of governmental expenditures." But Obama quickly fixed the bank panic with free deposit insurance for the banks, and the economy began to recover, with unemployment dropping from 25% to 17%. But as Keynes had to remind him, he had not increased government spending, so unemployment shot back up to 22%. After two-and-a-half years, Obama passed Obamacare (similar to Social Security), but it only took in money for the first few years while providing no healthcare, and it was deliberately sexist and racist.

Early in his second term, Obama got the unemployment rate down to 11%, so he decided the economy no longer needed much support and cut government spending. That sent unemployment back up to 20%. At the start of his third term, America was attacked by Iran, so he put 110,000 Muslims—whole families—in concentration camps for three years. And when Michelle, taken by surprise, protested to Barack about the concentration camps, he said he did not wish to discuss the subject with her!

Obviously, Obama did nothing like this and was a vastly more progressive president than Roosevelt. But substituting Japan for Iran and Eleanor for Michelle, FDR did all of them. He was on the side of the common man, but he was more of a politician than a radical, and the times were different. That's how you get things done.

Because FDR is such a bugaboo for socialists, I'm sure Sanders is well aware of all this. So it cannot be that he vastly prefers FDR to Obama because Roosevelt was more progressive. So why does Sanders give the ultra-establishment FDR a pass and pretend to worship him?

The story of LBJ, another one of Sanders' heroes, is not so different. He wasn't born filthy rich, but he made his $100 million through government corruption involving the FCC and radio stations that his wife owned. Plus, of course, he brought the Vietnam War to a peak, and its death toll, both foreign and domestic, was 10 times that of Bush's Iraq war. And he was an establishment politician if there ever was one.

What's Up with Sanders' Hypocrisy?

So why would Sanders replace his hero, the most-loved American Socialist, Eugene V. Debs, with a staunch anti-socialist, ultra-elite, ultra-establishment, somewhat-racist politician from the party he has despised for his entire life?

I'm not condemning FDR. I'm not a socialist, and I don't judge people by purity tests. And I do take into account the times in which they lived and that everyone has their good sides and their bad sides. It doesn't bother me at all if you're from the top 0.1% or from the political establishment, as long as you're on our side. So I look at FDR and see him as a hero who is just as flawed as most every other hero.

My point is that Sanders goes around condemning people for their money, for their position in the Democratic Party, for getting only halfway to universal health coverage and for wanting to reform capitalism rather than throwing it out. But he does that only when it's to his political advantage.

When it's to his advantage to break every one of his political taboos and break them with a vengeance, he doesn't think twice.

In the case of FDR and LBJ, he needs to claim them as his own in order to obscure his socialist past. And he needs to define them as socialists so that when well-informed Democrats reject socialism, they will be attacked by his misguided followers.

This is a brilliant strategy for Sanders, and I'm afraid also a brilliant strategy for electing Trump—even though Sanders probably won't get the nomination.

I would also note that although Sanders' supposed heroes, FDR and LBJ, were strongly opposed to socialism, they have long been unfairly attacked as socialists—that's called "red baiting," and it's something Sanders vehemently opposes. Yet Sanders has now proclaimed that the red-baiters have been right all along about FDR and LBJ—they really were socialists.

Conclusion

People should not be judged by wealth or social position any more than they should be judged by their race or sexual orientation. To do so is pre-judging, otherwise known as prejudice. People should be judged as individuals, by their words and by their actions.

If we were to accept the rantings of Sanders and his fellow radicals against the 1% and the "entire political establishment" right down to the "local party leaders," we would have to condemn Franklin Roosevelt to the lowest circle of political hell.

This is not a path toward progress but a throwback to a darker age. Sanders is not in FDR's lane, which has its roots in the American progressive movement. Sanders is still a socialist, and although less dogmatic than most, he operates with a cold expediency masked by self-righteous anger.

- FDR was ultra-elite and at the pinnacle of the political establishment.
- This does not prove FDR was evil. It proves Sanders' purity tests are evil.

CHAPTER 26

The Myth of the Bully Pulpit

I have always been fond of the West African proverb "Speak softly and carry a big stick; you will go far."
—Teddy Roosevelt

"There are two dominant views," according to Robert Reich, "about how presidents accomplish fundamental change." He was making the case for Sanders over Clinton. "The first might be called the "dealmaker-in-chief"—he saw that as Clinton's approach.

"The second view about how presidents accomplish big things," the approach he prefers, is "by mobilizing the public to demand them." Teddy Roosevelt, he continued, won great victories "not because he was a great dealmaker," but rather because he used "his 'bully pulpit' to galvanize political action."

C‿‿‿‿ɔ

The Democratic Party has split between these two dominant views of what's most effective—dealmaking or preaching. Two candidates, Elizabeth Warren and Bernie Sanders, represent the bully-pulpit view, and their followers sneer that the others are establishment dealmakers. But the dealmakers are less polarizing.

As I argued in the Introduction, the bully-pulpit myth has been believed until recently even by political scientists, but the evidence against it is persuasive. Still, the question is far from settled among nonspecialists and has a huge influence on how people think about candidates and our presidents.

Getting this wrong slows progressive change and causes many to condemn our presidents for not doing impossible things. This further polarizes the party and weakens us.

The Bully Pulpit Myth

The term "bully pulpit" was coined by President Teddy Roosevelt sometime early in his first term, perhaps in 1902. "Critics will call this preaching," he told his preacher friend. "But I have got such a bully pulpit." At that time, "bully" meant "first-rate."

Of course, TR did make fundamental changes, and he did love to campaign for office more than any president before him. His personal popularity was, at times, enormous. So a myth has grown up that he accomplished what he did mostly by preaching from his bully pulpit.

Robert Reich served under Presidents Ford, Carter and Clinton. He is now Chancellor's Professor of Public Policy at U.C. Berkeley. To support his conclusion, in a 2016 op-ed Reich listed four accomplishments that he said resulted from TR's use of the bully pulpit. "Teddy Roosevelt got:

1. A progressive income tax,
2. Limits on corporate campaign contributions,
3. Regulation of foods and drugs, and
4. The dissolution of giant trusts."

The first two of these were already discussed in some detail in the Introduction, and it turned out that neither supports the bully-pulpit myth. The progressive income take was unconstitutional while TR was in office, and he did not push for it. And he was opposed to limiting corporate campaign contributions.

Let's Keep Checking

It would be unfair to dismiss the bully-pulpit myth because it failed in the case of just two examples. So let's continue by checking the last two bully-pulpit accomplishments suggested by Reich.

Regulation of food and drugs. Upton Sinclair's blockbuster novel, *The Jungle*, was released January 25, 1906, and has never gone out of print. The book's hero worked in a meat-packing plant and became a socialist. Incidentally, the book described the unhealthy conditions in the slaughterhouses.

According to a popular but completely fictional story of the time, Roosevelt was "reading it at breakfast when he suddenly cried, 'I'm poisoned,' started throwing his sausages out the window and became a vegetarian." In reality, Roosevelt was slow to catch on. After reading the book, he wrote to Frank Doubleday, the publisher, and berated him for publishing "such an obnoxious book." A strange way to lead the progressive movement from your bully pulpit.

Doubleday, and eventually TR's inspectors, confirmed the book did in fact accurately portray the meat-packing industry. The public outcry caused by Lewis' book was so great that in 1906, Congress passed both a new Meat Inspection Act and the long-dormant Pure Food and Drug Act. Sinclair Lewis mobilized the public, not Roosevelt.

The "dissolution of giant trusts." TR did have his justice department file 44 lawsuits based on the Sherman Antitrust Act of 1890. Two of the most well-known of these suits busted the biggest railroad holding company and Standard Oil. But where did the public pressure for such actions come from? The short answer is Ida Tarbell—not Teddy Roosevelt.

In a series of 19 lengthy articles published in *McClure's Magazine* starting in November 1902, Tarbell exposed the Standard Oil Trust. But it was her focus on John D. Rockefeller that won her a huge national audience. In 1904, she concluded, "We the people of the United States and nobody else must cure whatever is wrong in the industrial situation."

The Outlook, a publication aligned with TR, proclaimed Tarbell "a Joan of Arc among moderns," crusading "against trusts and monopolies." *The Washington Times* said she had "proven herself to be one of the most commanding figures in American letters." *The Washington Post* facetiously suggested "that Mr. Rockefeller would be glad to pay the expense if some man should win Miss Ida Tarbell and take her on a leisurely tour of the world for a honeymoon." She was the star of this show. She used *McClure's Magazine* as her bully pulpit, and she galvanized public opinion.

Ultimately, Roosevelt sued Standard Oil, but not until 1906. This time Roosevelt did get on the progressive bandwagon. And this time Reich may have a bit of a point, although I found no evidence of this while reading *The Bully Pulpit*, by Doris Kearns Goodwin.

Searching for Other Evidence

Although Reich's evidence for the efficacy of the bully pulpit falls flat, there may still be a case to be made. If there is, we might expect to find it in Goodwin's biography. However, while Goodwin made an excellent choice for the title, it may have been an afterthought.

On the second page of the preface, she makes her case: "The essence of Roosevelt's leadership, I soon became convinced, lay in his enterprising use of the 'bully pulpit.'" That's it—no evidence, just an assertion. (This is not meant as a criticism of her book, which is highly informative and a joy to read.)

In the body of the book, the term "bully pulpit" is only mentioned once (thank you, Kindle search feature) with regard to Roosevelt: "He created the Palisades Park and used his bully pulpit to promote it." That's an awfully weak case for the power of the bully pulpit.

Besides this example, Goodwin's book does provide two other examples that clearly show TR's effective use of the bully pulpit, although she does not call these out.

Bully pulpit use #1. Roosevelt preferred corporate regulation to trust-busting. To achieve this, he created the Bureau of Corporations. He did so by relentlessly employing his legendary dealmaking skills. But in the end, that was not enough. So he tricked the press into believing that Rockefeller had sent six threatening telegrams to Congressmen. Though no telegrams were ever discovered, the resulting scandal tipped the balance and pushed Congress to pass his bill.

No preaching was involved, but he did use (or misuse) the press very effectively, and without radio, they were his bully pulpit.

Bully pulpit use #2. Roosevelt's most memorable use of the bully pulpit occurred when he prompted the press to coin the term "muckraker," which we now apply as a badge of honor. But at the time, he was more than a little annoyed at the direction progressive journalism had taken. As explained in the next chapter, he took journalists to task in his famous "Man with the Muck Rake" speech. The conservative press exaggerated his criticism and basically put an end to the era of progressive investigative journalism. His most famous use of his bully pulpit was to accidentally sabotage the progressive movement. This is not what Reich had in mind.

A Firsthand Report. Ray Baker, a colleague of Ida Tarbell at *McClure's* magazine and perhaps the most politically astute of the era's investigative journalists, summarized Roosevelt's relationship to the public as follows:

> The reforms he has advocated are really our reforms, not his. He has voiced them valiantly and fearlessly.
>
> For Roosevelt never leads, but always follows. He acts, but he acts only when he thinks the crowd is behind him. His understanding of us leads him rarely astray; and when he goes astray, he instantly acts in the opposite manner—and gets in with the crowd.
>
> Railroad reform was imminent in many states before he took it up. ... The Standard Oil Company and other trusts had been exposed before he framed the governmental machinery for exposing them.
>
> Roosevelt has been an instrument in letting off a Revolution quietly in the form of evolution.
>
> —Ray Baker, *The American* magazine, 1908

Goodwin's example. Concerning the Hepburn bill which enabled the government to set maximum rates on railroads, an unprecedented step toward regulation, Goodwin wrote:

> However astute Roosevelt proved in dealing with Congress, he would doubtless have failed to secure a meaningful bill without a galvanized public behind him. The combined efforts of Baker and his fellow journalists had generated a widespread demand for reform.

Note that she credits Roosevelt with being astute in dealing with Congress, while the journalists, not Roosevelt, had "galvanized the public behind him." This is the opposite of Reich's claim that "mobilizing the public" was done by Roosevelt using his "bully pulpit to galvanize political action."

According to Goodwin, the mobilizing was done by "hundreds of magazines and newspapers following every aspect of the debate and clearly outlining what was at stake." And by Ray Baker, who "published the most consequential piece in his railroad series, an exposé of the techniques the railroads employed to malign and falsify the Hepburn bill. ... The sensational article heightened public demand for regulation." Goodwin spends over a page describing how this article galvanized the public.

After the bill's passage, Roosevelt himself wrote to Baker, saying: "It is through writers like yourself, Mr. Steffens and Miss Tarbell, that the country as a whole is beginning to understand." And the press gave Roosevelt full credit for all the dealmaking and compromising it took to get the bill passed. Goodwin spends five pages describing Roosevelt's dealmaking and not one sentence on his use of the bully pulpit.

In other words, fundamental change occurred because there was a progressive movement with its own leaders and lots of support from the press. Ray Baker had long conversations with Roosevelt, resulting in a more effective bill. And Roosevelt used his political talents to push the bill through Congress. That's how fundamental change usually happens—as Reich says in the title of his op-ed, "It Takes a Movement." It also takes a dealmaking politician that the movement trusts.

In a letter to muckraker Lincoln Steffens, Roosevelt reminded him that results "must be gotten by trying to come to a working agreement with the Senate and House and therefore by making mutual concessions."

The Political Science of the Bully Pulpit

As discussed in the Introduction, President Reagan, aka the Great Communicator, completely failed to move public opinion in his direction during his eight years in office. This was demonstrated by the results of 10 years of research presented in *On Deaf Ears: The Limits of the Bully Pulpit* (2003) by political scientist George Edwards.

The bottom-line conclusion from all this research and much more is that presidents can sway members of their own party a bit, but the other party sees what they're up to and heads in the opposite direction.

After learning this the hard way, Obama was careful not to mention a payroll tax cut in the run-up to the November 2010 midterm elections. But after the election, it appeared in the tax deal. Obama's senior advisor explained: "We didn't put the payroll-tax cut into our speeches [because] if we included it in our rhetoric it might impair our chances of getting it done after the election."

In short, political science tells us that using the bully pulpit gets in the way of dealmaking—and dealmaking is usually the only path to progress. It does require a movement, but not one led from the presidential bully pulpit.

Conclusion

Teddy Roosevelt was a great "dealmaker-in-chief," and proud of it. And we should be proud of him for being who he was. Modern political science has proven his approach correct.

In a primary, there is no need of or chance for dealmaking, but Warren and Sanders can shift their followers' expectations to the left. This gives them the appearance of power, without any need to show they can actually get results. But if one of them were to become president, they would prove less able to get results than those with real political skills.

Why You Will Find Teddy Roosevelt on Mount Rushmore

Don't judge Teddy Roosevelt by today's far-left mythology. Judge him in his own historical context. He grew up as an elite conservative, and he transformed himself into a progressive who could operate effectively inside the system. He did this through tough-minded honesty that was as rare then as it is now.

He did not approach politics through the lens of socialist economic analysis: "My problems are moral problems, and my teaching has been plain morality. ... People are going to discuss economic questions more and more ... I am not deeply interested in them."

He applied his "square deal" standard equally to the rich and the poor. In his context, that was the way to make progress. He railed against the populists, socialists and independents as much as against the Republican bosses. Those like the strident Wisconsin populist La Follette, who fought "the system in the abstract," Roosevelt said, accomplished "mighty little good."

According to Ray Baker, a journalist and confidant of Roosevelt, "Roosevelt never leads; he always follows." That was a smart strategy, which strengthened his hand in the heart of the party of big business.

With a lot of help from the progressive movement, he shifted America's politics from a belief in laissez-faire economics and social Darwinism to a belief that the central purpose of government is to make society fair to all.

Taft may have been as good or better at moving Roosevelt's agenda forward once it was set in motion. But at that point in history, only the volcanic force of Teddy Roosevelt could have harnessed the power of the progressive movement to launch their programs from inside the party of big business.

CHAPTER 27

The Myth of the Overton Window

You win policy debates by crafting arguments for extreme positions—and then shifting the entire window of debate.
—DailyKos.com, 2006

The Myth of the Overton Window is a bit like the Myth of the Bully Pulpit, but you don't need to be president and you don't need to be thoughtful. Anyone can make the country more progressive just by saying extreme things on social media.

Perhaps you think I'm exaggerating. So let's check the video posted on Vox.com, the successor to *The Washington Post's* WonkBlog. "If you want to change what people think of as acceptable [inside the window], you shouldn't start here" explains the narrator, pointing to "Radical" as an idea located just outside the window. Then skipping over "Ridiculous," which is well beyond "Radical," he says, "You should start here" as he points to "Unthinkable."

This may just sound silly, but it's actually the key myth behind polarization, and once again, a major benefit for Trump. In a nutshell, extreme-left positions galvanize Trump's support and motivate them to vote. I'll come back to that toward the end of the book.

Returning to "unthinkable" positions, they have the advantage of requiring no thought. Just say something totally off the wall. Yet, as the narrator explains, "forcing people to consider the Unthinkable idea will make your Radical idea seem more acceptable." At least that's the myth. This way there's no need to actually come up with a reason for your Radical idea. That's brilliant! This video got 1.5 million views, and almost none of the comments note any problems with the concept. The concept has been popular for more than a decade with the radical left.

Who Was Overton Anyway?

When Joseph Overton died in 2004, he was in the process of trying to explain, in a fund-raising brochure for his think tank, how to move the policy window in the libertarian direction. Naturally, he thought his think tank could do that best.

His "window" idea, a least as his colleagues remember it, is simplistic but reasonable: "At any given time, in a given public-policy area, only a relatively narrow range of potential policies will be considered politically acceptable." He was arguing that think tanks were best equipped to shift this "Overton Window." And they should do this by making cogent arguments for ideas that were a bit outside the window in the direction they wanted it to move.

Thoughtful, cogent arguments—ideas that are just a little outside the window—none of that sounds like the Vox video. So how did such ordinary ideas, which started in a conservative think tank, end up as flamboyant nonsense on a progressive blog?

A Leap to the Left, then to the Right

Less than three years after Overton's death, his ideas somehow took a quantum leap over to the left-wing DailyKos website and mutated into "You win policy debates by crafting arguments for extreme positions—and then shifting the entire window of debate." As they explained it, "The GOP takes impossibly radical positions and makes them worthy of consideration just by talking about them," so the Democrats should do that too.

The Overton Window noise on the left soon drew the attention of right-wing radio talk show host Glenn Beck, the scourge of progressives (or "Crime Inc.," as he calls them). What a great scare concept—the left uses the Overton Window to take over the whole country. Beck wrote a thriller called, of course, *The Overton Window,* and it made it to #1 on *The New York Times'* hardcover fiction list on July 4, 2010.

The Myth and Reality

The myth is that taking extreme-left positions moves everyone left and extreme-right positions move us all to the right. Does that make sense to you? When Trump takes an extreme right-wing position, do you move right? No one on the radical left ever seems to ask that question.

Every four years, Gallup asks: "If your party nominated a generally well-qualified person for president who happened to be _____, would you vote for that person?" Between 2015 and 2019, Trump took extremely anti-Muslim positions. The result? Muslims became less acceptable to Republicans but more acceptable to Democrats.

Meanwhile, Bernie Sanders took positions that were extremely pro-socialist. Socialists became more acceptable to Democrats and less acceptable to Republicans. And for the country, there was no net change.

So the myth is just wrong. Taking extreme positions does have an effect—it polarizes the country. In fact, the extreme positions, of both the left and the right, are the primary force behind polarization.

A Tragic Example

Ida Tarbell, an investigative journalist, wrote a very non-extreme and incredibly well-researched article, "The History of the Standard Oil Company," that appeared in the November 1902 issue of *McClure's* magazine. (See chapter photo.) With it, Tarbell dramatically shifted the Overton Window of acceptable views regarding trusts, the giant monopolies owned by the robber barons. This cleared the way for Teddy Roosevelt to begin suing them under the Sherman Antitrust Act and breaking them up—part of his famed trust-busting.

This part of the story fits with Overton's view (not the myth) that careful arguments made by think tanks can shift public opinion. Tarbell out-researched most modern think tanks using only one assistant.

But other progressive journalists thought if her non-extreme ideas were this powerful, wouldn't more-extreme ideas be even more powerful? The Overton Myth is actually a very old myth. Soon all kinds of magazines and newspapers were publishing "investigative" articles, which became ever more extreme and sensational, partly to gain publicity, but also out of a conviction that the more extreme, the more effective.

Only three-and-a-half years after Tarbell's first Standard Oil article appeared, the reaction struck with a vengeance. Tarbell's moderate steps shifted Teddy Roosevelt's opinion, but when the ideas became unthinkable, he put an end to the entire business, or nearly so. And the result is celebrated to this day, although the meaning has been inverted.

We now call Ida Tarbell and her fellow journalists "muckrakers" and think of that as a badge of honor. But when Roosevelt gave his famous

"Man with the Muck Rake" speech, it was meant and taken as harsh criticism.

William Randolph Hearst, who was then on the left wing of the progressive movement, had just published a series of articles called "The Treason of the Senate," which Roosevelt considered unthinkable. But Lincoln Steffens, who wrote for *McClure's*, was also part of the problem. He had claimed that Senator Aldrich was "the boss of the United States."

According to the Overton Myth, such a claim, which Roosevelt considered "absurd," should have shifted Roosevelt strongly towards Steffens' socialist views simply because the claim was extreme and on the socialist side. Instead, it caused Roosevelt to vehemently reject Steffens' views. So he gave his "Muck Rake" speech, which caused Steffens to conclude that Roosevelt had "put an end to all these journalistic investigations that have made you."

In this, Steffens was not far off the mark. *Life* magazine immediately published a devastating satire of *"McSure's Magazine,"* ridiculing "Ida Tarbarrel" and all the best muckrakers.

Certainly, Roosevelt had not intended this extreme result. But given the fact that there had been a widespread reaction against the increasingly extreme journalists, to the point where many considered their charges to be unthinkable, it was not surprising. In the final analysis, the death of the powerful and effective investigative journalism that was the beating heart of the Progressive Era can be laid at the feet of unthinking left extremists. They had bought into the Myth of the Overton Window a hundred years before anyone had heard of it.

Conclusion

Taking extreme positions, as advocated by the myth of the Overton window, is the hallmark, of most sources of polarization, and the cause of much of it.

A few unthinkable articles written by irresponsible radical-left journalists in 1906 triggered an unexpected and rather mild reaction from Teddy Roosevelt. But the right-wing press and their customers, who were just waiting for such an excuse, distorted what he said and blew it out of proportion.

So a relatively small amount of left extremism causes a much larger reaction from the right. You can say the right should not have done that, but that won't stop them. Worse yet, radicals often choose positions that are designed to provoke the biggest possible reaction.

And when that reaction comes, even moderate Democrats see the right-wing reaction as unreasonable, so they tend to side with the left radicals who caused the problem. That encourages the radicals to say even more unthinkable things. You can see where this is going. Just remember, the radicals thrive on this dynamic—it "proves" they are right about how bad the other side really is.

- Overton was right: Thoughtful arguments for ideas that are a little bit radical can succeed. But taking extreme or unthinkable positions simply polarizes the country.

PART 5

Identity Politics

*"We hold these truths to be self-evident, that all men are created equal, that they are endowed by their Creator with certain **unalienable Rights** ..."*
—Declaration of Independence, July 4, 1776

Identity politics used to take the equal-rights approach. That includes the antislavery movement, the women's suffrage movement, the civil rights movement, and the gay rights movement. The new identity politics includes such diverse concepts as microaggressions, triggers, intersectionality, queering and feminist glaciology (sic). The *equal-rights approach* to identity politics brought two centuries of progress. The *new* "identity politics" approach mainly helps Trump.

Equal Rights

Perhaps the most important idea of the Enlightenment was that ordinary people—not just nobles and clergy—had basic human rights. Our Declaration of Independence marked a turning point.

In 1791, Thomas Paine published *The Rights of Man* in England. Later that year, our Bill of Rights was ratified. The next year, Mary Wollstonecraft, one of the founding feminist philosophers, wrote *A Vindication of the Rights of Woman*.

Starting in the 1600s, humanism (another Enlightenment idea) led to criticism of slavery for violating natural rights. In 1848, the Seneca Falls Convention passed a resolution to secure for women their "sacred right to the elective franchise."

During the Civil War, ex-slaves fought alongside Whites to procure for Blacks the most basic human right—freedom. In 1920, the 19th Amendment gave women the right to vote. In 1944, Franklin Roosevelt proposed his Second Bill of [economic] Rights.

Between 1955 and 1965, Blacks and Whites worked together to pass the Civil Rights Acts of 1957, 1960 and 1964—followed by the Voting

Rights Act of 1965. More recently, gays and lesbians have gained many new rights.

From Rights to Privileges

The new identity politics rejects nearly four centuries of equal-rights identity politics. The start of this rejection was the "White privilege" idea of Noel Ignatin, a Marxist-Leninist White guy who sold the idea to the New Left in about 1969. As he put it, "We intend to keep bashing dead White males, live ones, and females too, until the social construct known as 'the White race' is destroyed."

The White privilege idea works like this. If Blacks but not Whites are subject to arbitrary arrest by police, the equal-rights approach would demand equal rights for Blacks—no arbitrary arrests. But the White-privilege approach tries to make Whites feel guilty for not being arbitrarily arrested. But then what? Should the "guilty" Whites demand to be arbitrarily arrested?

Or what if only Whites have the privilege of eating in a certain restaurant. Should we take away that guilty privilege so no one can eat there, or should we give Blacks equal rights? For a few decades, this bizarre approach of taking away "privileges" that should be rights remained on the fringes. But now the White-privilege approach is back in force as part of the new identity politics.

The Birth of 'Identity Politics'

The founding document of what we now call "identity politics" is the Combahee River Collective Statement, written in April 1977. It declared: "This focusing upon our own oppression is embodied in the concept of identity politics."

The Combahee River Collective was a Black feminist lesbian collective, many of whom were college-educated writers. One member, Chirlane Irene McCray (no longer a lesbian), is now the wife of New York City Mayor Bill de Blasio. The Collective's statement provided a groundbreaking description of various sources of oppression: Whites, men, heterosexuals and capitalism.

They explained their strategy: "We believe that the most profound and potentially most radical politics come directly out of our own identity, as opposed to working to end somebody else's oppression." That "somebody else" was aimed first at White women, then Black men, and a little at straight Black women.

This foreshadows the fragmenting nature of the new identity politics. Identities were already being defined by "intersectionality." Once all the identity groups that you belong to have been listed, that combination is your intersectional identity.

Three years later, the Combahee River Collective disintegrated. Seemingly, it died of exclusivity. But this was only the beginning.

Courage versus Outrage

These first two currents, intersectional identity politics and anti-White-privilege politics, soon merged with the new Critical Race Theory that was an offshoot of postmodern politics, which has its roots in European neo-Marxism. By the mid-1970s, postmodernism was taking over the humanities and social sciences in American universities. This combination was incredibly powerful and produced the identity politics we see today.

The next chapter compares the courage of the old civil rights movement to the victim mentality of the new identity politics. Then I explore different strains of identity politics and finally drill down to find its roots.

As it turns out, the new identity politics is now at the heart of the culture war, which powers Trump's base. And it may be providing more motivation for Trump's get-out-the-vote efforts than even the fear of socialism.

Synopsis of Part 5

Chapter 28. When the Klan Went Low, SNCC Went High. Identity politics protesters trying to (literally) whitewash an anti-racist mural are contrasted with the Freedom Riders of the civil rights movement.

Chapter 29. What's Identity Politics? How you can get fired for a microaggression even if it's not an act of aggression at all.

Chapter 30. Identity Politics—the Dark Side. How a Black Lives Matter activist was easily duped by Sanders' dirty-tricks strategist.

Chapter 31. Cultural Appropriation. Why *Cosmopolitan* doesn't think little White girls should dress as Moana for Halloween.

Chapter 32. The Microaggression Hoax. Microaggressions theory amounts to vigilante-style prosecution of invisible crimes.

Chapter 33. The Roots of Identity Politics. How French postmodernism grew from German and Italian neo-Marxism and guided the development of the new identity politics.

Chapter 34. Postmodernism: The Anti-Truth. The sexual reproduction of glaciers and other postmodern identity-politics fantasies.

Chapter 35. The Ultimate Con Game. The seven major godfathers of postmodernism and their anti-Enlightenment heritage.

CHAPTER 28

When the Klan Went Low, SNCC Went High

A people without the knowledge of their history, origin and culture is like a tree without roots.
— Marcus Garvey, Jamaican political activist

In 1961, hundreds of civil rights activists, many just out of high school, rode buses to Jackson, Mississippi, knowing they would spend weeks or months in one of the South's worst jails. They ended segregation in the interstate bus system and won enormous respect for the civil rights movement.

But identity politics has changed twice since then. First, the Black power movement rejected King's nonviolence and ethics but retained the bravery exhibited by nonviolent direct action.

Second, the new identity politics replaced bravery with demands for protection from exaggerated perceived threats, even when there's no actual threat. An example would be the "threat" of a little White girl dressing as Moana (Disney's Polynesian princess) for Halloween.

Only a small minority of the left engages in the outrage politics and cancel culture used to enforce the demands of the new identity politics. However, this small but growing band, which has sometimes self-identified as "social justice warriors," increasingly inflicts damage on the Democrats and generously fires up Trump's base.

The purpose of this chapter is to make clear the dramatic differences in tactics and objectives between the civil rights movement and today's new identity politics. Its main focus will be the Freedom Riders of the 1960s, whose nitty-gritty realities tend to be forgotten. But to make the contrast as clear as possible, I will start with a current incident, with roots in the past, that threatens to destroy a valuable piece of progressive history.

Throwing Ink on the Mural

By 1968, African-American students at George Washington High School (GWHS) in San Francisco, many of whom were Black Panthers, were angry about the school's anti-racist 1,600-square-foot mural. (Yes, anti-racist; just hang on a minute.) They wanted it gone, replaced with a mural depicting their current heroes. (Spoiler alert: They actually got the mural they wanted, and the original mural was preserved as well—the perfect ending.)

The "Life of Washington" mural was commissioned in 1936 by Franklin Roosevelt's Federal Art Project to match the school's name. The artist, Victor Arnautoff, was already famous for other murals in the city, including a set in Coit Tower on Telegraph Hill—a landmark tourist attraction to this day. Arnautoff happened to be a student of the most renowned modern muralist, Diego Rivera. And like Rivera, he was a Communist.

Being a Communist meant he took care to show great respect when painting workers, slaves, and Native Americans. In contrast, he painted the White settlers in black and gray as they walked past the dead Plains Indian (with no visible wound). The daring aspect of the mural showed the country's first president as a slave owner and complicit in the near destruction of the Native American nations.

Now the hero of this story is Dewey Crumpler, a Black art student just out of high school. In 1968, the Black students at GWHS asked him to paint a mural for their school, but the Art Commission said he was too inexperienced (he was) and the students should paint one themselves. That's when they splashed ink on Arnautoff's mural (it's still there). In the meantime, Crumpler went to Mexico, where he studied mural painting and also learned about Arnautoff.

When Crumpler returned from Mexico, he said he would not be a party to destroying the mural but offered to paint a "response" mural. The students agreed and the Art Commission accepted the project in 1970. After 30 meetings with students over the design, he finally painted his mural in 1974.

By then, most of the students agreed with saving the Arnautoff mural. At the dedication of Crumpler's mural, one of the student leaders got up and said, "Mr. Crumpler, I believe your murals are important. But I want this audience to know that if I had understood what Arnautoff was doing, I would never have reacted in the way that I did."

Woke Identity Politics

Amy Anderson, a Native American, took her eighth-grade son Kai to visit GWHS in 2016. She was horrified to see the dead American Indian. But Kai wanted to go to GWHS for the music program and told his mom he would walk into school with his head down every day so he would not have to see the murals on the wall.

Later, he said that during his entire freshman year, "I remember not having the emotional capacity in me to look up." It is hard to imagine a Black Panther or a Freedom Rider reacting this way. They had been taught to be tough and proud, not traumatized.

Because Kai was being traumatized by not looking up, his mother and her fellow indigenous activist Mariposa Villialuna drafted a resolution in the fall of 2018 and sent it to the school board. This resulted in the creation of the district's Reflection and Action Committee, and on June 25, 2019, the board voted unanimously to destroy the mural.

This move was justified, the committee stated, because Kai and unspecified others were being traumatized, and some, according to Villialuna, were experiencing post-traumatic stress disorder (PTSD), something usually associated with extreme battlefield traumas. The board felt it needed to make the school a safe place for the students.

Some have a different view

"Why try to hide the reality of our history, which is a terrible one?" asked Alice Walker, the first African American to win the Pulitzer Prize for fiction. "They should leave the mural and explain it to the children. I think that this feeling that everybody is now so tender-hearted that they can't bear to know the history is ridiculous." Walker is part Native American. Her daughter attended GWHS and suffered no trauma or PTSD in spite of having both African and indigenous heritages.

Willie Brown, California's most famous Black politician, said, "I'm the father of a Washington High graduate. My daughter was never traumatized by Arnautoff's painting—as a matter of fact, it generated conversations at home that otherwise would not have occurred. It was a learning experience for her, and for me."

The San Francisco president of the NAACP, Rev. Amos Brown, also spoke out for saving the mural, stating, "There comes a time you need to do some deeper thinking, not sound bites."

Internationally acclaimed Black actor and activist Danny Glover attended GWHS and compared destroying the mural to "book burning." Dewey Crumpler, who still wants the mural preserved and displayed, said, "Today's students aren't taught to interpret artistic imagery. Arnautoff's goal for the work was to expose America's first president for who he was, warts and all." The GWHS alumni association has also gone on record supporting preservation of the mural.

Who's Been Colonized?

According to Willie Brown, there's no greater authority on Arnautoff than Robert Cherny, who "literally wrote the book on the artist." And Cherny reports that "during the public comment section of the school board meeting, those seeking to destroy the murals described the defenders of the murals as representing the perspective of 'the White supremacy culture.' They described the American Indians, Latinos, African Americans, and Asian Americans who defended the murals as having been 'colonized.'"

So there you have it. Alice Walker, Willie Brown, Rev. Amos Brown, Danny Glover, Dewey Crumpler, and the GWHS alumni association have been "colonized." No need to listen to their brainwashed arguments.

The root of the problem is ignorance protected by what I will show later is postmodern ideology. This ideology denies there is any reason to look into what an artist meant—a notion called "the death of the author." This is why Crumpler is right when he states: "Today's students aren't taught to interpret artistic imagery." The result, he says, is that "they are trying to look at images literally."

According to this ideology, when the Reflection and Action Committee sees Washington owning slaves, members think Arnautoff was saying that's a good thing because they believe that artists only paint what they approve of. I know that may sound like I'm exaggerating their ignorance and confusion, but the written conclusion of the committee states:

The mural glorifies slavery, genocide, colonization, manifest destiny, White supremacy, oppression, etc.

It's amazing that Danny Glover attended GWHS for four years and missed this completely. But lucky for us, Kai's Native American mom, Amy Anderson, understood this the minute she laid eyes on the mural. And the rest of these Black cultural luminaries did no better than Glover, all because they let themselves be colonized by White supremacists.

Thankfully, there's a good chance the school board will not get away with this, but there is no hint yet that they will do anything to help the students understand the murals.

Lessons from the Civil Rights Movement

Two differences to keep in mind between then (the Sixties) and now as we turn to the civil rights movement are first, students are currently being taught to be traumatized rather than brave, and second, today's new identity politics picks fights that completely miss the serious racial issues that still exist.

A few of the Freedom Riders booked in Jackson, Mississippi

John Lewis has been a member of the House of Representatives from Georgia since 1987. But on May 9, 1961, he was on one of the two buses making the first Freedom Ride from Washington, D.C., to Jackson, Mississippi. Al Bigelow, another Freedom Rider, was a 55-year-old White man. He had graduated from Harvard in 1929, studied architecture at MIT and designed buildings for the 1939 World's Fair in New York. In WWII, he served as commander of a submarine chaser and a destroyer escort.

As one of the buses carrying the Freedom Riders crossed into South Carolina, the first deep-South state, it made a stop in Rock Hill. As Lewis reported in his 1998 memoir, *Walking with the Wind:*

As Al Bigelow and I approached the "WHITE" waiting room in the Rock Hill Greyhound terminal, I noticed a large number of young White guys hanging around the pinball machines in the lobby. "Other side, Nigger," one said. He pointed to a door with a sign that said "COLORED."

"I have a right to go in there," I said, speaking carefully and clearly, "on the grounds of the Supreme Court decision in the *Boynton* case."

"Shit on that," one of them said. The next thing I knew, a fist smashed the right side of my head. Then another hit me square in the face. As I fell to the floor I could feel feet kicking me hard in the sides. I could taste blood in my mouth.

"I figured Southern women should be represented so the South and the Nation would realize all Southern people do not think alike."

—Genevieve Hughes

At that point Al Bigelow stepped in, placing his body between mine and these men. It had to look strange to these guys to see a big, strong White man putting himself in the middle of a fistfight like this, not ready to throw a punch, but not frightened either.

They hesitated for an instant. Then they attacked Bigelow, who did not raise a finger. It took several blows to drop him to one knee. At that point, Genevieve Hughes, who had also been on the bus, stepped in the way and was knocked to the floor.

Fifty years later, Elwin Wilson, the man who twice smashed the 21-year-old John Lewis in the face, remembered it like this:

What happened was, after he was beat and bloody and all, the policeman came up and asked him, he said, "Do y'all want to take out warrants?" He said, "No." He said, "We're not here to cause

trouble." He said, "We're here for people to love each other." ...
The thought, it comes in my mind so many times, what he said he
wasn't out to harm nobody.

A little earlier, Wilson had called the local paper in Rock Hill, confessed to the 1961 beating and said he wanted to apologize. He did apologize to two local civil-rights groups. Lewis read about this and invited
Wilson to Washington. Wilson told Lewis that he had tried to block the
incident out of his mind for years but just couldn't. He apologized to
Lewis, who commented, "I think it takes a lot of raw courage to be willing to come forward the way he did."

Birmingham. When John Lewis' bus arrived in Birmingham, Alabama,
well-known CBS anchorman Howard K. Smith was on the scene to report on what became known as the Mother's Day Riot. "The riots have
not been spontaneous outbursts of anger," he reported in one broadcast,
"but carefully planned and susceptible to having been easily prevented or
stopped had there been a wish to do so."

White Freedom Riders were singled out by the mob for especially se-
vere beatings. Jim Peck, a longtime White pacifist who was in charge of
this first phase of the Freedom Ride, was knocked unconscious and refused treatment at the all-White hospital but was eventually treated at
another. The "rule of barbarism in Alabama," said Smith of CBS, must
bow to the "rule of law and order—and justice—in America."

Diane Nash. The Freedom Riders were making their point effectively,
but the Congress of Racial Equality (CORE), which had organized the
Rides, decided they had become too dangerous. Attorney General Bobby
Kennedy's man on the scene, John Seigenthaler, arranged a flight for
those who wanted to continue to New Orleans, their intended final desti-
nation.

Diane Nash wasn't having it. Nash felt that if violence was allowed to
halt the Freedom Rides, the movement would be set back years.

A founding member of CORE, she had orchestrated the 1960 Nash-
ville lunch-counter sit-ins that first desegregated those spaces in the
South. Trained in Gandhi's nonviolent direct action, as head of the Fisk
University branch of the Student Nonviolent Coordinating Committee
(SNCC), she had recruited John Lewis and other Freedom Riders.

"
We presented
Southern white
racists with a new
set of options. Kill us
or desegregate.
"

- Diane Nash
Leader in fight for desegregation

Nash convinced CORE of her position that they should continue by bus, and soon Bobby Kennedy got word of this. Here's how Seigenthaler remembers what happened next:

My phone in the hotel room rings and it's the attorney general. "Who the hell is Diane Nash? Call her and let her know what is waiting for the Freedom Riders." So I called her. I said, "I understand that there are more Freedom Riders coming down from Nashville. You must stop them if you can."

Her response was, "They're not gonna turn back. They're on their way to Birmingham and they'll be there shortly." ... I felt my voice go up another decibel and another and soon I was shouting, "Young woman, do you understand what you're doing? Do you understand you're gonna get somebody killed?"

And there's a pause, and she said, "Sir, you should know, we all signed our last wills and testaments last night before they left. We know someone will be killed. But we cannot let violence overcome nonviolence."

Montgomery. The Freedom Ride continued from Birmingham, protected by the Alabama State Highway Patrol, until it reached the city limits of Montgomery, Alabama. Then all protection vanished. As the Freedom Riders disembarked in Montgomery, all was quiet—until they were ambushed from all sides by a mob led by the Klan.

The mob brutally attacked John Lewis and Bernard Lafayette. William Barbee was beaten unconscious and suffered injuries that would later shorten his life. Two White women were pulled from a cab as they tried to escape and were beaten by the mob.

John Seigenthaler, who was there as an observer, tried at one point to help one of the female Freedom Riders being pursued in the street. He was pulled from his car and beaten with a tire iron. His skull fractured, he was left unconscious in the street.

James Zwerg, a White student from Wisconsin and a friend of John Lewis, was beaten unconscious by the mob. While unconscious, three men held him up while a woman kicked him in the groin. He spent five days in the hospital, the first two, unconscious.

But as Zwerg recalls, "If you want to talk about heroism, consider the Black man who probably saved my life. This man in coveralls, just off of work, happened to walk by as my beating was going on and said 'Stop beating that kid. If you want to beat someone, beat me.' And they did. He was still unconscious when I left the hospital. I don't know if he lived or died."

The Outcome. As discussed in Chapter 3, thousands joined in the Freedom Rides. More than 300 Freedom Riders spent much of the summer in jail in Jackson, Mississippi. Finally, on Nov. 1, 1961, the Interstate Commerce Commission issued a ruling to enforce the Supreme Court's Boynton decision.

But the larger impact was the change in public understanding. The national news had been filled with images, reporting, and commentary that exposed the nature of Southern segregation. It suddenly became clear to millions of Americans that not only was segregation part of the South's legal system but that such laws were enforced—and not just by the terrorism of the Klan. The Klan had the active support of state and local governments.

Perhaps even more shocking to the larger White community was the fact that this terrorism would be, and was, directed at any Whites who openly advocated changing Jim Crow laws. Even a close friend and assistant to Attorney General Robert Kennedy would be beaten unconscious and left in the street when he dared to help a young woman, a Freedom Rider, who had done nothing illegal or offensive.

Is the Mural Like the Klan?

Are the critics right that the mural "glorifies slavery, genocide, colonization, manifest destiny, White supremacy, oppression, etc."? If so, then the mural is a little bit like the Ku Klux Klan enforcing segregation in the

South, and it is right that students are being traumatized and right that the mural should be permanently whitewashed.

Art can be hateful. Roger Ebert deemed *The Birth of a Nation*, which revived the Klan, "a great film that argues for evil." So in principle, the critics of the mural could be right that it is traumatizing students.

But if the mural's critics are wrong, and the mural condemns slavery and genocide, as Black community leaders familiar with the mural say, then students are not being harmed, and the critics are falsely accusing many good people of being "colonized"—brainwashed into supporting White supremacy.

The two sides make their case in completely different ways. The mural's critics make an identity-based argument, and the supporters make a fact-based argument. The critics pretend to use facts—that a dead Native American and slaves appear in the mural. But the mural could either glorify these facts or condemn them, and the critics make no argument that the mural glorifies them. So they have facts, but no *argument* based on facts.

Should we buy the identity-based or the fact-based argument? The civil rights movement was fact-based. They argued that discrimination was harmful and unfair based on obvious facts. And they excluded identity-based arguments. They did not say "only Blacks see the harm, and they are virtuous and should be believed." Civil rights meant equal rights for all regardless of identity.

The critics' argument. Arnautoff's critics claim that their own identity gives their claim priority. But why should Black identity critics have priority over Black supporters of the mural making fact-based arguments? The critics' implied answer is circular: Our identity is pure because we are "woke," but supporters' minds are impure because they have been "colonized." We know we are woke because our identity is pure.

The supporters' arguments. These can best be understood by listening to Dewey Crumpler. When Crumpler, a young art student, first saw it, he perceived its images of Blacks as "horrible." But after learning more, he said, "Arnautoff put slaves next to Washington, and it was that contradiction when I first saw the mural that threw me." As Crumpler explained, "Most students including myself never knew that George Washington owned slaves. Never." Other radical Black students came to the same conclusion once the mural was explained.

A second argument is that exposing the extent and evils of slavery has long been a goal of the anti-slavery and anti-racism movements, so Arnautoff was painting to support these movements, not racism. This was also the intent of the famed TV series, *Roots,* which was highly acclaimed by the Black community even though it was vastly more violent and traumatizing than the mural. The final episode was watched by 100 million Americans, and the series was deemed to be highly educational.

The only violence depicted by the mural is a battle between two Indians and a four-man White militia. One White appears to be dead. This indicates the dead American Indian was a brave fighting for his people. And the Westward settlers walking by the dead American Indian are painted in black and gray—a mark of disapproval. So on its face, the mural is anti-racist.

Then there is the fact that Arnautoff was a student of Diego Rivera, perhaps the world's most famous muralist, who was a member of the Mexican Communist Party. To think Rivera would have approved of Arnautoff if he had celebrated genocide and White supremacy is simply absurd.

The same is true of Alice Walker, Willie Brown, Rev. Amos Brown of the NAACP and Danny Glover. All of them understand the mural and racism and know it is absurd to blindly see it as racist.

Conclusion

The critics of the mural claim a position of privileged knowledge based on their identity and "wokeness." And based on this, they have condemned some of the most trusted and knowledgeable people in the Black community. They are attempting to destroy an anti-racist mural that is a landmark of FDR's New Deal, created by one of our greatest muralists.

While they are "well-intentioned"—they are, as the proverb says, "paving the road to hell"—by attacking *anti*-racism. They are the antithesis of the civil rights movement in almost every way.

Where civil-rights protesters braved beatings and jail, identity-politics protesters claim to have been traumatized by glancing at a progressive mural.

Where civil-rights protesters shoved the brutality of racism in the nation's face, the identity protesters seek to obliterate even the memory of its early years.

Where civil-rights protesters targeted the country's most racist elements, the mural protesters target some of our most progressive elements.

Where civil-rights protesters showed respect for their racist opponents, the mural protesters express outrage and moral condemnation of their progressive opponents.

All told, this typical example of the new identity politics shows that its advocates have forgotten the hard-won lessons learned over decades. And they have forgotten that the luxury they have to bicker over the political correctness of progressive murals was won for them by the dedication of the heroes of the civil rights movement.

- The civil rights movement fought bravely and respectfully against racist laws and for equal rights regardless of identity.
- The new mural critics use outrage against other progressives to enhance their status in the "woke" community.

CHAPTER 29

What Is Identity Politics?

It's not just a matter of it not being polite to say nigger in public. That's not the measure of whether racism still exists or not.

—President Barack Obama, June 22, 2019

The civil rights movement of the 1950s and '60s was a form of identity politics that was passionate, effective and brilliantly strategic. The new "identity politics" is still passionate, but it has lost its way. Fortunately, this new politics has not completely taken over.

Just what is today's new identity politics? The concept comes from radical-left academics, but you may have heard some of its jargon on the news—microaggressions, safe spaces, triggers, trigger warnings, White privilege and cultural appropriation. If you've paid attention, you may have also heard about intersectionality, essentialism, cisgender and queer theory. We'll meet several of these later on, but for this chapter, microaggressions will suffice.

Colleges and universities had no identity-studies programs when Congress passed the Civil Rights Act of 1964 or the Voting Rights Act of 1965. But now, if you don't have a "studies" program dedicated to promoting your identity, you're not even on the map.

Black Studies was the first, but to that has been added: Chicana/o (Chicanx), Mexican-American, Native-American, Asian, Critical Race, Ethnic, Feminist, Women's, Gay and Lesbian, Gender, LBGT, Queer, Postcolonial, Cultural, Disability, (anti-) White, (anti-) Science and Fat Studies. But the most important identity politics in the U.S. still concerns Black racism.

Here's one real-life story of how the new identity politics played out in Kansas in 2015. It's the story of how one accidental, microscopic aggression traumatized one person and derailed another person's life. Everyone was, as usual, "well-intentioned."

Microaggressions in Kansas

After a town-hall meeting on racism at the University of Kansas, 10 students met for a graduate seminar with Dr. Andrea Quenette. They steered the discussion to the question of how to discuss the town-hall issues with their own undergraduate students. According to a public letter some of them published, Dr. Quenette said, "As a White woman I just never have seen the racism … It's not like I see 'Nigger' spray-painted on walls…"

Gabrielle Byrd, the only Black student in attendance, told *The Washington Post* that she almost couldn't believe what she'd heard. "I was incredibly shocked that the word was spoken, regardless of the context," said Byrd. "I turned to the classmate sitting next to me and asked if this was really happening. Before I left the classroom, I was in tears."

Byrd had suffered a microaggression. It was unintended, but in microaggression theory, that doesn't matter. Quenette had not used the n-word as a slur but had, in fact, implied that its use against a person or group would be completely unacceptable. Twenty years earlier, her statement would have been seen as anti-racist, which was her intention.

But don't blame Gabrielle Byrd. Her behavior was the result of "microaggression theory," which is now taught at most major colleges and universities in the U.S.

Back to the Freedom Riders

Now compare Byrd's reaction to the incredible mental toughness and bravery of the first Freedom Riders. Many of them were students no older than Byrd. They had received training in nonviolent direct action—how to withstand deliberate, violent levels of aggression, not just barely detectable microaggressions or micro-nonaggressions.

Instead of being taught that even an unintended slight could do them great psychological harm, they were taught how to withstand intense personal, physical violence. They knew how to expose it and win against it. And they did.

Had the Blacks and Whites of the civil rights movement been brainwashed by the academics now pushing microaggression phobia, there could not have been a civil rights movement.

Some Microaggressions Are Real

Microaggressions—minor slights, slurs, and insults—certainly happen to all of us, and they can be damaging. Moreover, racism, sexism and other forms of discrimination often include the systematic use of such small insults, and this is a problem that should be openly addressed. Even unintended slights should be understood and avoided.

This is nothing new. Back in 1970, as I was training to teach junior high school in a part of California where half my students would be Mexican American, I was shown a training film that helped us understand cultural differences and avoid accidentally hurting each other's feelings. The instructor in the film was Mexican American, and nearly 50 years later, I still remember his warmth and humor. He made me want to be like him. Outrage would have had the opposite effect.

Microaggression Dogma

The problem with microaggression theory is the "theory" part. This so-called theory predicted that saying "America is the land of opportunity" might be more damaging than a hate crime. Actual research, however, revealed that 93% of Blacks and 89% of Latinos were not offended by "the land of opportunity." Quite likely no one saw it as more damaging than a hate crime. Microaggression theory consists of four dogmas:

1. Intent does not matter even if the "perpetrator" is intending a compliment.
2. Microaggressions can be more harmful than "hate crimes by the Klan" (according to its leading proponent).
3. If the recipient feels hurt, almost any level of retaliation short of physical assault is justified (and in a few cases, even that).
4. People should be treated as members of their identity group, not as individuals.

With this in mind, let's return to the incident in Kansas.

Back to Kansas

Recall that the Quenette incident was preceded by a town-hall meeting on racism. In a report that was entirely sympathetic to the KU students, Slate.com noted that at the meeting, students complained that faculty members had insulted them. Slate gave only two examples. The faculty had been caught "complimenting them for being (1) well-spoken and (2) intelligent." You read that right.

The idea is that the professors had secretly been thinking, Hey, you're intelligent like everyone else, even though you're Black. So the compliment part—"you're intelligent"—meant nothing, and the professor was only sending the invisible message, Blacks aren't intelligent.

So what's a professor to do? There are only two ways to avoid this microaggression—only compliment Whites but never students of color. Or never compliment any students. Neither outcome of this "theory" is acceptable.

I'm not saying Whites never compliment Blacks sarcastically or out of racism. Sometimes they do, and that's abhorrent. What I'm saying is: Don't apply microaggression dogma #1. It does matter whether the speaker is a sarcastic racist or simply someone doing their damnedest to improve race relations but not getting it exactly right according to the latest identity fad. Treating one like the other is just going to make things worse.

I don't want to blame the students. This mode of thinking—that the speaker doesn't matter, only the listener's interpretation—didn't start with people of color. It was developed and introduced as "deconstructionism" in America's top universities beginning in 1968 by Jacques Derrida, a French philosopher who ironically was a highly privileged White male. I'll get to him later.

Martha and the N-Word

Martha Stewart said the n-word. Yes, that Martha Stewart, who you may not realize has been co-hosting Martha & Snoop's Potluck Dinner Party since 2016. Yes, that Snoop—rapper and Rastafarian Snoop Dogg. So a couple of years after Dr. Quenette said the n-word, Martha and Snoop were taping a show with bubble-gum rapper and teen idol Lil Yachty when the production hit a snag. They didn't have clearance to show Yachty's album cover. The Doggfather, according to Fader.com, "appropriately referred to Yachty's album cover as 'this nigga's shit.'" It was then that Martha leaned over and asked, "Yachty, does it upset you when Snoop says 'nigga shit?'"

According to the Los Angeles Times, "The room filled with every imaginable reaction: anger, horror, embarrassment, laughter, joy, pain." Throughout the exchange, Martha did not seem to understand what the big deal was. Yachty's reaction? A huge smile.

No one person could agree with all the contradictory reactions in that room, but those reactions have one good thing in common. Not only was Martha not severely punished, she was not punished at all. I'm not saying she didn't make a mistake. I'm saying we shouldn't punish people for honest mistakes—

mistakes made with no ill intention, an intention that we ourselves would not condemn.

Unfortunately, that's probably not the reason Martha got off scot-free. She basically owns that show. And besides, most rappers are in a pretty poor position from which to criticize the use of the n-word.

Kansas Again

Andrea Quenette was essentially powerless. Her students were able to force her to take an unwanted immediate leave of absence and forced the university to try her in administrative hearings. After five months, she was found innocent. Despite that, and despite being backed by her department, Quenette was fired, although with a built-in, one-year delay.

This is a good example of the part of the dogma that argues that if the recipient feels hurt, almost any level of retaliation is justified. The students saw Quenette's slip as justification for immediate termination of her career. Saying the n-word was their primary complaint, and the only one they backed up with evidence.

I must emphasize that this is what is being taught at many colleges and universities. As usual, everyone has "good intentions." They are trying to end our greatest and most enduring political evil—racism. My point is simply that this approach is counterproductive. It makes the problem worse. And it hurts a lot of innocent people in the process.

Once More, Only Crazier

At a high school in the very "woke" Madison, Wisconsin school district, on October 9, 2019, Marlon Anderson, a Black security assistant, was asked to help the assistant principal escort a student from the school grounds. The student was yelling and pushing the principal and began calling Anderson the n-word. At first, Anderson asked him to stop, but without using that word. When the student continued, Anderson said, "Don't call me nigger."

The school administration thought this over for a week and then fired Anderson, who had worked for the school for 11 years. They were so brainwashed by postmodern thinking that after a whole week, the lot of them could not figure out the most obvious moral problem. The Madison School District explained that "racial slurs will not be tolerated ... no matter what the circumstances ... no matter the intent." Note dogma #1 above—intent doesn't matter.

Had the school district administrators known English, or perhaps tried using a dictionary, they could have saved themselves a lot of trouble. A slur is "an insulting or disparaging remark." Anderson did not make an insulting remark. He did not slur the troublemaker and did not use a racial slur against him. Saying "he's a bastard" is a slur. Saying "Don't call me a bastard" is not. Anderson didn't use or make a slur. It's that simple.

The students quickly realized their administrators had taken leave of their senses, and two days later, 1,500 students and staff walked out on strike, led by Anderson's son, president of the Black Student Union. Three days later, Anderson's firing was rescinded and two weeks after that he was back at work.

Conclusion

Nonviolent direct action, as implemented by leaders like Diane Nash, Martin Luther King Jr., and John Lewis, massively changed White attitudes for the better and produced reforms so fundamental that reversing them today would likely cause another civil war. (Of course, we still have a long way to go.)

The techniques used then were the exact opposite of those used in today's new "identity politics." So are the results.

CHAPTER 30

Identity Politics—The Dark Side

*This idea of purity and you're never compromised and
you're always politically 'woke' and all that stuff. You
should get over that quickly.*
—President Barack Obama, October 29, 2019

About a week before the Democrats' 2016 Super Tuesday primaries,
Black Lives Matter (BLM) organizer Ashley Williams spent $500 on a
ticket. "I shut down a private Hillary Clinton Fundraiser last night in
Charleston, South Carolina," bragged Williams as she recounted her notorious escapade.

"She [Clinton] said that 'we need to bring them to heel.'" To Ashley,
this proved that Clinton was "pathologizing, demonizing and also crimi-
nalizing Black youth." She added, "I found these comments really racist," apparently after having watched the viral version of a video that had
been stripped of context.

The new identity politics targeted Hillary Clinton, who got 94% of
the votes cast by Black women, only 2% shy of Barack Obama's percentage. Those four-million Black women knew what they were doing.

Bill Maher said at the time of this incident, "You people [William's
supporters] need to learn the difference between an imperfect friend and
a deadly enemy. You want to tear Hillary Clinton down? Great, then enjoy President Trump." The new identity politics has escaped from the
campus and is damaging Democratic and national politics. Its adherents
have good intentions but don't know what they're doing.

That's not the only reason this is the dark side of identity politics. The
Williams/BLM attack on Clinton was likely the result of a setup by a
high-powered political consultant who was able to manipulate the dark
dynamics of identity politics. I'll return to that shortly. First, let's see
how Williams and BLM went wrong.

The Clinton Attack

Soon after the confrontation at the Clinton fundraiser, Williams appeared in a seven-minute segment on MSNBC. She told the host, Tamron Hall, "We cannot continue to pretend that Hillary Clinton wasn't involved in laying the foundation for mass incarceration in our society." (Actually, that was done by Richard Nixon in 1972.)

Ashley Williams, just like Bernie Sanders and Ta-Nehisi Coates (see chapter 7), quotes some of Clinton's words, but they are completely out of context. Then she interprets them as racist, asserts evil intentions and finally charges Clinton with causing mass incarceration.

Clinton's accusers concluded that Clinton was deliberately being evil to further her and her husband's political careers. That's right, Williams and Coates believed that the Clintons grossly insulted Blacks—the most loyal part of their base—and effectively sent a million to prison in order to win racist votes.

The only thing missing? Evidence.

Evidence

I've made some strong claims: Hillary Clinton did not call Black people super-predators, nor did she lay the foundation for their mass incarceration. To avoid the failing I accuse Williams of, I must back up these claims with solid evidence. That's only fair. So bear with me as I check Williams' three assertions during her interview. These are:

1. **Clinton called Black people in general super-predators.**
    o "You called Black people 'super-predators.' I'm not a super-predator, Hillary Clinton."
2. **Clinton used that term in** 1994 (which implies she did it to support the crime bill).
    o "I know that you called Black youth super-predators in 1994."
3. **Clinton is responsible for mass incarceration.**
    o "We want you to apologize for mass incarceration." Hillary Clinton was "involved in laying the foundation for mass incarceration in our society."

Assertion 1: Super-predators. In her 1996 news conference, Clinton referred to gangs, then mentioned "the mob" (mainly Italian) and drug cartels (mainly Latin American) and then said, "They are not just gangs of kids anymore. They are often the kinds of kids that are called super-predators." She never once mentioned race, and only spoke of super-violent kids, not kids in general, and certainly not nonviolent adults as Williams implied when she said, "I'm not a super-predator, Hillary Clinton."

But why was "super-predators" even a topic? The reason is the crime wave that underlies this story.

Between 1985 and the early 1990s, a dramatic violent crime wave really did sweep through both White and Black communities. It hit males under 25, particularly teenage males under 18. This was largely the result of a crack cocaine epidemic and easier access to guns. The results can best be seen in the Bureau of Justice's homicide statistics.

Homicide Rate per 100,000 for males under 18 (DOJ)				
	Offending Rates		Victimization Rates	
	White	Black	White	Black
1985	10	53	4	24
1993	23	253	9	76

As the table shows, for males under 18, White homicides and White homicide victims more than doubled in eight years, which is horrible enough. But the Black community, which started out with much higher crime rates, saw the homicide rate nearly quintuple and the victimization rate triple.

As a result, everyone from Jesse Jackson to the FBI to academics and Hillary Clinton became focused on teenage violence. Of course, inner-city Blacks were most distraught about their children killing and dying for drug gangs. That's why Clinton was talking about federal programs to bring this situation under control. These programs were generally supported by Black communities. But where did she get that awful term, super-predators?

Visiting New Jersey's maximum-security prison, John Dilulio, one of the more sensationalist academics, spoke to a life-term Black inmate who told him, "I was a bad-ass street gladiator, but these kids are stone-cold predators." Dilulio took this vivid phrase, "stone-cold predator" and turned it into the comic-book moniker, "super-predator."

Dilulio used his new term in the title of his November 1995 essay, "The Coming of the Super-Predators." *Newsweek* picked it up for a December 1995 issue and used it again a month later. Just days later, Hillary Clinton used it at a press conference.

Dilulio acknowledged the problem was worst for inner-city Black communities. But he also pointed out that there were 200 teenage Latino gangs in L.A. and that some White working-class fathers in Philadelphia were asking their district attorney what she was "going to do to control their children." I cannot find any evidence of anyone using the term as a code word for Blacks in general or even for Black children or violent Black children.

The modern concept of "super-predator" as a code word for all Black children or, as Ashley Williams implied, for all Blacks, may have originated with Bernie Sanders and his high-paid campaign strategist—I'm coming to that soon.

Assertion 2: Was it 1994? When Williams "shut down" Clinton's fund-raiser, she accused Clinton by saying, "I know that you called Black youth super-predators in 1994." Broadcast journalist Tamron Hall echoed this on MSNBC, saying, "Ashley Williams confronted Hillary Clinton over the word [super-predator] … when *she was advocating for a landmark crime bill* signed in 1994 by then-President Bill Clinton."

To illustrate this, Tamron showed the same video clip I discussed in Chapter 7 with reference to Ta-Nehisi Coates. As you will recall, the clip clearly shows the date as 01-28-96. So both disruptor Williams and MSNBC host Tamron were off by two years. Neither *The Atlantic* nor MSNBC did even the simplest fact check of a damning but obviously wrong claim. That is how the new identity politics gains traction.

Hillary Clinton could not have used the term to lobby for the crime bill, as the term had not been invented yet. Besides, in 1994, she was totally absorbed with her attempt to pass universal healthcare.

Assertion 3: Mass incarceration? Williams said, "We [BLM] want you to apologize for mass incarceration." Then on MSNBC, she said, "Tamron, we cannot continue to pretend that Hillary Clinton wasn't involved in laying the foundation for mass incarceration in our society."

It's not a matter of pretending. Clinton played no part whatsoever in "laying the foundation for mass incarceration" for any number of reasons, including:

- Mass incarceration started 20 years before she arrived.
- Mass incarceration quadrupled before the 1994 crime bill, and the combined federal and state imprisonment rate for Blacks (but not for Whites) stopped increasing five years after it passed.
- Hillary did not persuade any members of Congress to vote for the bill.
- Joe Biden had been working on the bill for two years before Bill Clinton was elected.
- Had the Democrats not passed the 1994 bill, it is absolutely certain the Republicans would have passed a bill with more money for prisons and less for inner-city programs.

All that Williams and BLM seem to know about mass incarceration is that (1) it happened, and (2) it's a bad thing.

Enter the Dark-Side Consultant

Tamron twice asked why Sanders was not getting equal treatment, considering that he actually voted for the 1994 bill. Williams twice gave a scripted non-answer. Here's the real story.

You may recall Tad Devine from Chapter 18. He worked for Paul Manafort, Trump's campaign chairman, in support of a Ukrainian dictator. Then Devine became Sanders' chief strategist. In an October 2015 article, *Bloomberg News* reported "he [Devine] is already familiar with the array of issues that Sanders might soon deploy against Clinton" and that the "Sanders camp has also been combing the record of Clinton's statements."

Devine himself said at that time, "Her remarks back then about the evils of urban gangs filled with 'super-predators' with 'no conscience, no empathy' are unlikely to endear her to the Black Lives Matter movement." Tad Devine and Bernie Sanders, in October 2015, were already thinking about using Black Lives Matter to attack Clinton.

Three months later, Sanders came out with his "Racial Justice" position paper—a perfect title for attracting racial-justice activists. That paper stated, "We must address the lingering unjust stereotypes that lead to the labeling of Black youths as 'thugs' and 'super-predators.'" Apparently, Ashley Williams, a Sanders supporter, took the bait.

Sanders' Roles in 1994 and 2016

Disturbingly, Sanders knew the score. He knew that most Blacks supported the 1994 bill, including two-thirds of the Black Congressional Caucus. He knew that he himself had spoken on the floor of the House multiple times in support of the crime bill.

- "Many of us are in agreement that the 100,000 new police officers are going to be a real help."—Sanders, January 14, 1994
- "The State of Vermont will receive ... $6.5 million for drug and crime enforcement; $3 million for our cities and towns ..."—Sanders, April 11, 1994

When Sanders first ran for the U.S. Senate in 2006, his campaign website declared:

> BERNIE SANDERS' STRONG RECORD OF SUPPORTING
> TOUGH ON CRIME LEGISLATION
> **SANDERS: STRONG ON FUNDING POLICE AND ANTI-
> DRUG PROGRAMS**
>
> ...
>
> Sanders Has Voted for Over $186 Billion for the Justice
> Department to Fight Crime.

Note that $186 billion is six times the size of the 1994 crime bill. On the floor of the House, arguing for the bill, he had said:

> "It is my firm belief that clearly there are **people in our society who are horribly violent, who are deeply sick and sociopathic**, and clearly these people must be **put behind bars** in order to protect society from them."
>
> —Sanders, April 13, 1994

The term super-predator had not yet been invented, and I'm not saying Sanders was wrong, but this is not much different than what Clinton said, except that his "put behind bars" is harsher than her "brought to heel." And Sanders actually was using "deeply sick and sociopathic" to help sell the 1994 crime bill.

In April 2016, at the Apollo Theater in Harlem, Sanders was asked what he thought about Bill Clinton defending his wife's use of "super-predator." Sanders replied, "We all know what the term meant in the context that it was said years ago. We know who they were talking about." Someone in the audience yelled, "Black people." And Sanders said, "That's exactly right."

But it wasn't right, and he knew it. He knew the term referred to violent kids of any ethnicity caught up in murderous violence and not to "Black people." Bernie Sanders lied. It's that simple.

Once again, a White guy and his megabucks political trickster had conned a Black audience. It's well worth noting that nationally, few Blacks fell for such nonsense.

Conclusion

MLK's civil-rights-based identity politics and today's new "identity politics" are polar opposites. One built alliances with liberals to fight against society's most conservative forces, and the other—"identity politics"—attacks liberals. One moves us forward; the other polarizes us.

Because the new identity politics is so often focused on finding fault with "imperfect friends," it's easy for dark-side political strategists like Tad Devine to use it against even the best Democrats. Once again, polarization only hurts democracy and helps Trump.

CHAPTER 31

Cultural Appropriation

*Those who can make you believe absurdities can make you
commit atrocities.*

—Voltaire

"Maybe Don't Dress Your Kid Up As Moana This Halloween?" That
leading question was a *Cosmopolitan* editorial headline the week before
Halloween in 2017. The subhead avoided a direct answer: "It's on you to
teach your kid not to be racially insensitive." So I'll say it in plain English: "If your little girl is White, and you let her dress up as Disney's
Moana, you're being racist," according to *Cosmo*.

Obviously, that could upset some little girls and their mothers, so
Cosmopolitan has thoughtfully provided instructions for how mothers
can console their disappointed daughters.

> "Encourage them to take a step back and realize that they're awash
> in privileges that the real Moanas and Tianas of the world will
> likely never see because the world is full of racist assholes."

I'm sure that will make "the real Moanas and Tianas," as well as your
kid, feel much better.

Identity politics has escaped the campus, infiltrated the Democratic
Party, and as "cultural appropriation," now shows up on a regular basis
in women's magazines—*Cosmopolitan, Vogue, Teen Vogue, Redbook,
People, Glamour, Allure*. The first time I looked it up, Google handed
me a piece in *Teen Vogue* explaining that White girls should *not* wear
cornrow braids.

Although never labeled as such, "cultural appropriation" is just another type of microaggression. And being micro, its unintended hidden
message is that racial and ethnic oppression has diminished to such a
microscopic level that a White girl rocking cornrows is now near the top

of the list of racial concerns, so we can rest easy. That unintended message is itself racist (I said the "message," not those sending it).

Fortunately, there are still sane voices being heard, for instance, Whoopi Goldberg's: "If you're going to talk about appropriating, we're all in deep doo-doo, because we're doing it to each other constantly." When Stevie Wonder was asked about singer Bruno Mars being accused of cultural appropriation for covering Black songs, he commented, "God created music for everyone to enjoy. So we cannot limit ourselves by people's fears and insecurities. He [Mars] has great talent. So the other stuff is just bullshit."

Auli'i Cravalho is the Hawaiian/Polynesian actress who spoke and sang for Moana, the Polynesian Princess, in Disney's 3D animated musical, and Disney was widely praised for its cultural sensitivity when choosing Cravalho. In spite of being Polynesian herself, she had a different take than the White corporate magazine editors when it came to anyone dressing up as Moana.

> I think it's absolutely appropriate. It's done in the spirit of love and for the little ones who just want to dress up as their favorite heroine. I'm all for it. Go for it! Parents can dress up as Moana, too.

So what was the "logic" of the *Cosmo/Redbook* editors?

> "To pretend to be Moana when you're not makes light of [Polynesian] history—and reinforces a deeply problematic power dynamic, wherein White people use, then discard, pieces of cultures they've subjugated for centuries just because they can."

In other words, if your little girl wants to dress up as Moana for Halloween, she is actually trying to subjugate other cultures just because she can. Stevie Wonder was right—that's just bullshit. No one with the power to subjugate cultures has ever dressed up as Moana. That's not how power operates. And they certainly are not little girls, White or otherwise.

The obvious point that usually gets lost is an old piece of folk wisdom: Imitation is the sincerest form of flattery. When a little girl dresses as Moana, she's saying she loves Moana. And that helps her remember a bit about Polynesian culture. When Bruno Mars covers a Black song, he's saying he loves that song, and he's complimenting the culture it came from. No one ever ate pizza in order to deprive Italy of its culture. We just love pizza. That makes us like Italians more, not less.

It Came from the Ivory Towers

So where did this nonsense come from? Academics, of course. Who else can twist their thinking into such intellectual pretzels?

Two years before the Moana hoopla, administrators from 13 multicultural centers and offices at Yale University sent the student body a two-page memo advising them on how to choose their Halloween costumes. They hoped that people would avoid any circumstance that "disrespects, alienates or ridicules segments of our population based on race, nationality, religious belief or gender expression." Fair enough.

But, in addition, students were warned that even if they were "*not intending* to offend," they could fall so far short of the mark that no apology could undo the damage. To sort this out, students should ask themselves five fairly ambiguous questions, the last of which was, "Could someone take offense with your costume and why?" As we know, the answer to that is always: Yes, *someone* could! If the self-appointed culture police choose to take offense, that by itself makes you guilty.

A number of students approached the master and associate master, Nicholas Christakis and Erika Christakis, respectively, at Silliman College, one of Yale's 12 residential colleges, and expressed their concern and frustration with these instructions.

The great 'offense.' In response to this concern, Erika Christakis sent an email to the students at her college, in which she said, "As a former preschool teacher, for example, it is hard for me to give credence to a claim that there is something objectionably 'appropriative' about a blonde-haired child's wanting to be [Disney's animated Chinese princess] Mulan for a day." She also suggested that students might want to handle the costume question on their own rather than letting the university's establishment "exercise implied control over college students."

The 'brave' response of 150 Yale students was to publicly confront college master Nicholas. A video taken toward the end of the confrontation shows a female student yelling, "Be quiet! In your position as master, it is your job to create a place of comfort and home for the students who live in Silliman. You have not done that." Silliman College, with its indoor basketball court, dance studio, gym, movie theater, film-editing lab, billiard tables, and art gallery, sounds far more comfortable than what 99% of college students experience, not to mention what urban Black kids experience.

Then the student demands, "By sending out that email, that goes against your position as master. Do you understand that?!" He replies calmly and quietly, "No, I don't agree with that." Standing a foot away, she explodes, screaming:

> Then why the fuck did you accept the position?! Who the fuck hired you?! You should step down! If that is what you think about being a master, you should step down! It is not about creating an intellectual space! It is not! Do you understand that? It's about creating a home here. You are not doing that!

This too is a dark side of identity politics. This is about intimidating your intellectual opponent when you have no reasonable argument. It's not about "creating a place of comfort and home," as she claims. Otherwise, she would not be so eager to destroy that in order to enforce her ideology.

The student's demand is an extension of the standard identity-politics demand for "safe spaces" on campus. These spaces, safe from those who might question the logic or ethics of identity politics, are now provided on most campuses. The student's rant is a demand that the residence college itself should count as a safe space—safe from points of view that differ from her own.

Although the Christakises apologized for unintended racial insensitivity, they would not disown the views expressed in their email. The thought police were not pleased. Nearly 1,000 students and faculty signed a petition asking for Nicholas and Erika Christakis to be immediately removed from their campus jobs and campus home. Some students demanded advanced warning of Erika's appearances in the dining hall so they wouldn't be traumatized by the sight of her. This is the sort of thing that gets them labeled "snowflakes."

None of the politics enforcers saw the least problem with screaming curses in Nicholas Christakis' face. That could not be a microaggression because he is White.

Seven months later, at Silliman College's graduation ceremony, some students refused to accept their diplomas from Nicholas. Two days later the two resigned from their posts at the residential college.

The View of a Black Marine. I have no data as to the majority view of Blacks regarding Halloween costumes, so-called cultural appropriation or open discussion on college campuses. But the view of one Black Marine who commented on the situation in a letter published in *The Atlantic* seems to me to put things in perspective better than anything else I've read.

> My name is Chris Martin. I was in the U.S. Marine Corps Infantry from 2007 to 2011. After combat deployments to Ar Ramadi, Iraq, and Marjah, Afghanistan, ... I attended Denison University, a liberal arts college in Ohio, where I was a Phi Beta Kappa graduate in economics.
>
> Violence, the prospect of violence and fear always seem to grab peoples' attention more roughly than almost anything else. The world grieves for ISIS' victims this past week, as they ought to.
>
> During these recent tragedies, and the student protests sweeping campuses across the U.S., I find myself intrigued by the term "safe spaces."
>
> In the military, I firsthand witnessed occasional racism. At college, I again heard of racial tensions between student groups. I wholeheartedly acknowledge and support the causes that the students at Mizzou/Yale/Ithaca/CMC/Amherst and other colleges are fighting for. Their cause is just and needed.
>
> It is difficult for me to reconcile the idea that campuses are not "safe spaces" for students. ... A member of my unit, Kyle Carpenter, was awarded the Congressional Medal of Honor for diving onto a hand grenade to save his friend. That kind of environment, to me, constitutes an "unsafe space."
>
> Again, I do agree that there is racism in academia.
>
> My Millennial peers who are still on college campuses do their causes disservice by claiming conversations about inappropriate Halloween costumes cause them to fear for their safety. Talk to a student veteran about fearing for your safety before invoking such hyperbolic terms.

Conclusion

The standard "proof" of cultural appropriation's harm is blackface. But if some frat brats put on blackface to ridicule Blacks, this is neither a microaggression nor a cultural appropriation. It's simply a highly offensive insult. Blackface is not some important part of Black culture; it is purely an offensive artifact of White culture.

Most "cultural appropriations" fit the definition of microaggressions perfectly. The offense, if it exists, is generally small by objective standards—Whoopi Goldberg, Stevie Wonder, and Auliʻi Cravalho could detect no offense at all. In microaggression theory, it doesn't matter if borrowing the culture is intended as a compliment. As I've pointed out before, if someone decides their feelings are hurt, almost any level of retaliation is justified.

When someone borrows from another culture because they respect it, admire it, enjoy it or simply think it's cool, this is not an act of aggression, micro or otherwise.

CHAPTER 32

The Microaggression Hoax

The only way for prejudiced people to change is for them to decide for themselves that all human beings should be treated fairly. We can't force them to think that way.

—Rosa Parks, 1997
Initiated the 1955 Montgomery bus boycott

"The invisibility of microaggressions may be more harmful to people of color than hate crimes or the overt and deliberate acts of White supremacists such as the Klan." So claims Dr. Derald Wing Sue, the leading "expert" on microaggressions. Yes, he claims that a microaggression—that's micro as in microscopic—can be "more harmful" than a hate crime, which the Department of Justice says is "often a violent crime, such as assault, murder, arson or vandalism." To drive this home, he mentions the Ku Klux Klan.

As previously discussed, microaggression are real, and in areas of prejudice, they often follow systematic patterns that amplify their harm. But as Sue admits, they are so small it is often impossible to even be sure they happened. This is no excuse for ignoring them. Instead, the point of this chapter is that Dr. Sue's solution just makes race relations worse.

Dr. Sue popularized "microaggressions," which he described as subtle "slights and insults" in a 2007 paper that provided a list of 51 examples that the president of the University of California distributed to its 10 campuses with a quarter-million students. Unfortunately, Sue's paper provides no evidence for his list.

"America is the land of opportunity." That's one possible microaggression listed by U.C. But this claim was checked by a Cato Institute/YouGov survey in 2017, which found that 93% of Blacks and 89% of Latinos did not find this assertion offensive, let alone "more harmful" than a Ku Klux Klan hate crime.

They're Invisible

Sue believes that "microaggressions hold their power because they are invisible," but offers no evidence of power due to invisibility. Generously, he says microaggressions are committed by "well-intentioned White folks who are unaware." (People of color cannot commit them.)

The belief that invisible "slights and insults" may be more harmful than "hate crimes" is polarizing. Microaggression accusations usually follow Sue's analysis of racism and target "White liberals." The right-wing press plays this up because polarization is their mission. Their message seems to be, "If the radical left is attacking liberals as racist, think how they would treat us." This may help explain why 71% of Republicans view Democrats as moderately to extremely racist.

Dr. Sue and the 'Racist' Flight Attendant

The toxicity of microaggression theory is confirmed by Sue's own story of what happened when he applied his own theories to a possible microaggression aimed at him. By all indications, he should be the one person in the country most capable of using microaggression theory to reduce racism and soften the blow to the victim. Here's what happened.

Sue, an Asian American, has a Ph.D. in counseling psychology, and by the time he wrote his landmark paper, he was the country's leading expert on how to handle microaggressions. His 2007 paper provides only this one example of how his microaggression theory works in practice.

Sue and a Black colleague were asked to move to the back of a small plane "to distribute weight on the plane evenly." Three White men seated in front of them were not asked to move. There were no other passengers.

Sue could feel his "blood pressure rising" and his "face flush with anger," and he asked the flight attendant, "Did you know that you asked two passengers of color to step to the rear of the 'bus'"? The flight attendant correctly perceived this as an accusation of racism (because Sue said "bus," not "plane") and indignantly denied it.

I'm no psychologist but accusing someone of being a racist is not the best way to start a productive conversation, especially when, as he later concluded, the flight attendant was well-intentioned. In fact, I would call Sue's opening remark more than a microaggression, as it was made in anger and was certainly not "invisible" to either of them. It was just a normal-size, nasty, verbal aggression, which Dr. Sue seems to find acceptable since he never acknowledges it.

He persisted in trying to get her to recognize her racism, but as he explains, "For every allegation I made, she seemed to have a rational reason for her actions. Finally, she broke off the conversation and refused to talk about the incident any longer. ... For the rest of the flight, I stewed over the incident." So he definitely didn't help the victim (himself) feel any better.

The flight attendant's view? Now let's try to see this from the flight attendant's perspective. Something Dr. Sue never attempts, perhaps because he defines microaggressions to be actions that can only be "perpetrated" by Whites.

In spite of his anger, Sue was eventually "convinced that she was sincere in her belief that she had acted in good faith without racial bias." Nonetheless, he is sure that her "actions and their meaning were invisible to her." He's saying she could not understand her own actions or what they meant, but he could. It is entirely possible that Dr. Sue is correct. But ...

Sue notes that "balancing the weight on the plane seemed reasonable." Quite likely it was more than reasonable. The FAA's *Weight and Balance Handbook* indicates that the flight attendant may have had more on her mind than Sue realized. It's crucial "that the center of gravity is slightly *ahead of* the center of lift."

Had the flight attendant moved the three White men to the back of the plane, that would have shifted the center of gravity even *more* toward the back than moving Sue and his colleague. According to the FAA, having the center of gravity too far back makes "the airplane unstable and difficult (or even impossible) to recover from a stall," which means the flight ends somewhat ahead of schedule and not likely at an airport. That could be even worse than a microaggression.

Had the flight attendant considered the situation in her own microaggression terms, she might have thought, This privileged male college professor thinks he can read my mind, but he's just 'mansplaining' and has no idea what I'm dealing with. Plus he has the chutzpah to suggest that I'm racist.

Conclusions? What we know for sure is that Sue was very unhappy with the outcome. Surely the flight attendant was too. On top of that, both parties probably ended up thinking worse of the other race. And this is in fact what has happened in every microaggression encounter that I've read about.

So this is how it turns out when the country's leading expert in fixing microaggressions tries to solve the problem using his own theories. Dr. Sue apparently considers this outcome normal since he used this as his main example for years.

Microaggression Theory

As mentioned, Dr. Sue believes that "microaggressions hold their power because they are invisible." But would Sue have felt better if the flight attendant visibly discriminated against him, and they both knew it? Sue never considers that question. Possibly because an honest answer would contradict his theory.

If someone is well-intentioned and unknowingly says something that offends you, it may be best not to get angry but to explain politely why it upsets you. Generally, a well-intentioned person will be embarrassed by their mistake and do their best to avoid it in the future.

If Daryl Davis could win over dozens of Klansmen, surely Derald Sue should have been able to successfully deal with one well-intentioned flight attendant.

Because microaggressions, such as "You are so articulate," cannot be verified as aggressions by the recipient and are invisible to the "perpetrator," they are an open invitation to acrimony. The supposed "perpetrator," being unable to see what's wrong, will likely view the "victim" as inventing a crime.

This doesn't mean there's no problem. It just means that vigilante-style prosecution of invisible crimes is not the way to solve the problem.

In a later chapter, we will see that Sue's paper mentions that microaggression is based, in part, on "critical race theory." The first two contributors to that theory that he lists are a French philosopher who doesn't believe in truth and the founder of the Italian Communist Party. Perhaps we should not be surprised that Sue's theory seems rather odd.

The Stereotype Threat to Black Students

Fortunately, there are many other approaches to dealing with racism and its lingering effects. After a little online searching, here are a few experiments I found interesting. Surely there are even better ones that I did not discover in my brief quest. My point is only that solid, innovative research is being pushed aside by ideological claptrap derived from the likes of Jacques Derrida, a postmodern charlatan, and Antonio Gramsci, a 1920s Italian neo-Marxist, whom we will soon meet.

Stereotype threat means being at risk of confirming a negative stereotype about one's group. It's like being on a team that's viewed as a bunch of losers and not wanting to mess up because that would help confirm the negative stereotype of you and your teammates. Of course, this threat is mainly felt when you're under pressure to perform—for example, on a final exam.

There is a lot of evidence (although there's still some doubt) that this stereotype threat damages Black academic performance. There is also evidence of the same problem for women and their performance on difficult math tests. Here's one of the many pieces of evidence.

Black and White college students were given a difficult verbal test in an experimental setting. For some participants, both Black and White, it was described as "diagnostic of intellectual ability." This was expected to produce a stereotype threat for the back students who would worry about performing well as representatives of their race. Other participants, both Black and White, were told the test was simply "a laboratory problem-solving task that was nondiagnostic of ability" in order to reduce any stereotype threat. The same test was given in all cases. With the stereotype-threat description, Whites outperform Blacks, but with the threat-reducing description, Blacks and Whites performed equally well.

Compared to microaggression theory, this result points to a workable approach to making things a little better. There are many reasons for the negative academic stereotypes of Blacks. Some are microaggressions, and all trace back to White prejudice. Tracking down all the aggressions, the microaggressions and the self-doubt now built into the Black community is hopeless. Fixing them all individually is even harder.

It makes more sense to focus on finding the most effective ways to counteract and repair the damage. This will have the benefit of helping to break the vicious cycle. Success will tend to breed more success. Self-confirming approaches have led to dramatic changes in sports, television, movies, and politics, as has happened since the civil rights movement.

There are many ways out of the stereotype threat. But undoubtedly the best ones have not yet been found, and few have been implemented. To show something of the breadth of possibilities, here's another interesting experiment.

Four groups of students (two White groups and two Black groups) were assigned to write letters to disadvantaged kids who lived far away to encourage them in their educational pursuits. But two groups, one Black and one White, were instructed to use a special argument and were provided with evidence to support the theory that minds can grow and develop—that you can actually increase your intellectual ability.

The experiment had little effect on three groups. But for the Black students using the special argument, the effect was dramatic. They became happier with their own studies, and at the end of the semester, their grades were dramatically higher.

This result did not surprise the experimenters because they had designed the special argument to indirectly relieve some of the effects of the negative academic stereotype. It worked. Having Black students argue the case themselves was the best way to convince them they could increase their intellectual abilities.

And one more example. A number of studies have found that one of the strongest predictors of college GPA for African-American students is the number of White friends they have. That's after taking into account the obvious confounding factors. One theory is that such connections tend to contradict the negative stereotype and thereby lessen its impact. It seems that a deliberate effort in this direction might well succeed.

Conclusion

By stereotyping "liberal Whites" as the common enemy, Sue drives a wedge between people of color and many who would be their best allies inside the dominant culture. Historically, such allies have always been helpful—if not essential—for progress. Just think back on the decades-long abolitionist and anti-slavery movements that led up to the Civil War. Think of the hundreds of thousands of northern Whites who died fighting against slavery. Think of the White Freedom Riders of the 1960s. Think of JFK and LBJ.

No, allies are not perfect. But as we will see shortly, the upper-class, White, male neo-Marxists and postmodernists who are the fathers of Sue's "critical race theory" are far less trustworthy than the "well-meaning White folks" who Sue claims are perpetrators of "invisible" microaggressions that can be worse than hate crimes.

CHAPTER 33

Roots of the New Identity Politics

The Democrats, the longer they talk about identity politics, I got 'em. ... If the left is focused on race and identity ... we can crush the Democrats.

—Steve Bannon, former Trump strategist

The Wachowski sisters were brothers back when they wrote and directed their cult film, *The Matrix*. So it may not surprise you that their latest project, the TV series *Sense8,* has been described by one reviewer as a "no holds barred exploration of identity politics."

Now this is going to sound as spooky as the plot of *The Matrix,* but what's cool is that it's true. The Wachowski brothers hid the key to identity politics in that movie. Where? The hero, Neo, hides his computer disks in a book—*Simulacra and Simulation*—the pages of which have been hollowed out just as reality has been hollowed out by a computer simulation called *The Matrix.*

Now comes the strange part. *Simulacra and Simulation* is a real postmodern philosophy book from 1981, and the Wachowski brothers saw it as central to their worldview. It was so important to them that they tried to get its author to appear in the film, and forced Keanu Reeves, who plays Neo, to read the actual book! That must have been painful.

❧

Now, I don't expect you to believe that proves anything, so I'll take a factual approach. But here's where we're headed. Postmodernism is the primary root of both the new identity politics and the Matrix view of reality that's been adopted by the alt-right wing of Trump's base. I'll begin by showing how postmodernism underpins identity politics. Then I'll let Michiko Kakutani, the former chief book critic at *The New York Times,* explain why "some Trump allies invoke the iconography of the movie *The Matrix.*"

Let me show how to track down the source of the new identity politics, which unexpectedly lies in Europe—in the German and Italian neo-Marxism of the 1920s and some French "philosophers" of the 1960s.

Finding the Roots

Dr. Derald Wing Sue, the popularizer of microaggression theory, published a textbook in 2015, *Multicultural Social Work Practice,* covering microaggressions and related topics. In Chapter 2, he states:

> Critical race theory (CRT) ... began as a movement in law departments during the 1970s and 1980s and has spread to ... political science, ethnic studies, postcolonial studies, education, and social work ... with specific influence from **Antonio Gramsci, Jacques Derrida** ...

He is absolutely correct. Microaggression theory grew out of **critical race theory (CRT)** and the two main godfathers of CRT are Gramsci and Derrida. Antonio Gramsci was a founder of the Italian Communist Party in 1921. Jacques Derrida is the father of deconstructionism, the original core of postmodernism, a French "philosophy" that was brought to America in 1968.

But just because Dr. Sue writes about CRT in his book, does that make it the root of his microaggression theory? It's good evidence, but conclusive evidence comes from his 2007 paper, which provided the foundation of microaggression theory and related identity politics. That paper cites only one actual study of microaggressions, and the name of that paper is, you guessed it, "Critical Race Theory, Racial Microaggressions, and Campus Racial Climate."

CRT led to microaggression theory, and Dr. Sue tells us that CRT is based on neo-Marxist Gramsci and on Derrida, the godfather of postmodernism. Gramsci saw that Marx had made fundamental mistakes so he developed a new version of Marxism, a neo-Marxism, to correct them. Microaggression theory comes from CRT which has one root in Gramsci's Italian neo-Marxism.

Similarly, note that German neo-Marxism flows through postmodernist Derrida and then into CRT and on to microaggressions and identity politics. In Frankfurt in 2001, Derrida received the Adorno Prize. Adorno is one of the two leading proponents of "Critical Theory" and a leader of the "Frankfurt School" of German neo-Marxists, founded in 1923. And by the way, Critical Race Theory is a type Frankfurt-School Critical Theory. Here are the main roots of identity politics:

The new identity politics

- Critical Race Theory
  - Italian Neo-Marxist Antonio Gramsci
  - Jacques Derrida
    - The neo-Marxist Frankfurt School
  - Kimberlé Crenshaw
    - Gramsci and the Postmodernist, Michel Foucault

- Third-wave feminism
  - Judith Butler
    - Postmodernists Derrida and Foucault
    - the neo-Marxist Frankfurt School
  - Kimberlé Crenshaw

We will meet Kimberlé Crenshaw and Judith Butler soon and meet Butler again in Chapter 35. As Dr. Sue points out, Critical Race Theory, a major component of the new identity politics, has spread to law, political science, education and social work departments—and to ethnic studies and postcolonial studies—at most American universities. And all of these have roots in campus-based postmodernism, which itself is rooted in European neo-Marxism.

Double-Checking the Roots

Many try to deny these roots, so to double-check this, I turned to JSTOR, a huge, searchable collection of academic articles.

A check of JSTOR turns up 70 articles that discuss both "cultural appropriation" and the Italian neo-Marxist Gramsci, who died in 1937. That strong a link between problems like Halloween costumes and the founder of the Italian Communist Party can't be mere coincidence.

Cultural appropriation and Derrida turn up together in 304 articles. "Michael Foucault," currently the most popular postmodernist, and cultural appropriation turn up together in 370 articles.

Gramsci is linked with identity politics in 1,247 articles. Derrida is linked with identity politics in 2,601 articles. And "postmodernism" shows up together with "identity politics" in 4,049 articles.

So European postmodernism and neo-Marxism are indeed the root of the new identity politics. Who would have guessed? (Actually quite a few have. I didn't discover this myself.)

What is Postmodernism?

Because the new identity politics grows out of postmodernism, we need to know a little about that. I will explain quite a bit more in the next two chapters, but for now, this will do. Postmodernism is actually a mish-mash of closely related "isms" with no agreement on where the boundary lines are. For convenience, non-devotees usually just lump them together, as I will.

Most importantly, postmodernism rejects the ideas and ideals of the Enlightenment—truth, reason, science, and democracy. I know that sounds hard to believe, but stay with me and in the next two chapters you'll see that postmodernists are quite open about this. Strangely, these negative ideas were first brought to the U.S. by Derrida and introduced into the literary criticism departments of Cornell, Johns Hopkins, and Yale universities in the late 1960s.

Derrida's new idea was called "deconstructionism," and it was based on a concept called "the death of the author." This meant that when interpreting a literary text, one should ignore the author's intended meaning. The reason for this is the neo-Marxist idea that everyone (except elite postmodernists) is brainwashed by capitalism, so authors don't understand their own true intention—their intentions are invisible to them.

As you've heard, to someone with a hammer, everything looks like a nail. Similarly, to postmodernists, all forms of communication look like literary texts in need of deconstruction. And deconstruction means rejecting the intentions of the author, whether the "author" is a painter of a mural, someone who makes a microaggression or a mother who dresses a little girl in a costume. This is why we find:

1. Dr. Sue telling us that the flight attendant's "actions and their meaning were **invisible** to her."
2. Yale telling its students that in "many cases, the student wearing the costume has not **intended** to offend, but [that's no excuse]."
3. The University of California telling students that something is a microaggression if it is perceived as a slight "whether **intentional or unintentional**."

4. Dr. Andrea Quenette being fired for saying something that was perceived as offensive, although she quite clearly had no such intent.

5. The Madison School District stating that the n-word is grounds for dismissal **"no matter the intent."**

6. *Cosmopolitan* telling us that if a little girl dresses as Moana, she is "mocking other people's cultures" no matter what she thinks she's doing.

7. In the San Francisco School District's mural controversy, the artist's intent is not even considered by those who want to destroy it. One such person said that **"intent no longer matters."**

In every case, the "author"—that is, the speaker, the artist or the little girl dressing up—is judged without any consideration of his/her intentions. That's like judging someone who trips and accidentally steps on your toe as if they had done so intentionally. It's like judging someone who sincerely compliments a haircut that you don't like as if they had deliberately ridiculed you. We might judge them harshly by accident, but none of us would make it our policy to do so.

I'm not saying everyone gets a pass for having "good intentions" no matter what they do. Far from it. But if they are trying to do something that *we ourselves* think they should be trying to do and they simply fall short or make a mistake, we do not refuse to consider their good intentions.

The only historical exception to this rule that I know of is the treatment of Blacks in the South during the age of lynchings. In that era, a Black person was judged by the offense taken by a White person. The law didn't matter, and the intention of the Black person counted for nothing. Only the view of the accuser mattered.

Ignoring all intentions comes from postmodernism's "death of the author" dogma, which is explained in *Death of the Author* (*La mort de l'auteur*), by Roland Barthes (1967).

The Postmodern Matrix

As I have mentioned, the "death of the author" concept springs from the theory that we are all brainwashed by capitalist culture. This neo-Marxist idea—that we're all brainwashed—is not only the deepest root of the new identity politics, but it also plays a surprising role in Trump's assault on truth. It's worth a closer look.

Marx's economic determinism led to his most famous prediction: Societies would progress from feudalism to capitalism to socialism. But in the 1920s, some more thoughtful Marxists noticed that the first socialist revolution took Russia directly from feudalism to socialism (skipping capitalism) and that Germany and Italy seemed to be heading from capitalism to fascism. Marx's economic determinism had gone off the rails at the first opportunity.

That intellectual crisis led to various neo-Marxisms. The Frankfurt School decided that Marx had missed the "culture industry," a part of capitalism that blinded workers to their economic self-interest. Gramsci decided that Marx had missed "cultural hegemony," which is pretty much the same idea as missing the culture industry.

The postmodernists then took these ideas and sensationalized them to the point where they no longer made any sense. Everything people say and do, they say, is **"socially constructed**." That includes your political views, your sexual orientation, and even science. All of that is dictated by capitalistic social pressures, and neither your own thinking nor your own biology has anything to do with it. This has had a strong influence on a new strain of feminism.

Of course, if you're a postmodernist, you believe neo-Marxism and that frees you from such effects. In non-academic, identity-politics jargon, you're "woke." The rest of us are presumably asleep. This metaphor was powerfully embraced by the 1999 sci-fi, cyberpunk action film, *The Matrix*. As Michiko Kakutani, the author of *The Death of Truth,* explains:

> Some Trump allies invoke the iconography of the movie *The Matrix*—in which the hero [Neo] is given a choice between two pills, a red one (representing knowledge and the harsh truths of reality) and a blue one (representing soporific illusion and denial).

In the film, the entire population, except for Neo and a small band of (woke) rebels, are completely unaware of reality, and their perceptions are controlled by the artificial intelligence of the Matrix. The Matrix is a perfect metaphor for the postmodern concept that everything is socially constructed or the neo-Marxist concept of a capitalist culture industry.

Far Left and Right Converge. *The Matrix* can easily be seen as a radical-left critique of capitalism, and Neo can be seen as a neo-Marxist revolutionary hero. In this case, being "red-pilled" would mean the same thing as being "woke." But that's not how it turned out. Being "red-pilled" has come to mean just the opposite—being converted to anti-woke (alt-right) crypto-fascism.

In her book, *The Death of Truth,* Kakutani points out that the red-pill meme has been taken up by "members of the alt-right" and that "some aggrieved men's rights groups talk about 'red-pilling the normies.'" This means they've slipped a normie (one of us) a red pill (some "facts" we didn't know), and the normie has their eyes opened. Liberals and progressives, they say, live in a world of delusion—we are asleep in the Matrix.

In this view, *The Matrix* teaches that Neo is a hero who is waking people to the truths of Trump and the alt-right. Why would the alt-right find a film by the Wachowski brothers (now sisters), who embrace the new identity politics, so compatible with their own worldview? Well, consider the main clue to the film's philosophical parentage—the hollowed-out book, *Simulacra and Simulation.* (Another clue is that fact that the Wachowskis even asked its author, Jean Baudrillard, to appear in a sequel to The Matrix.)

Baudrillard started out as a Marxist and then became, according to the *Stanford Encyclopedia of Philosophy,* "a major guru of French postmodern theory." The year after *The Matrix* was released, Baudrillard informed us: "We must adopt a delirious point of view. We must no longer assume any principle of truth." His book opens with an unacknowledged fake quote from the *Bible:* "It is truth that hides the fact that there is none." In other words, there is no truth. That's the very essence of Trump's worldview.

Postmodernism leads to the new identity politics and supports the crypto-fascist right's denial of facts and truth.

Third-Wave Feminism

Feminism has always been a key part of identity politics. According to Vox.com, third-wave feminism is generally linked with Kimberlé Crenshaw, who coined the term "intersectionality," and with Judith Butler, one of the two founders of "queer theory." Are they linked to postmodernism?

Crenshaw, a lawyer, was also one of the founders of Critical Race Theory, which Dr. Sue told us was influenced by Gramsci and Derrida. So "yes" as to Crenshaw's identity-politics connection.

Judith Butler, a professor at both U.C. Berkeley and Harvard, was awarded $1.5 million by the Mellon Foundation in 2008, which she used to fund a Critical Theory Institute at U.C. Berkeley. (Recall that Critical Theory was developed by the neo-Marxist Frankfurt School.)

Butler's queer-theory book, *Gender Trouble: Feminism and the Subversion of Identity* (1990), has become a feminist classic, cited in scholarly literature more than 57,000 times. The very first person the book mentions is Michel Foucault, one of the earliest postmodernists and currently the one most in vogue. Third-wave feminism is quite postmodern.

Conclusion

What is now called "identity politics" does not derive from Martin Luther King Jr. and the civil rights movement. Instead, it derives from a French pseudo-philosophy called postmodernism, which is largely derived from neo-Marxism.

Postmodernism: The Anti-Truth

We must no longer assume any principle of truth.
—Jean Baudrillard, "postmodern guru," 2000

"Call it relativism, critique or postmodernism. The idea is the same: *Truth is not found but made.* And making truth means exercising power." So explained postmodernist Casey Williams in a 2017 *New York Times* opinion piece. At the time, Trump had him flummoxed. Williams could see Trump exercising power by "making truth" for his base, and he did not like the truth Trump was making.

Under the headline "Has Trump Stolen [postmodern] Philosophy's Critical Tools?" Williams had to admit, "Trump has stolen our ideas and weaponized them." (Again, we see Michiko Kakutani was right.) Williams was writing to console himself and to assure us that even though postmodern ideas fit Trump like a glove, it was okay—because postmodern tools are good, and we need them to fight Trump. No, that doesn't make sense to me either.

The crux of the matter is this: According to postmodernism, truth does not exist, and we cannot even rely on "hard facts." Williams comes right out and says so.

> Some liberals ... insist on the existence of truth and the reliability of hard facts.

Yes, some liberals (actually, almost all of us) still do insist on the existence of truth and of hard facts. For example, Trump famously claimed he won the popular vote if you "deduct the millions of people who voted illegally." Here's the truth: There weren't millions of illegal votes and Trump lost the popular vote. That truth exists. It's a fact. To be redundant, it's a true fact, a hard fact. Another fact: Trump was president during 2019. There are actually millions of hard facts. But postmodernists always refuse to look obvious facts in the eye—kind of like Trump.

It's crucially important that we say what's true, and that we convince people Trump is a liar. No, that's not a silver bullet, but the postmodern approach of telling everyone that truth doesn't exist, and that hard facts are not reliable, is just evil. It's exactly what Trump, Putin, and long ago, Hitler wanted their publics to believe. That's what keeps (or kept) them in power.

Truth is Found, Not Made

Williams' claim that "truth is made, not found" is a strange one. Nonetheless, it's worth looking into because it's at the heart of the postmodern befuddlement. Say you want to know a fact—how much a new Tesla would cost you. First, you try the postmodern approach—just make it up. May as well make up a price you like, say $15,000. That would make a great fact.

Then you go down to the Tesla dealer and *wham*. Truth, existing truth, the hard truth, hits you smack in the face. What happened? You *found* the truth. What is Williams thinking?!

Well, he sorta tries to explain. "People who produce facts ... (maybe they're white, male and live in America) ... They rely on non-neutral methods (microscopes, cameras, eyeballs) and use non-neutral symbols (words, numbers, images)." Whoa! They're even using non-neutral symbols like words and numbers? Who would have guessed that even White American males would stoop so low? But it was in the New York Times, so it must be true ... well, except "true" is not a thing anymore, is it? This is confusing.

His idea is that people (even scientists) try to discover facts using microscopes, numbers and other bad stuff like that. But they blow it every time. Instead, what happens is they end up "making facts," "producing facts" ... that are not true. Usually because they're White, male Americans. Hold on, what's that got to do with it?

Williams pretends to be making some deep philosophical argument about how it's theoretically impossible for anyone ever to discover a true fact. But he can't help showing us the ax he's grinding. In fact, the whole argument is just made up to fit a hidden agenda—to trash the Enlightenment and all that dominant White male stuff.

This is ridiculous. Couldn't we trash White males without throwing out truth, reason, and science? Ironically, postmodernism was entirely cooked up by a bunch of not-so-nice European White guys.

Science, Too?

Yes, of course. Once you trash the idea of finding the truth, science is dead in the water. Williams reports that "Bruno Latour had made a career questioning 'scientific certainty.'" Latour is the #2 postmodern science wizard, and Williams quotes him as saying:

> Entire [postmodern] Ph.D. programs are still running to make sure that good American kids are learning the hard way that facts are made up.

There you have it: Postmodernism says that scientific facts are just made up. As an example of what goes wrong with postmodern science criticism, consider the following quote from Encyclopedia Britannica's entry on postmodernism. (To appreciate this entry, understand that the "mechanics" (motion) of solid objects is relatively simple, but there is a $1 million prize offered for making progress on fluid mechanics because it's so tricky.)

> The French [postmodernist] philosopher and literary theorist Luce Irigaray, for example, has argued that the science of solid mechanics is better developed than the science of fluid mechanics because the male-dominated institution of physics associates solidity and fluidity with the male and female sex organs, respectively.

Irigaray is obviously bonkers, but this is no barrier to being a postmodern guru. Even if we did think physics is mainly guided by an interest in sex organs, what is she thinking? That male scientists are more interested in male than female sex organs? No, they're not all gay! That was 1985, but don't worry, you can still get a postmodern Ph.D. for similar "contributions" to postmodern science. Here's proof.

Feminist Glaciology

M Jackson (M is her first name) has come out with her fourth book on glaciers, *The Secret Lives of Glaciers* (2019). She holds a doctorate from the University of Oregon in geography and glaciology. Top climate activist Bill McKibben blesses her as a "noted scientist." I watched her TEDx Talk from 2017 in which she explained:

> "Female glaciers, they move quick. They give off more water. They're usually blue or white. Gender identification is crucial in

this part of the Karakoram [mountain range in Pakistan] because here villagers breed their own glaciers. They take the seeds from male glaciers ... [and] combine them with seeds from female glaciers and they make a brand new glacier. Some glaciers are farmed for just a couple of years and some are farmed for centuries, all to provide stable water in the dry season."

Believe it or not, she was completely serious. However, one problem did get Dr. M's knickers in a twist: "The majority of glaciological knowledge that we have today stems from knowledge created by men, about men within existing masculinist stories." Umm ... are we sure those men (and a lot of women, by the way) aren't creating knowledge about *glaciers* using amazingly sophisticated science and not just "masculinist stories."

Jackson studied under Mark Carey, a dean and postmodernist professor of history at the University of Oregon. The two of them recently published a paper on "Feminist Glaciology" that they wrote under a five-year, $412,930 grant from the National Science Foundation.

Not surprisingly, the right wing, from the *Wall Street Journal* to DailyCaller.com, had a field day. "FEDS PAID $709,000 TO ACADEMIC WHO STUDIES HOW GLACIERS ARE SEXIST," shouted the DailyCaller. (That amount is right because Dean Carey has gotten three grants from the National Science Foundation.) What an embarrassment for all the women who are real scientists.

How Trump Uses Postmodern Anti-Science

In his *NYT* opinion piece, Williams told us: "Latour observed that conservatives had begun using the methods of critical theory to muddy debates around issues, like climate change." Here's how that works.

In October 2018, Leslie Stahl, interviewing Trump about climate science, asked, "What about the scientists who say it's worse than ever?" Trump replied, "You'd have to show me the scientists because they have a very big political agenda, Leslie."

That's the postmodernist line exactly. They claim, as Williams does, that you can't trust scientists because:

People who produce facts—scientists—do so from a particular social position that influences how they perceive, interpret and judge the world.

While it's true that anyone can be biased, even scientists, it's also true that your smartphone works, and if the science had just been made up, it would not even glow in the dark.

The essence of science is skepticism, and the central requirement for getting results accepted into the scientific canon is cross-checking by others. Postmodernism, on the other hand, has no ethic of skepticism about its own beliefs, is highly suspicious of logic and is disdainful of any attempt to be objective.

Conclusion

Helping Trump disparage science has no upside. Trump doesn't read postmodern philosophy, and that's the scary part. How did it reach him and his base? Postmodernism has been diffusing into popular culture unnoticed for 50 years. It has now reached every political corner, from the notorious crypto-fascist troll, Mike Cernovich ("Look, I read postmodernist theory in college"), who is spreading "alternatives to the dominant narrative" to the National Science Foundation, which is funding fake feminist glaciology.

It gains access to popular culture through colleges and universities by claiming to be radically left. But as the next chapter shows, it was derived from the philosophies that underpinned Hitler's Third Reich. Postmodernism is not itself fascist, but its anti-truth, anti-reason philosophy serves the right wing in America just as it did in Germany and now does in Russia.

Addendum (optional and wonkish)

Because postmodernism has made such a hash of the language and the concepts of truth and fact, and because I enjoy clarity and logic, I thought I would provide a clear overview of the basic concepts of truth and reason. It's wonkish but simple, so that's your warning, served with some encouragement.

Logic concerns statements, implications, and truth. The classic example is: Socrates was a man. All men are mortal. So Socrates was mortal. That's logical. But for now, just notice that logic deals with *clear* statements that can be either true or false. OK, here goes:

About true statements:

- **A true statement is called a fact.**

  ○ You can say it's a true fact or a hard fact, but it's all the same. Facts are facts.

- **If you know a fact, that's knowledge and also (some) truth.**
- **Some facts do exist.** (In other words, true statements exist. Truth exists.)

  ○ Two Proofs: 2 + 2 = 4. Trump became president.

- **You can learn (or find) facts, that you didn't know.**

  ○ Proof: If you don't know what state Mount Rushmore is in, ask Google. You'll find a fact.

- **You cannot make up a brand new fact.**

  ○ It's either already true (not new) or not true; saying it's true won't make it a fact if it's not one already.

About false statements:

- Everyone thinks some things are true that aren't. We call those mistakes.
- Some people call things truth when they know they are false. We call those lies.
- "There are no facts" is a false statement. If it were true, it would prove *this fact*: "There are no facts." So there would be at least one fact. So the statement cannot be true. It is false.

It all boils down to this: Some statements are true, and some are false. The false ones can be mistakes or lies. Other statements are unclear and neither true nor false. Sometimes we can tell which category a statement is in, and other times we can't. If we use our heads, we can get better at telling which is which. That's what science does, and that is what Trump and postmodernists most want to prevent.

CHAPTER 35

The Ultimate Con Game

Dare to know! That is the motto of enlightenment.
—Immanuel Kant, 1784

Today's campus protests share many similarities with those of the 1960s. But something is weirdly different. To me, that difference seems best captured by the Yale student's rant:

> Being a master [of Silliman College] ... is not about creating an intellectual space! It is not! It's about creating a home here. You are not doing that!

This undergraduate is literally screaming to have the university supply her with an ultra-protective parent. Unthinkable. In the 1960s, the point of college was to get out on our own, think for ourselves and escape anything that seemed the least bit paternalistic. "Don't trust anyone over 30" was our mantra. But this is not a generational issue; this is an identity politics issue that affects those of any generation who subscribe to postmodern identity politics.

The "anti-racist" protests on the Evergreen College campus, perhaps the most "progressive" campus in America, were instigated by a joint faculty-administrative committee. And then there was the microaggression fatwa handed down to the entire University of California system from its president.

Although some students are willing accomplices, the real instigators now hide in faculty offices. They, not the students, are truly the snowflakes sitting in safe spaces while their students, social justice warriors, protect them by harassing faculty who have not drunk this postmodern Kool-Aid.

I won't explore the tactics used for intra-departmental warfare. But note that most academic identity politics is associated with "critical theories"—critical race theory, critical feminist theory, critical gender theory, critical legal theory and such. "Critical Theory," as it happens, is a neo-Marxist, Frankfurt-School system of thought that "seeks to liberate human beings from the circumstances that enslave them."

So, postmodern professors see themselves as political activists seeking to free the enslaved minds of their students and colleagues. With such a noble calling, much can be justified. Meanwhile, normal academics are focused on their research and don't put up much of a fight. Recall from Chapter 33 that Judith Butler, whom we will soon meet again, was given $1.5 million by the Mellon Foundation to fund a *critical theory* institute.

But to better understand this takeover of higher education's soft underbelly, we need to explore the ideas and strategies of those who launched this modern, anti-Enlightenment counterrevolution.

Postmodern Godfathers

Two highly controversial philosophers, Nietzsche and Heidegger, inspired Foucault and Derrida, the two most well-known postmodernists. I will introduce these four, plus three postmodernists—de Man, Lyotard and Lacan—who I selected from among the first tier. Here's the list:

- Friedrich **Nietzsche** (1844–1900): German philosopher and uber-elitist. A Nazi favorite.
- Martin **Heidegger** (1889–1976): German Nazi philosopher.
- Michel **Foucault** (1926–1984): French historian who preferred torture to prisons.
- Jacques **Derrida** (1930–2004): French philosopher of deconstruction who opposed logical argument.
- Paul **de Man** (1919–1983): Belgian literary critic, con man, and promoter of Jacques Derrida.
- Jean-François **Lyotard** (1924–1998): French anti-science philosopher.
- Jacques **Lacan** (1901–1981): French psychoanalyst and pseudo-mathematical charlatan.

Friedrich Nietzsche

Michel Foucault, now the most influential of the postmodern godfathers, claimed that Nietzsche influenced him more profoundly than any other philosopher.

Hitler gave a copy of Nietzsche's works to Mussolini, and some crypto-fascists love Nietzsche. But Nietzsche wasn't a fascist. Fascism is a kind of right-wing populism, and Nietzsche was an elitist. A close friend of Franz Liszt and the Wagners, his favorite *Übermenschen* (Supermen) were Goethe and Beethoven. But that does not begin to scratch the surface of his elitism.

In 1859, Darwin disrupted the philosophical world with his concept of evolution. That transformed Nietzsche's philosophy. He became convinced that man had evolved, and God had nothing to do with it. "God," he proclaimed, "is dead ... and those born after us ... shall be part of a higher history." What would that look like?

Friedrich Nietzsche   Karl Marx   Martin Heidegger

Antonio Gramsci   Max Horkheimer   Theodor Adorno

The European Great-Godfathers of the new identity politics
Top: the philosophers, Bottom: the neo-Marxists

The "New Party of Life," according to Nietzsche, "would tackle ... the breeding of humanity to a higher species, including the merciless extirpation of everything that is degenerating and parasitic." Life would be organized into three castes: Olympian men, guardians, and laborers.

Somehow, everyone would be ranked and assigned according to his "quantum of power and the abundance of his will." He elaborated: "We must agree to the cruel-sounding truth that slavery belongs to the essence of culture … the wretchedness of struggling men must grow still greater in order to make possible the production of a world of art for a small number of Olympian men."

As for feminism, try this Nietzschean gem: "Man shall be trained for war and woman for the recreation of the warrior. All else is folly. ... Thou goest to woman? Do not forget thy whip." Has there ever been a more despicable "philosophy"?

Michel Foucault   Jacque Derrida   Paul de Man

Jean Baudrillard   Jean-François Lyotard   Jacques Lacan

The European Godfathers of the new identity politics
Top: the originals, Bottom: second generation

Michel Foucault

Turn now to Foucault, both because he was inspired by Nietzche and because he is the most influential postmodernist. He is mentioned the most in academic articles and in Google searches. In fact, he is mentioned more than "postmodernism" itself.

For Nietzsche, "the test of truth" is "the feeling of power." Foucault's view is similar: "Truth is linked in a circular relation with systems of power." More often, Foucault speaks of "knowledge" rather than "truth," so his famous concept is "power-knowledge."

Foucault may be wrong when he interprets Nietzsche as saying that "all knowledge rests upon injustice" and that "the instinct for knowledge is malicious." But Foucault accepts these views, which lead him to see power-knowledge as concentrated in "the carceral network"—"prisons, factories, schools, barracks, hospitals, which all resemble prisons."

Compare that to the progressive view that we should "speak truth to power" because truth is the antidote to power, which often hides the truth. In Foucault's view, it's the other way around. Knowledge/truth hides power, so truth is "malicious."

Better feudalism than Enlightenment. Under feudalism, Foucault believes "knowledge" (he means something like a myth that obscures power since he doesn't believe in *true* knowledge) was absent, so raw power was exposed. He supports this view in *Discipline and Punish* (1975) which disparages the Enlightenment because it substituted prisons for torture. Yes, you read that right.

To make this point, Foucault contrasts pairs of anecdotes, one from the Enlightenment with one from feudalism. *Discipline and Punish* opens with such a pair. A spectacular and horrifying torture-execution in Paris in March 1757 is contrasted with a timetable for the House of Young Prisoners from 1838. Foucault implies that the regimen of the timetable is worse for young prisoners than execution by torture.

His ally and close friend, Gilles Deleuze, tells us that in this work, the scenes of torture are "lovingly rendered." Foucault, he says, "always managed to illustrate his theatrical analyses in a vivid manner"—"the red on red of the tortured inmates contrasts with the grey on grey of prison."

Foucault found the idea of torture so attractive that he decorated his college dormitory room with images of torture from the Napoleonic Wars. From the early 1950s, he practiced sadomasochism. He frequented sadomasochistic bathhouses in San Francisco in the 1980s and praised sadomasochistic activity in interviews with the gay press. Once, when hit by a car, he thought he would die but described the sensation as one of intense pleasure.

But it was only in the last few years of his life that he publicly revealed this side of his personality. Before that, he was one of the main proponents of "the death of the author," the concept that we should not look at the author of a work when interpreting it. You can see why. Examining his "philosophy" in light of his personal preferences would quickly call it into question.

Case closed. I am not saying that he was a dreadful person or that he said nothing worthwhile. But his politics are not to be trusted.

Why Foucault Matters. Foucault has been a darling of the radical left since the beginning of the anti-psychiatry movement in the late 1960s and is currently the most influential postmodernist, bar none. His ideas have undoubtedly lent force to the misguided "New Jim Crow" myth.

When Ta-Nahisi Coates, in an *Atlantic* blog post from 2012, listed authors he has read, the only author he said he loved was Michel Foucault. When Coates talks about the "carceral state," I would lay good odds that he got that from Foucault. I'm sure that neither Coates nor most of Foucault's fans imbibe much of his distorted view, but even a little is likely too much.

Foucault's theory of universal control by invisible power-knowledge feeds left and right conspiracy theories, similar to *The Matrix* and The Deep State.

Foucault's attitude towards power and his view that when it comes to prison reform we should "question the social and moral distinctions between the innocent and the guilty" reinforce calls to abolish the police and ICE. Foucault's politics are perfect for a get-out-the-vote campaign—if you're working for Trump.

Martin Heidegger

Despite being a dues-paying Nazi from 1933 to 1945 (card number 312589), Heidegger was the primary source of philosophical inspiration for Jacques Derrida's deconstruction of Western philosophy, the very foundation of postmodernism.

"The Jews, with their marked gift for calculating," Heidegger wrote, "have lived for the longest time according to the principle of race, which is why they are resisting its consistent application with utmost violence." After the war, he never admitted to the existence of the Holocaust.

He told his students, "Let not theories and 'ideas' be the rules of your being. The Führer himself and he alone is German reality and its law." To a colleague, he wrote: "The individual, wherever he stands, counts for nothing. The fate of our people in their State is everything."

He wrote to a friend in 1974 saying, "Europe is being ruined from be-low with 'democracy.'" This was a direct result of Heidegger's life-long, anti-Enlightenment philosophy.

Jacques Derrida

Derrida's "deconstruction" was even more complete than Heidegger's "destruction" (*destruktion*) of Western philosophy. And Derrida picked up his antipathy towards "Logocentrism"—a focus on logical argu-ment—from Heidegger.

When Derrida died in 2004, *The New York Times* wrote, "No thinker in the last 100 years had a greater impact than he did on people in more fields and different disciplines." Sadly, that could be true in America. But the French saw it differently. When 600 French intellectuals were asked in 1981 to name the three most influential living French intellectu-als, Derrida's name was not even mentioned. Meanwhile, in American literary-criticism departments, his popularity was skyrocketing.

When *Heidegger and Nazism* was published in 1987, the postmodern-ists circled their wagons around Heidegger with Derrida as his principal defender. Derrida attributed Heidegger's support for Hitler to a misguid-ed "metaphysical humanism," which he thought Heidegger corrected by 1938 (while he was still paying Nazi dues).

The main postmodern excuse for relying on Heidegger's philosophy is that it is completely separate from his Nazism. But this contradicts Derrida's view, which blamed his Nazism on an error in his philosophy. Shouldn't Heidegger's philosophy, if it had any value, have led Heidegger to at least admit the Holocaust happened?

Derrida's main postmodern contribution, however, was to provide the first "proof" of Nietzsche's claim that "There are no facts, only interpre-tations." This was the purpose of his deconstructionism. His proof con-tradicts itself, however, because Derrida claims to prove, in effect, that it is a fact that there are no facts.

The damage done by Heidegger/Derrida and their rejection of the En-lightenment, which leaves nothing of value in its place, is immense and continuing.

Paul de Man

Paul de Man began promoting Jacques Derrida in 1971 from his perch in Yale's Department of Comparative Literature. Eventually, de Man became chairman of the department. From there, deconstructionism took over nearly every literature department in the U.S.

But four years after de Man's death, it was learned that he had published more than 100 articles in *Le Soire*, a newspaper that had been seized by the Nazis. He had also worked for two other Nazi-era, German-controlled media companies. After the war, all three media companies were found treasonous, as was his uncle Henri de Man, who served as Prime Minister of Belgium for a year under the Nazi occupation. Henri was a father figure to Paul de Man.

De Man fled to the U.S. in 1948 and was prosecuted in Belgium in absentia. He was found guilty on 16 counts of fraud, forgery, and swindling, and sentenced to five years in prison. In the process, he nearly bankrupted his father and became a lifelong fugitive.

He soon conned his way into a teaching position at Bard College, where he married one of his students without letting on that he had sent his Belgian wife and two children to Argentina.

After de Man's Nazi connection became known, Derrida performed a deconstructionist reading of de Man's most anti-Semitic and collaborationist texts and claimed they were anti-fascist. He then concluded that those who denounced de Man's collaboration were applying Nazism's "exterminating gesture" to de Man. Yes, to excuse de Man's Nazi collaboration, he compared exposing de Man to the Holocaust!

Deconstruction, you see, can "prove" anything. As the French had figured out, Derrida was a con man. Paul de Man, his chief promoter, was worse.

Jean-François Lyotard

Jean-François Lyotard was thrilled to learn that the Conseil des Universités of Quebec had asked him to produce a report on the state of knowledge in the Western world.

What had been bugging Lyotard and other postmodernists was that their horse, Marxism, had lost the race so decisively that the other horse, the Enlightenment, looked sure to win. But Lyotard had the answer: "Metanarratives are not credible." That view he defined as postmodernism—a hip term previously applied only to art and architecture.

Marxism is a "metanarrative"—a grand collection of stories about how societies always evolve—and it had already been sent to the "dustbin of history."

Lyotard's target was the Enlightenment—and its crown jewel, science. Science, he said, couldn't legitimatize itself. "What we have here is a process of delegitimation fueled by the demand for legitimation itself ... There is no other proof that the rules are good than the consensus of the experts." Not trusting experts, he recommended himself instead and decided the rules of science were not legitimate.

Lyotard never noticed what actually proves science is legitimate—it works! For example, Fleming discovered in 1928 that penicillin kills some bacteria and logically concluded it might cure some diseases. It worked. Because it worked, it became part of science.

Ironically, postmodernism's view of science is exactly backward. The problem is not that science is stuck in ambiguities and circular logic. The real problem is that it's so good at its job that it often gives humanity powers we are not ready for.

Lyotard's nonsense wouldn't matter, except that 40 years later his anti-science has spread through the new "identity politics," and it makes the Democrats look a little bit ridiculous. For example ...

Time out for some performativity. Lyotard tells us that in science, "the goal is no longer truth, but performativity." So now we find Professor Judith Butler of Harvard and U.C. Berkeley defining "gender" to be purely "performative."

> We act as if being a man or being a woman is actually an internal reality or something that is simply a fact about us.

> *Yes, most of us do.*

> But actually, it's a phenomenon that is being produced all the time and reproduced all the time.

> *I perform as a male and have a Y chromosome. That's just a coincidence?*

> **So to say gender is performative is to say that nobody really is a gender from the start.**

> *Nobody? Get out of here! Maybe true for you.*

> I know it's controversial, but that's my claim.

> *Controversial, yes—a necessary postmodern career move.*

Butler claims that no part of gender is determined biologically. Gender, she says, is just a set of performances passed from generation to generation. Pure codswallop!

She might benefit from a stroll up to the botanical garden behind her university. There she could watch a male hummingbird perform his death-defying courtship dives at speeds exceeding 45 mph only to make a U-turn at the last second to display his brilliant gorget precisely in front of the female. Next, Butler should ask a biologist if this natural-seeming masculine gender behavior is "culturally constructed" or might there be some other explanation?

Oh, wait, that would be sc**nce. Scientists just make up the fact that gender performance is hugely correlated with sex in every vertebrate species. Well, not really. And we all know that for humans, society also plays a role; nothing new about that.

Foucault felt no strong need to explain his attraction to torture because it fit his personal psychology, and a similar observation suggests itself for Butler. She seems to feel no need to examine evidence for innate attraction to the opposite sex. Might this be because, as a lesbian, she has not experienced it?

Now, back to Lyotard. Eight years after the publication of Lyotard's report, *The Postmodern Condition*, Lyotard came clean in an interview for the Italian magazine, *Lotta Poetica*:

> I referred to a number of books I'd never read. Apparently, it impressed people. It's all a bit of a parody ... I wanted to say first that it's simply the worst of my books, they're almost all bad, but that one's the worst ... it belongs to the satirical genre."

Judith Butler seems not to have understood Lyotard's satirical performance.

Jacques Lacan

Lacan, a member of the postmodernist inner circle, was a surrealist before becoming a Freudian psychoanalyst. When he was disbarred as a Freudian in 1953, he began mixing abstract math jargon with his psychoanalytic theories.

We find him lecturing in 1970: "One can show that a cut on a torus corresponds to the neurotic subject, and on a cross-cut surface to another sort of mental disease." For the record, a torus is a mathematical shape like an inner tube.

"May I ask," begged audience-member Harry Woolf, "if this fundamental arithmetic and this topology are not a myth or merely at best an analogy?"

Lacan responded with a large helping of topo-psycho gibberish and finished it off with: "This torus really exists and it is exactly the structure of the neurotic. It is not an analogon (sic); it is not even an abstraction, because an abstraction is some sort of diminution of reality, and I think it is reality itself." I love math, but no, a neurotic does not, in reality, have the exact structure of an inner tube. Once a surrealist, always a surrealist.

What is shocking here is not Lacan, it's his postmodern audience. Every field has its lunatics, but in no other part of academia are they numbered among the most revered.

Lucan had learned many new mathematical buzzwords by 1977—irrational and imaginary numbers, compact sets, open covers and so on. Unfortunately, he could not distinguish irrational from imaginary and had little, if any, idea what any of it meant. Yet he was able to conclude:

> Thus, the erectile organ comes to symbolize the place of *jouissance* [enjoyment] ... that is why it is equivalent to the square root of minus one [an imaginary number]."

But of course! Is such brilliance the reason Butler, in her book, *Gender Troubles*, makes heavy use of Lacan and his *"jouissance,"* referring to him nearly a hundred times? Butler also relies heavily on Irigaray, she of the fluid mechanics and sex organs, and of course on Foucault as well.

The Ultimate Con Game

There have been many strong attacks on the postmodernists, but for 50 years they have continued to mutate and reproduce at an ever-increasing rate. They employ an array of clever defensive and offensive tactics. Foucault said Derrida employed a "terrorism of obscurantism: He writes so obscurely you can't tell what he's saying. [Then he says,] 'You didn't understand me; you're an idiot.'"

But I think there's a more powerful force at work—affinity fraud. This is usually financial, for example, Bernie Madoff targeting fellow Jewish clients. But Nobel economist Paul Krugman has extended the concept of affinity fraud to politics and defines it as:

People are most easily conned when they're getting their disinformation from someone who seems to be part of their tribe, one way or another.

Postmodernists claim to be radical progressives, and I'm sure most really believe they are. So Democrats, quite naturally, see them as part of the greater Democratic tribe. And they do share many views with us. They hate Trump. They want greater equality. They think "the system" is oppressive.

They're not after our money. They just want us to trust them and become loyal members of their cult.

Because Democrats (myself included) tend to be open, trusting, big-tent sorts of folk, it's pretty easy for those we see as similar, even superficially, to suck us in. But taking a closer look shows postmodernist politics may be less progressive than classic conservative politics. Classic conservatism at least shares our belief in the Enlightenment—truth, reason, science, and democracy. And all that is non-negotiable.

The postmodernists reject progressive accomplishments as delusions and claim the Enlightenment has been a failure and only made things worse.

Conclusion

Postmodernists do not belong to the Democratic tribe, although they share certain similarities in appearance. Their ancestry is a mix of Marxism, neo-Marxism, Nietzsche's elitism, Heidegger's fascism, and deconstructionist chicanery. Their rejection of truth makes them accidental allies of Trump. They do, however, have good intentions and would be worth winning back to the progressive cause. But don't hold your breath.

The affinity fraud they are committing has conned more good Democrats than any other political hijacking in our party's history. The only antidote is to open our eyes, think for ourselves and be brave enough to say what we see. That is not an easy task in the face of the postmodern outrage culture.

PART 6

Wrap-up and Overview

Reason is non-negotiable.

—Stephen Pinker

Trump rules the Republican Party with autocratic power, a power given to him by his fanatically loyal base. Democrats are nearly as loyal to their party but rightly reject autocratic leadership. That comes at a cost to unity. So, while heading into an election that could destroy American democracy, we find ourselves divided. On one side is the radical approach—demanding a utopian transformation—and on the other, a liberal approach, which proposes strategic compromises for steady progress.

To choose between them, I will rely on historian Michael Kazin. There is no voice more sympathetic to radical utopian dreams and no one more expert on the history of radicalism than Kazin. Yet, he concludes, "Radicals in the U.S. have seldom mounted a serious challenge to those who held power," and he finds no example of their success. His claim is that they slowly "transform the moral culture," which eventually pressures opportunistic liberals to implement fundamental changes.

Even if this were correct, it would not bode well for success in the present emergency. Where Kazin is most helpful is in identifying the radical mode of thought, the radical "ethic" as he calls it. Understanding this leads to a unifying vision that covers most of the material in this book. Using this framework, it becomes possible to look back over nearly two hundred years of political history and see how social progress has been made. Of course, this is a broad view that only answers one question, but it is a most important question.

Synopsis of Part 6

Chapter 36. Radical-Left Mythology. The Green New Deal is a utopian vision. Striving to achieve it in 10 years is apocalyptic millennialism.

Chapter 37. The Tragic Paradox of Radicalism. Radicalism is powered by the utopian ethic that forbids compromising some utopian dream. This often damages the radical cause unnecessarily.

Chapter 38. How Progressive Change Happens. Lincoln, Teddy Roosevelt, FDR, and LBJ were all radical liberals—not radicals—strategic liberal politicians with vision who compromised to make progress.

Chapter 39. Putting the Pieces Together. Purity tests, which lead to emotional polarization, result from using the radical ethic. The antidote is the art of strategic compromise.

CHAPTER 36

Radical-Left Mythology

So convenient a thing is it to be a rational creature, since it enables us to find or make a reason for everything one has a mind to do.

—Benjamin Franklin

"Why are you so optimistic?" I ask my radical friends. Of course, they deny it. As Bernie Sanders tells us, they believe these are the worst of times. They understand Alexandria Ocasio-Cortez (AOC) when she says her "entire generation came of age and never saw American prosperity," and we are all pessimistic about climate change, Donald Trump and the extreme polarization of the country.

So of course, they are right to say they're ever so pessimistic. But does that mean they're not optimistic? Quite the contrary. Most of the radical left believes Sanders' revolution started three years ago and is proceeding at lightning speed by historical standards. Brand New Congress was going to completely revolutionize Congress in two years. AOC says that "change is a lot closer than we think," and she has spelled out that change in her Green New Deal, or "green dream" as Nancy Pelosi more aptly calls it. All three of these changes are billed as more fabulous than any political change the U.S. has ever seen.

∼

This strange combination of extreme present-day pessimism and even more extreme future optimism, joined by a tipping point when we suddenly turn the corner, is nothing new. In fact, it's a pre-biblical "ism" that has been tried hundreds of times, sometimes with astounding results. I will describe this shortly and then show how this ism organizes most of the radical-left mythology.

∼

To be clear about the level of optimism, examine the Green New Deal, which will "secure for all people of the United States *for generations to come*" a guarantee that every economic need will be met and every injustice and harm to the environment will be eliminated. Of course, this will only be done to the maximum level that is technically possible—sparing no expense. And all of this will be accomplished in the space of only 10 years. Here's a taste of what radicals guarantee you could look forward to in 10 years:

1. 100-percent renewable electricity.
2. All buildings upgraded to max-tech safety and durability.
3. Massive growth in manufacturing.
4. Max-tech removal of all pollution.
5. Threatened or fragile ecosystems restored and protected.
6. High-quality education and higher education for all.
7. A job with a family-sustaining wage and retirement security.
8. Freedom from unfair competition for every businessperson.
9. High-quality health care and affordable housing.
10. Economic security, affordable food and access to nature.

Of course, all programs will be developed through inclusive collaboration with vulnerable communities, labor unions, worker cooperatives, civil society groups, academia, and business. And that's not all ...

It will be a struggle to win Congress and the Presidency, and it will cost a lot, but the economy will boom immediately with great new jobs. And in only 10 years we'll reach the promised land, where we can live in peace and harmony "for generations to come." That last phrase, written into House Resolution 109 and signed by 67 Democrats, is a key indicator of millennialism.

Millennialism Defined

No, millennialism is not the ideology of the millennial generation. And no, it's not about end-of-world catastrophes in the year 1000 or 2000. It's an ism named after what may be the most powerful and disturbing *Bible* story, recently retold in *Left Behind,* a series of 16 best-selling religious novels, seven of which made it to #1 on *The New York Times* bestseller list. Yes, millions of people on the right still believe in Christian millennialism. The end of this epic story gave this ism its name:

An angel … laid hold on the dragon, that old serpent, which is the Devil, and Satan, and bound him a thousand years.

—Book of Revelations

"Mille" is Latin for a thousand, and "millennial" denotes a thousand years. So **millennialism** is an ideology that strives to catapult us into a time when the devil will be bound for 1000 years, and we can all live in peace and harmony—a sort of biblical Green New Deal.

But isn't this just a Christian story that has nothing to do with progressive politics? Actually, you would be amazed by how many times and places this ism has taken hold. Of course, non-Christian versions usually don't claim that the good times will last for exactly 1,000 years, but as long as they last for a very long time, it's still called millennialism.

To convince you that millennialism is a powerful human tendency, let me tell you about a few of the hundreds of known examples. It started at least 3000 years ago, perhaps with Zoroaster, aka Zarathustra, a Persian religious leader who taught that there would be 1,000-year epochs ending in catastrophe until a great king fixes everything for all future generations.

Eugène Delacroix—Liberty Leading the People, 1830

There were many millennial movements during the Middle Ages and Renaissance. For example, Müntzer, an Anabaptist leader, taught that if the common people were to place group interests above those of the individual, they would be able to transform society (sounds rather socialistic, no?). He led 8,000 peasants into what he may have thought was the final battle between good and evil. The result was that they were massacred on May 15, 1525.

Hong Xiuquan, the self-proclaimed brother of Jesus Christ, led a rebellion from 1850 to 1864 against the Qing dynasty to establish the Taiping Heavenly Kingdom. This resulted in 20 to 70 million deaths.

The French Revolution formally began on May 5, 1789, and as a delegate to the Estates-General (a national congress) wrote: "The lower classes of the people are convinced that ... we will see a *total and absolute change* ... in conditions and income." The French New Deal? The Bastille fell in July, and in August the National Assembly abolished feudalism and de-established the Catholic church. This was a secular millennial movement, and it was on a roll.

French people everywhere stood up and replaced the collapsing feudal establishment by building new organizations from the bottom up. According to millennialist scholar Richard Landes, "In this magical moment of forgiveness and reconciliation, vast assemblies met throughout the land, holding festivals and enacting a kind of social contract until the climax with the great commemorative festival of July 14, 1790."

Then things began to get complicated. By 1793, Robespierre the Incorruptible felt compelled to impose the Reign of Terror, which then guillotined him on July 28, 1794. Roughly 300,000 lives were lost in the extremely brutal war to put down the counterrevolution. Nonetheless, the revolution ended in failure.

There have, of course, been many more examples. Russia's socialist revolution had millennial characteristics, and Nazism had even more. Germany was to be "the champion of the Final Empire," and the Third Reich was to be the *Tausendjähriges Reich*—the Thousand-Year Reich—or you might call it the Millennial Reich.

The Dynamic of Millennialism

Millennialism is a fundamentally irrational group dynamic that takes many paths. If I have understood Richard Landes correctly, the relevant dynamic for today's radical-left politics is transformative, apocalyptic millennialism. "Transformative" because the millennium will come due to a change of heart, not by a violent revolution. "Apocalyptic" because the change is presumed to occur through an imminent quick struggle and not in the distant future—"closer than we think," as AOC says.

Bernie Sanders, AOC, and Elizabeth Warren are all charismatic leaders announcing this type of millennial message. As with all millennialisms, their message says that change will come about through a struggle between good and evil—in this case, the 99% against the 1%.

This type of millennialism typically evolves through three stages if it ever takes off:

1. A charismatic leader promotes apocalyptic thinking.
2. An intense struggle is followed by disillusionment.
3. The movement loses power and the old way returns.

We should pay the most attention to the first stage because the rise of a charismatic leader can lead to dynamic forces of group thinking (aka groupthink) which are so strong that little can be done to change course.

The first stage is powered by a sense of catastrophe. Things have (or seem to have) gone from bad to worse and, although everyone is trying individually to escape this trend, most are failing. This opens the door for a charismatic leader to propose an apocalyptic solution—one that will work quickly. To become powerfully viral, the solution should:

- Promise more than seems possible (to induce awe and excitement).
- Be untested (so there is no obvious counterevidence).
- Require that almost everyone participates (to induce intense peer pressure).

The more extreme the present catastrophe, the more extreme the solution can be. If reality is not catastrophic, the charismatic leader must make it seem that it is. This is why we find Sanders claiming (see Chapter 24) that not even counting climate change or Trump, these are the worst times since the Great Depression. And this is why AOC claims she has never seen prosperity (even though no generation has been richer).

The Basic Radical-Left Myth

The basic myth of the radical left is not one of the myths discussed in *Part 4: Mythology Traps*. Instead, it's the simpler "Our Revolution" myth discussed in Chapter 16. That's the notion that "pretty soon" the 99%—both Democrats and Republicans—will realize they're all on the same side against the 1%, and they'll stage a political revolution. The "People's Party" will sweep Congress and the presidency in 2020. That's Robert Reich's millennialist dream.

Interestingly, this view is just a tamer version of the conclusion to Marx's *Communist Manifesto* (1848): "Workers have nothing to lose but their chains. They have a world to win. Workers of the World unite!"

And there you have it. The charismatic leader, Karl Marx, tells his potential followers that their situation is catastrophic—they are slaves in chains. Then he tells them (following bullet-point #1) that they can rule the world—that's the Marxist version of the 1000-year Millennium. Then, using bullet-point #2 above, he gives them the untried solution—unite (for a revolution). And as Lenin said, the revolution requires "the sympathy and support of the overwhelming majority of the working people"—bullet-point #3.

The basic radical-left myth is straight-up apocalyptic millennialism. The mythical part of Marx's millennialism is, as always, the notion that his solution—a socialist revolution—would bring workers to the promised land. Instead, it took them to Russian, China, North Korea, Cambodia, and most recently, Venezuela.

The Five Supporting Myths

Because the basic myth keeps failing, as millennial myths always do (after 170 years, there is still nothing remotely close to a Marxist worker paradise), it has needed updates to keep it going. Some of these are the neo-Marxist theories discussed in Part 5, but the supporting myths of Part 4 are the bread and butter of today's radical left. Here's how they support the basic myth of a political revolution leading to the promised land "for generations to come."

The Democratic Socialism myth (Ch. 23) addresses the main problem of sustaining socialist millennialism—170 years of failing to reach the political revolution, the apocalypse that will overthrow the capitalist elite. Sanders deals with this dismal history by obliterating it from popular consciousness. Although he's squarely in the socialist lane with Karl Marx, Eugene V. Debs, Norman Thomas, and Michael Harrington, he never mentions them. Instead, he pretends the socialist lane consists of Teddy Roosevelt, Franklin Roosevelt, and Lyndon Johnson.

So it looks like there have been three near-misses, but we keep getting closer. The one Sanders emphasizes is FDR's 1944 Second Bill of Rights speech. Unfortunately, FDR died months later. Bernie's ad claims: "Some say it can't be done again. But another native son of New York is ready: Bernie." (Ch. 25) The apocalypse has been delayed, but the time is almost here. That's typical millennialism.

The Myth of the Utopian Savior (Ch. 24), holds that we have had several such saviors whose failure is due only to bad luck or nefarious plots.

This myth is needed because most of us tend to doubt the existence of saviors.

The myth claims that such saviors really do exist, and we must be careful not to miss the next opportunity. These "saviors," all of whom are grossly misrepresented by the radicals, include Teddy Roosevelt in 1912, Henry Wallace in 1944 (Ch. 12), George McGovern in 1972 and even, according to Oliver Stone, JFK, who he claims had an epiphany just before he was assassinated. But if we just elect Sanders, he'll bring us the revolution we've been waiting for.

The Establishment Myth (Ch. 25) is needed because the Democrats' heroes, the two President Roosevelts and LBJ, were each establishment figures (gold-plated one-percenters). But that contradicts the millennial myth that the 1% is entirely evil. Millennialism pits good against evil.

The Bully Pulpit myth (Ch. 26) supposedly explains how it's possible for the charismatic leader to usher in the millennium once elected to the presidential bully pulpit.

The Overton Window myth (Ch. 27) provides followers with an easy way to participate. Giving them a role (even though it doesn't work), especially a conspicuous role, cements their commitment to the cause. As noted, in normal times their extremist rhetoric is likely to backfire. But if and when the apocalyptic dynamic gains legitimacy, extremist positions may well add to the growing hysteria.

In conclusion, from the Communist Manifesto to the present, the radical-left strategy has focused on launching an apocalyptic millennial movement. In America, this has never taken off, but recent developments could change that. Climate change and Donald Trump both add significant real dangers. Disguising their millennial aspirations as FDR's liberalism provides much-needed cover for the radicals while also damaging their chief competitors—real FDR liberals.

The danger is not that the radical left will lead us over the cliff into authoritarian socialism, as Republicans like to imagine. The danger comes from the very nature of millennial movements. To succeed, they must completely dominate the political views of their base. There is no room for give-and-take with Green New Deal millennialism. It's an ideology that says perfection is technically possible so any compromise must be condemned as immoral. Here's how AOC put it at the South by Southwest festival:

The New York Times said, and I quote, "The Green New Deal is technologically possible. Its political prospects are another question." That, to me, is the biggest condemnation of where we're at … our biggest obstacle is political!

AOC doesn't see herself as political. She is simply right. This polarizes the Democratic Party. There is no room for disagreement. You either accept her religion, or you are an infidel. Of course, this weakens the party. It also polarizes the country with the message that if we do win, we will impose on Trump's base every single point of our agenda in its purest form.

Just as they have done in the past, the radical left is weakening the liberal side and inadvertently strengthening the most reactionary forces on the right.

Myths Behind Postmodern Identity Politics

Identity politics does not fit the pattern of millennialism so closely. It focuses more on the evils of the past and present, and simply implies that when these are eradicated, we will arrive at the promised land. It differs from socialist millennialism, which diagnoses the present evil as income and wealth inequality caused by capitalism. Instead, identity politics blames European culture, particularly the Enlightenment, which it sees as White male culture.

We should expect the myths needed to support the implied millennialism of identity politics to focus on how terrible the present is and who is to blame rather than on a utopian future. This is enough, given the tacit assumption that once the evil forces are defeated, all will be right with the world.

The central microaggression myth is one of the myths supporting the idea that the evils of colonialism and slavery have continued nearly unabated. That myth holds that microaggressions "may be more harmful to people of color than hate crimes," and that "microaggressions hold their power because they are invisible."

But a more elaborate myth, the Space Traders Myth, will better serve to illustrate how the mythology in postmodern identity politics focuses on identifying the forces of evil.

Critical Race Theory. Derrick Bell was a prodigious civil-rights lawyer who supervised more than 300 school desegregation cases, including the famous fight that got James Meredith admitted to the University of Mississippi. But in 1992, he told *The New York Times* that he believed his career in civil rights was misdirected and that Blacks were worse off and more subjugated in 1992 than at any time since slavery!

By 1995, he was saying that "the concept of rights is disutile [useless]." In other words, the idea of "civil rights" was useless nonsense.

Back around 1980, Bell had been sucked in by postmodernism and "critical legal theory" and had gone on to become the most prominent founder of critical race theory. Postmodernism taught him to indoctrinate people with myths. "People ... will often suspend their beliefs, listen to the story, and then compare their views, not with mine," he said, "but with those expressed in the story." This method of deceit ultimately comes from the corrupting influence of the elite European godfathers of postmodernism (see page before Ch. 35). Notice that Bell employed this method mainly to deceive Black students.

Here's his favorite story, one he made up and told over and over for years. A Google search for "Derrick Bell" and "space traders" yields more than 11,500 results. He used this story in teaching his students critical race theory.

The Space Traders. "Aliens from outer space visit America on New Year's Day in the year 2000. They promise wealth in the form of gold, environmental-cleansing material and a substitute for fossil fuels. If accepted, their gold and space-age technology will guarantee another century of prosperity for the nation. In return, the space traders want to take back to their home star all Black people. Given two weeks to decide, Americans debate the offer and vote to accept it by 70% to 30%.

"The last Martin Luther King holiday that the nation would ever observe dawned on an extraordinary sight. In the night, the Space Traders had drawn their strange ships right up to the beaches and discharged their cargoes of gold, minerals, and machinery, leaving vast empty holds. Crowded on the beaches were some 20 million silent Black men, women and children, including babes in arms. As the sun rose, the Space Traders directed them, first, to strip off all but a single undergarment; then, to line up; and finally, to enter those holds which yawned in the morning light like Milton's 'darkness visible.'

"The inductees looked fearfully behind them. But on the dunes above the beaches, guns at the ready, stood U.S. guards. There was no escape, no alternative. Heads bowed, arms now linked by slender chains, Black people left the New World as their forebears had arrived."

Interpreting Space Traders. Bell is making the point that almost all Whites (they were then about 70% of the population) are just like the slave traders who sold Africans into American slavery (before some Whites outlawed the slave trade in 1808). To Whites, this slander is a baseless microaggression that it is of no consequence because we know it's ridiculous.

But for some Blacks, this story perpetuates a harmful myth—that all American Whites were guilty of the slave trade, and most Whites alive today would sell Blacks into slavery again today if given the chance. The myth is intended to be a source of paranoia and hostility. This does Blacks far more harm than it does to Whites. But sustaining racism harms both races and is the strongest force polarizing the country.

What makes the story stick is its emotional charge rather than reason or facts. Of course, using reason and facts would go against postmodernism, which rejection of logic.

Logic and facts would also be especially inconvenient in this case because nearly all of the Africans sold into American slavery (something like 90%) were sold by Black Africans, not Whites. Moreover, "Africans were selling African slaves to the Islamic world centuries before the Atlantic slave trade. And the Islamic slave trade lasted somewhat longer, in some places into the twentieth century" (from a review published in *The American Historical Review* of seven books on African slavery).

My point is not, in any way, to excuse any aspect of American slavery. Rather, my point is that condemning whole races is the problem, not the solution, and Critical Race Theory (aka identity politics) is contributing to that problem, which, as we know, hurts Blacks far more than Whites. Derrick Bell was well-intentioned and once did enormous good, but he was later captured by elite European postmodern "philosophy" and became a strong force for racial and political polarization.

Conclusion

Democratic socialism, the Green New Deal and even Elizabeth Warren's catalog of miraculous plans are all descriptions of different utopian dreams. Each is accompanied by the promise that we can, if we reject normal Democratic politics, capture the federal government in one or two elections and launch a utopia.

Identity politics holds out a more implicit promise: People of Color can quickly defeat White supremacy and take over the government. No plans or utopian vision is needed, but all will be well after that changing of the guard.

The myths of the first group are classic millennialism, and the last myth is close enough. All will fail, as all millennial movements do. None of that would matter if the hyper-optimistic dreamers were tolerant of those who did not share their optimism. Instead, they harshly judge any who do not swear allegiance to their changing dogmas.

But those of us in the pragmatic, FDR-liberalism camp must not let ourselves be silenced and must take heart in knowing that our past political heroes were, every one of them, relentlessly down to earth. And in 2018, the pragmatic depolarizers won big. We can do it again if we can tame or bypass the well-intentioned, outrage-prone radicals in our own party.

CHAPTER 37

The Tragic Paradox of Radicalism

The spirit of liberty is the spirit which is not too sure that it is right; the spirit of liberty is the spirit which seeks to understand the minds of other men and women.

—Judge Learned Hand, 1944

To celebrate the Fourth of July, William Lloyd Garrison lit a match to the Constitution and, as it burned, exclaimed, "So *perish all compromises* with tyranny!" Several hundred people had gathered for the annual picnic of the Massachusetts Anti-Slavery Society in 1854. Speakers included Sojourner Truth, Henry David Thoreau, and Garrison, the most renowned radical abolitionist of the day.

Garrison's abhorrence of compromise led him to oppose the use of electoral politics and call for the North to secede from the Union. Rejecting compromise obviously leads toward polarization, and Garrison's radicals were both polarized and polarizing.

Understanding the radicals' rejection of compromise may be the key to understanding the source of polarization. And in fact, with the help of an expert radical, we will find that this antipathy to compromise comes from a radical "ethic," a kind of moral thinking that was first described by Max Weber, one of the founders of sociology. Conveniently, Weber also describes a second, contrasting ethic which I will call the strategic ethic and which provides a useful definition of liberalism.

But is the radical antipathy to compromise still at the heart of our problems with polarization? Recently, the House passed a progressive emergency-spending bill for the humanitarian crisis on the U.S.-Mexico border. The progressives had first passed a better one that failed in the Senate, and the Senate had sent back a compromise bill backed up by an 84-to-8 vote. There was no choice as funds would run out in under a week. So 129 House Democrats, led by Nancy Pelosi, passed it over the "no" votes of all 95 members of the Progressive Caucus.

The progressives simply refused to compromise, and Ocasio-Cortez's chief of staff slandered the compromising liberals as being as racist as the South in the 1940s. But the progressives felt no need to explain how not compromising would solve the problem that the Office of Refugee Resettlement, which cares for unaccompanied children, was going to run out of funding in four days. This is a perfect example of the radical ethic that I'll discuss shortly and that Weber described in 1918.

But would a radical agree with me that radicals, in general, refuse to tolerate compromise? For the answer, let me turn to Michael Kazin, the author of *American Dreamers,* a book that surveys 200 years of American radicalism in order to argue the case for radical thinking. He's a radical himself and a historian of American radicalism at Georgetown University.

Speaking of radicals before the Civil War, he tells us that "radicals refused to tolerate error, compromise, and moral backsliding." He also informs us that in 1904, Eugene V. Debs, Bernie Sanders' lifelong hero, preached that "Only Socialism will save ... the nation" and that the Socialist Party "would rather die than compromise." Kazin's view is unequivocal; radical detest compromise.

Radicals: Utopian Anti-Liberals

Kazin provides more insight into radical thought as he describes how 1960s radicalism fizzled out. "Most radicals," he is disappointed to say, returned to the Democratic fold and abandoned their radicalism as their "dreams of revolution dissolved along with other whims of youth" once Bobby Kennedy and George McGovern turned against the Vietnam War.

However, he finds that a "zealous" minority "refused to give up either their [1] ultimate ends or their [2] antagonism toward liberalism." By "ultimate ends," he means a "radically egalitarian transformation of society." Kazin also talks about "egalitarian dreamers," who are obviously the America dreamers referred to in his book title, who he also calls utopian dreamers.

His second characteristic of radicals—antagonism toward liberalism—is expected because liberals favor strategic compromises. Kazin confirms this, saying:

The challenge of *uncompromising* dissenters [radicals] made governing liberals and progressives appear to be problem-solvers.

In other words, "governing liberals" only appear to be "problem-solvers," and they only gain that appearance because *uncompromising* radicals "challenge" them into solving problems. So in Kazin's view, the radicals deserve the credit for pressuring the liberals to act but then the liberals get the credit because they "appear to be" the problem-solvers. The radicals are then antagonistic to liberals because they see the no-good liberals as standing in the way of progress and then getting credit for the progress that only happened because radicals pushed them.

The Ethics of Radicals and Liberals

Kazin digs deeper to find the ethics that underlie his description of radicals. He does this by looking at a revealing split that occurred in the radical abolitionist movement that helped lead to the formation of the Republican Party.

> The schism of 1840 did reveal an inescapable aspect of left tradition: the ongoing clash between self-righteous purists [radicals] and anxious opportunists [liberals].

In this case, the radicals were Garrison's radical abolitionists and liberals were some compromisers who were splitting off to form the Liberty Party. Their "vital compromise," Kazin tells us, was to "stop demanding, for the present, the abolition of slavery where it existed."

It may seem surprising that he calls his favorites, the radicals, "self-righteous purists." But as we will see in the next chapter, he has a theory for how they are the essential ingredient for social change in spite of this character flaw.

To explain the "inescapable aspect of left tradition" revealed by the schism of 1840, Kazin turns to Weber, a founder of sociology.

> Max Weber would later point out, the difference between "*an ethic of responsibility*" and "*an ethic of ultimate ends*" is intrinsic to any enterprise in visionary politics.

The "ethic of ultimate ends" is the ethic of Kazin's radical, utopian dreamers. This is confirmed by Weber saying it applies to those with "pure intentions." So, for convenience, I will call this the utopian ethic. The "*ethic of responsibility*" is the liberal ethic, which I will describe as the strategic ethic. To summarize, Kazin endorses Weber's definitions of two opposing ethics:

- Radicals follow Weber's utopian ethic.
- Liberals follow Weber's strategic ethic.

These two ethics identified by Kazan and Weber explain a great deal about the troubles of the Democratic Party and our national polarization. And Kazin is persuasive when he traces this distinction from the 1820s to the present day.

Weber Explains the Two Ethics

Weber explains these "irreconcilably opposed" radical and liberal ethics in his well-known 1918 lecture, "Politics as a Vocation," cited by Kazin. According to Weber, the radical is, "in religious terms, 'The Christian does rightly and leaves the results with the Lord.' " The liberal ethic, however, requires that "one has to give an account of the foreseeable results of one's actions," taking into account the "*average deficiencies of people.*"

It may seem strange that Weber explains the radical ethic in Christian terms, but Kazin's history shows this makes perfect sense. In his chapter about the communist influence in the 1930s, he explains:

> From the perfectionism of the abolitionists [onward], *every sizable radical movement* in the past [before the 1930s] had articulated a version of social Christianity.

The Communists, who were opposed to organized religion, drove a wedge between the left radicals and organized religion, but that didn't change the radical ethic, which is still with us.

But Weber does not tie the utopian ethic to religion, and he illustrates this more fully with an example straight from radical-left politics.

> You may demonstrate to a convinced anarchist, believing in [the utopian ethic], that his action will result in increasing the oppression of his class—and you will not make the slightest impression upon him. If an action of good intent leads to bad results, then, *in the actor's eyes, not he but the world, or the stupidity of other men, is responsible for the evil.*

Even if you convince the (radical) anarchist that his action will "result in increasing the oppression of his class," he'll do it anyway if he considers the action to be righteous. (Remember that Kazin describes radicals as "self-righteous purists.") Of course, this kind of ethical thinking is quite destructive, and Weber's first comment on it is that "there is an abysmal contrast" between conduct that follows the radical ethic and conduct that follows the strategic ethic. And he makes it perfectly clear that it is the radical ethic that produces abysmal conduct. For reference, here are two compact definitions:

Utopian ethic: Do what is right according to your group's utopian ideals. Any evil that results is due to the stupidity or wickedness of others and you have no responsibility.

Strategic ethic: Do what causes the most progress toward your liberal ideals. You are responsible for taking into account the deficiencies of the real world as best you can.

Here's a modern example of the difference between the two ethics. Ralph Nader campaigned for president in 2000 in Florida. He and 100,000 Florida voters thought he was the right man for the job and "voted their conscience." Had 538 of them voted for Al Gore instead, Gore would have been president, and we would not have had the Iraq war, and that would have saved 100,000 lives, 4,424 of them American. That was the real-world consequence of their votes.

Nader completely denies responsibility for this outcome. All the Nader voters I have spoken with felt at the time that the Supreme Court was to blame, so his voters had *no responsibility*. Precisely as Weber predicted, "in the [voters'] eyes, not they but the stupidities of other men are responsible for the evil."

The "no responsibility" argument is so seductive that it's worth a closer look. If I'm supposed to put up the bulletproof shield to protect Al Gore but I don't bother to, and the court shoots him, the court is guilty— but so am I. Not *as* guilty, but guilty. Nader's voters failed to put up that shield of votes, not understanding this is how radicals hold on to their irresponsible utopian ethic. As long as they can point a finger at someone else, they think they must be completely innocent.

As I've admitted, I made this type of mistake in 1968. And several million Democrats made this same type of mistake in 2016 (compared with 2012, a million switched to Jill Stein and likely more than that stayed home; others voted for Johnson). We can't be sure they could have prevented Trump's win by voting strategically, but that's certainly a possibility.

Just as a reminder that the utopian ethic is alive and well, here are a few of the myriad possible examples of the radical utopian, no-compromise ethics currently in play:

- "Vote your conscience" regardless of electoral impact.
- Oppose all foreign interventions.
- Never use drones.
- Punish anyone how says the n-word, even if they are black and only defending themselves against a racist.
- Vote only for the best healthcare system, even if it can't pass.

Bernie Sanders refused to vote for Clinton's 1993 nearly-universal healthcare bill; that was a utopian vote. Although utopian rules often do no harm, their inflexibility is at times severely damaging.

Radicals vs. Liberal Thinking

Kazin calls radicals "uncompromising dissenters," "utopian dreamers," and "self-righteous purists." But how do they actually think when using their utopian ethic, and how is that different from liberal thinking?

The difference is that the utopian ethic is rule-based (for example, "vote your conscience") while the strategic ethic provides few if any rules. Instead, the strategic ethic requires the liberal to consider all the consequences of taking an action or not taking it and then compare the two sets of consequences. That process is the very definition of strategic thinking.

Of course, there are many rule-based ethical systems, including many religions, that have nothing to do with left political radicalism, so we need to say more. Utopian ethics specify rules (usually unwritten) that are interpretations of "Don't compromise your utopian dream." Also, note that a utopian ethic is a set of rules shared within a political group, such as radical abolitionists.

The strategic ethic says to compromise but only in ways that maximize progress toward one's liberal dream. Everyone is entitled to their own strategic views. Here's a short summary of the two types of thinking:

Radicals obey or outperform the group's rules. And to win righteousness points, they call out those who don't.

Liberals try to figure out the best strategy for maximizing progress toward a liberal or radical dream. They win points by demonstrating creativity in their strategic thinking.

Radicals are attracted to the rule-based approach for three reasons. They like to "know" they're right, know their opponents are wrong and, most importantly, have their group acknowledge their righteousness. These sources of satisfaction depend on having a set of rules shared by their group. Liberals give up those satisfactions for strategic flexibility. This is the fundamental divide in ethically-oriented political thinking:

> Liberals are strategic thinkers. But radicals, at least with regard to their utopian ideals, think in an uncompromising religious mode—as long as their own actions align with their radical dogma, they are not responsible for any damaging consequences.

The Paradox of Radicalism

Only simplistic rules will work for the kind of people who gravitate to rule-based systems. The rules may be numerous, but they must make it easy to see who's right and who's immoral.

A subtle one-rule utopian ethic that says "always use the best strategy" would completely miss the point. No one would be sure who was right. But the obvious problem with simplistic rules is that they often fail when applied to the complex real world. And sometimes, as when Ralph Nader threw the election to George W. Bush, they give disastrously wrong answers. This dangerous effect is what I call the paradox of radicalism. The best intentions can lead to the worst outcomes, even when this is foreseeable.

The paradox of radicalism: Following the utopian ethic leads to some dreadful consequences for the radical cause that could be avoided by thinking outside the rules.

Of course, any guiding principles can lead to drastic mistakes—stuff happens. The difference is that voting for Nader in Florida was a mistake *caused by an intrinsic flaw* in the utopian ethic. So the downside of the utopian ethic is that it suffers from both random mistakes—due to the unexpected—and mistakes that are built into any system of simplistic rules.

Historical Examples of the Paradox

"Radicals in the U.S.," Kazin explains, "have seldom mounted a serious challenge to those who held power." Instead, they've "carped from the fringes of national politics." But radicals sometimes do make headlines when they have a visibly negative impact—due to the Paradox of Radicalism. Here are a few major examples of that paradox.

The Anarchist's Bomb. The Knights of Labor blossomed in 1869, and by 1886 had grown to a membership of 700,000. That may have been the most radical year in labor history. Then, in Chicago, at 10:30 p.m. on May 4, 1886, an anarchist threw a bomb into a phalanx of police, killing one on the spot and prompting a shootout between those attending a labor rally and the police at Haymarket Square. Eight police and at least nine civilians were killed.

Immediately, the paradox of radicalism took hold. The country turned against labor organizations. Kazin reports that "a reputation for revolutionary terrorism sentenced the anarchist movement to an early death." The Knights of Labor was falsely accused of the bombing and began losing membership, never to recover. But the anarchists were celebrated by fellow radicals. (This might well have been the incident Weber was thinking of when he gave his "anarchist" example.)

Antifa radicals in Oregon, busy helping Trump

The Man with the Muck Rake. The height of the Progressive Era was catalyzed by a flood of still-unmatched progressive investigative journalism from 1902 to 1906. Ida Tarbell's *The History of Standard Oil* and Upton Sinclair's *The Jungle* are still in print. But their success drew in the radicals, whose "investigative journalism" became outrageous. That's when the paradox of radicalism took hold. In 1906, Teddy Roosevelt grew so upset with the radical fringe (and only the radical fringe) of that journalism movement that he gave his famous "Man with the Muck Rake" speech. That caused even Ida Tarbell to be ridiculed as a "muckraker" and essentially ended the era of progressive investigative journalism.

Atomic Spies. The Democrats won the presidency five times in a row from 1932 through 1948. But from its earliest days, the Roosevelt Administration had been infiltrated by members of the Communist Party USA. CPUSA agents were conducting espionage for the Soviets by 1942 or likely earlier, and by 1944 they had infiltrated the Manhattan (atomic bomb) Project. But in 1946, the U.S. started cracking Soviet diplomatic cables they had been collecting for a decade—the Venona cables. One of the first discoveries was the A-bomb espionage. But that was only the tip of the iceberg.

The Republicans were able to use the resulting scandals and spy trials to discredit the most progressive segment of the American left because more than 100,000 had been drawn into the CPUSA. Of course, Senator Joe McCarthy (and his sidekick and eventual Trump mentor Roy Cohn) was a despicable fanatic and deserves the blame he gets for gross exaggeration and false accusations. But this in no way excuses the fact that the CPUSA duped so many progressives about what it was really up to.

The Venona transcripts show that, at a minimum, 349 Americans, some high up in the federal government, had covert ties to Soviet intelligence agencies. Without the radical Communists' traitorous behavior and support for Stalin, the paradox of radicalism would not have taken hold. Hundreds of progressives would not have been sent to prison, and another 10,000 would not have lost their jobs. And America would not have shifted so far to the right.

War on the U.S. Government. "The Weatherpeople," Kazin tells us, "were perhaps the most inept terrorists on the planet," their worst act of destruction being to blow up their bomb factory in a Greenwich Village townhouse, killing three of their own. Nonetheless, they did set off 25 bombs. They worked in support of the Black Panthers, who sometimes initiated shootouts with the police.

As reported in Chapter 3, the turn to radicalism in the late 1960s contributed significantly to the loss of 20 million Democratic voters, a blow the Democrats have yet to recover from. Yes, other forces deserve blame, too. But the radical fringe made terrible mistakes, and liberals with radical sympathies—and I include myself—failed to distance ourselves from them. This was a result of following the old Communist "ethic" of "No enemies on the left," which came to mean never criticize radicals.

The Radical Root of Polarization

Radicals implement their utopian ethic—never compromise the group's utopian principles—as a set of simplistic rules. Like religious rules, these establish *a standard for purity* or righteousness—call it what you will.

That means every one of these rules is a purity test. To those subscribing to a particular radicalism, these rules are obviously true. So anyone who breaks them is doing something deliberately unethical and is, therefore, an immoral person. Falling for this moralistic conclusion is the purity trap discussed in Chapter 7. And that is the main source of emotional polarization inside the Democratic Party and a major source of national polarization.

The utopian ethic of radicals also explains the millennialism discussed in the previous chapter. Here's how: All millennialisms have a goal of achieving a utopian society, which is a crucial part of the utopian ethic. An apocalyptic form of millennialism avoids an incremental approach and instead tries to suddenly transform the system into such a utopian society. This is exactly what the uncompromising part of the utopian ethic is aiming for.

So the utopian ethic of radicalism, which is a religious mode of thought, is the source of left-wing millennialism. And as we saw in the previous chapter, most left mythology is designed to support such millennialism.

Conclusion

Have I overstated the case against radicalism? Again I turn to Kazin because he has checked into all the nooks and crannies of 200 years of radical *American Dreamers*. And no one can accuse him of being biased against them.

In his final subsection, "The Uses of Utopia," Kazin begins a paragraph stating, "Surely this is a time for awakening the better angels of our nature." But that paragraph concludes:

> In the United States no less than in the Islamic world, we need a moral equivalent of the passion that drives vengeful believers.
>
> —Michael Kazin, *American Dreamers*

Kazin bases his own call for radicalism on a religious model—vengeful Islam. There is something fundamentally wrong with an ethic that can so easily slide from our 'better angels" to the "vengeful believers" of the Islamic world. Note, too, that 9/11 was still a recent memory when he wrote this.

Surely, Kazin believes he can separate some good "moral equivalent" from the bloody radical "passions" that drive vengeful Islamic believers. But this is precisely the central flaw of radicalism—the belief that there is some form of righteous purity that is so right-minded and inspiring, that it will overcome the negative effects of an unthinking, rule-based set of purity tests.

In fact, this transition from better angels to vengeful believers is a perfect metaphor for the fate of all socialist republics. They start out seeking to build a utopia with better angels and end up with vengeful believers brutally enforcing a failed system. That this has happened time and again is not some unlucky coincidence. It is an inevitable result of the radical utopian ethic.

Radicals are locked into their belief system by the self-reinforcing nature of the radical ethic. Once you adopt it, you become convinced that questioning it is unethical. This is nothing new or unusual—it is found in most pre-Enlightenment ideologies and in every cult.

CHAPTER 38

How Progressive Change Happens

All progress is precarious, and the solution of one problem brings us face to face with another problem.

—Martin Luther King Jr.

The most fundamental social change in U.S. history was, without a doubt, ending the crime of slavery. Four-million slaves were freed at the cost of 400,000 *Northern* lives (about 40,000 of them Black), roughly the same number who died in WWII. The South suffered proportionally more.

This is one of four great fundamental changes that this chapter investigates to find out how progressive change happens—not in any detail but at the most essential level. Were these changes driven by politics based on the radical utopian ethic or the liberal strategic ethic? These are the "two fundamentally differing and irreconcilably opposed" ethics that Max Weber defined in 1918 and that Michael Kazin adopted in *American Dreamers* to describe the thinking of radicals and liberals.

In other words, according to both Weber and Kazin, this is the most fundamental and enduring divide in political thought.

As Kazin points out, the "governing liberals and progressives appear to be [the] problem-solvers." But his claim is that the "uncompromising" radicals have ways of pressuring the liberals, who are just "anxious opportunists," into taking the actions that solve the problem. And how do radicals do this? Specifically, Kazin claims that radicals are

> far better at helping to **transform the moral culture**, the "common sense" of society—how Americans understand what is just and what is unjust.

Kazin is proposing that even though it always *appears* that the liberals brought about a fundamental progressive change, it was really the radicals who caused the liberals (who are just "anxious opportunists") to take action. And without the radicals, the change would never have happened. Moreover, he claims that the controlling force of radicalism works through a slow, long-term transformation of "moral culture" that is difficult to trace.

Kazin's claim is far subtler than the standard radical claim that a millennial-style revolution is imminent (a very old radical claim). His claim is that radical influence works through cultural (not political) channels, such as books and songs, which come from sources that are hard to evaluate and which have invisible effects. In spite of these ambiguities, by looking at Kazin's own explanations for the four fundamental changes, we will be able to answer the most essential question about how progressive change happens:

Is fundamental progressive change brought about by following the radical utopian ethic or by following the liberal strategic ethic?

While in all four cases the obvious answer is that those following the liberal strategic ethic caused the change, we will need to check two aspects of Kazin's story—(1) were the liberals just "anxious opportunists," and (2) were radicals "far better at helping to transform the moral culture" in a way that led to the progressive change?

The four fundamental changes. Except for the end of slavery and the end of the Jim Crow era, which happened suddenly, almost all change has occurred incrementally—in thousands of tiny steps. When Social Security was passed in 1935, it looked nothing like it does today after myriad amendments. To find out how fundamental social change happens, we'll look at the two that were sudden and two that were dramatic turning points leading to a long series of incremental changes. These are:

- Abraham Lincoln's ending of slavery
- Teddy Roosevelt's ending of laissez-faire capitalism
- Franklin Roosevelt's launch of federal social spending
- Kennedy's and Johnson's ending of the Jim Crow era

These will provide the clearest lessons in the shortest space. And although these changes happened long ago, the old struggles for change show remarkable similarities to those now polarizing the Democrats and the nation.

The End of Slavery

By all accounts, Lincoln followed the liberal, strategic ethic—he proceeded cautiously, and each step was a compromise designed to increase his chance of success by not risking catastrophic failure. So Kazin is right that Lincoln, who "appeared" to solve the problem, was a liberal.

But did radicals "transform the moral culture" and apply the pressure that made Lincoln take the actions that ended slavery? Actually, that's not quite the right question. If the radicals did help inspire change but would have accomplished more by using the liberal ethic instead, then their radical utopian ethic actually made a negative contribution to social change—even though the radicals themselves may have made a positive contribution. If you fight with one hand tied behind your back, you may help win the battle, but that doesn't mean having your hand tied behind your back (by the radical ethic) is helpful.

In the previous chapter, we saw that Kazin used the example of the "Schism of 1840" to draw the distinction between the radical and liberal ethics. That schism occurred between Garrison's radical abolitionists, who would not participate in electoral politics, and those who compromised by forming the Liberty Party and putting their demand for immediate abolition on hold—Kazin called this a "vital compromise." And just participating in politics was another huge compromise with Garrison's radical views.

In any case, Kazin emphatically identifies Garrison's group as subscribing to Weber's "ultimate ends" ethic, which I call the radical utopian ethic, and just as clearly identifies the splinter group that formed the Liberty Party as subscribing to Weber's "responsibility" ethic, which I call the liberal, strategic ethic.

So the question is this: Did the radical ethic help the Garrison group accomplish more than it would have accomplished with the liberal strategic ethic? And the answer is "no" for two reasons. First, the Liberty faction, the political abolitionists, were strategically quite brilliant both in their Congressional lobbying and in working to build a party that was not dependent on Southern votes. This became the Republican Party. So the liberal abolitionist contribution to the struggle was immense and in the end decisive. And the actions they took would all have been prohibited under Garrison's radical ethic.

Second, although the radicals stirred up support, they also stimulated huge antipathy, which ended up damaging non-radical abolitionists as well as the radicals. And by refusing to join the liberal effort, they could make only the most tangential contributions to the party-building and lobbying efforts that eventually elected Lincoln. So while they may have made a positive contribution on balance, they could have contributed far more by joining the political abolitionists. That means their radicalism was a negative factor in ending slavery.

> As one example of the strategic contributions of the political abolitionists, consider how, for days on end, John Quincy Adams captured the House of Representatives and railed against pro-slavery interests in the federal government. He had been our fifth president, but, in 1842, he was serving Massachusetts as a representative in Congress. Each evening, he met with members of the Liberty Party to plan the next day's arguments. This went on for two weeks and made the national news in a way Garrison's radicals never could.

Finally, Kazin notes that "the popularity of *Uncle Tom's Cabin* dwarfed that of every other abolitionist production. Harriet Beecher Stowe's sentimental 1852 exposé outsold every other novel in the nineteenth-century United States." It also inspired "eight different stage versions." Stowe first published her book in *The National Era*, a newspaper dedicated to explaining "the leading Principles and Measures of the Liberty Party." As Kazin makes clear, Stowe was no radical.

So, for the biggest social change in our history—the end of slavery—is Kazin right that radicals were "far better at helping to transform the moral culture?" Given how much hatred they stirred up against their position, even in the North, and Kazin's report of Stowe's immense influence, I find that highly improbable.

But what about their political actions? Did burning the Constitution, rejecting electoral politics, and trying to prevent the political abolitionism that led to the Republican Party and the election of Lincoln do more good than they would have done using the liberal, strategic ethic?

From the success of the liberal abolitionists—capturing national headlines from Washington D.C., forming the Republican Party, and electing Lincoln—I would say, hands down, the liberals had the more effective approach. Had Garrison abandoned his radical, utopian ethic and gone with the liberal, strategic ethic, I cannot help but think that would have strengthened the abolitionist cause.

Garrison may well have played a positive role on balance, even taking into account his many negative contributions. But the radical, utopian ethic that Kazin advocates surely made him less effective, not more.

Was Lincoln an Anxious Opportunist? I will let Frederick Douglass answer that question. That liberals are mere opportunists is the other half of Kazin's theory of why radicals are the ones who really drive progressive change.

After having been partly taught but then forbidden to read, and then having taught himself on the sly—and after serving several masters, one of whom whipped him mercilessly—Frederick Douglass escaped slavery at the age of 20. As an abolitionist and renowned feminist, he was to become one of the greatest American orators of the 19th century. No one thought harder than Douglass about how to free the slaves.

Douglass parted ways with the radical abolitionists over their rejection of the Union and our Constitution sometime in the 1840s. Twice during the Civil War, when he felt that Lincoln was immorally compromising the interest of Blacks, he was able to discuss his views directly with Lincoln. In both cases, he came away satisfied with Lincoln's explanations.

Just days after Lincoln's assassination, Charlotte Scott, a former slave, decided Lincoln should have a memorial. She contributed her entire savings of $5 to start the process. Former slaves, primarily Black veterans, contributed the rest. Douglass delivered the oration at the dedication of the memorial.

He listed many of Lincoln's actions that seemed hostile to Blacks. Taken together, these would be considered the most immoral set of liberal compromises ever enacted. And many radicals still see them this way. But Douglass did not. Instead, he explained why they were necessary to gain the "earnest sympathy and the powerful cooperation of his loyal fellow-countrymen." He continued, "Without this, his efforts must have been vain and utterly fruitless." That's a powerful justification, and he expanded on it in the excerpts that follow.

> He was willing to pursue, recapture and send back the fugitive slave to his master ... after accepting our services as colored soldiers, he refused to retaliate our murder and torture as colored prisoners ...
>
> When we saw all this, and more, we were at times grieved, stunned and greatly bewildered; but our hearts believed while they

ached and bled. Nor was this, even at that time, a blind and unreasoning superstition.

We were able to take a comprehensive view of Abraham Lincoln and to make a reasonable allowance for the circumstances of his position. We saw him, measured him and estimated him; not by stray utterances ... but in the light of the stern logic of great events. [This logic is what the radicals' utopian ethic forbids.]

It mattered little to us what language he might employ on special occasions ... it was enough for us that *Abraham Lincoln was at the head of a great movement,* and was in living and earnest sympathy with that movement. [Note the importance of a movement and that Lincoln, the strategist, and not Garrison, the radical, was leading it.]

Had he put the abolition of slavery before the salvation of the Union, he would have inevitably driven from him a powerful class of the American people. ... measuring him by the sentiment of his country, a sentiment he was bound as a statesman to consult, he was swift, zealous, radical, and determined.

In his heart of hearts, he loathed and hated slavery. The man who could say the following gives all needed proof of his feeling on the subject:

> Fervently do we pray, that this mighty scourge of war shall soon pass away. Yet, if God wills it to continue till all the wealth piled by two hundred years of bondage shall have been wasted, and each drop of blood drawn by the lash shall have been paid for by one drawn by the sword, the judgments of the Lord are true and righteous altogether ...

I believe this speech is the most powerful and eloquent argument ever made for acting strategically, as Lincoln did so brilliantly, and for recognizing brilliant strategy, as Douglass did. Lincoln needed Douglass's help, and had Douglass not been open to strategic thinking—had he remained a radical—he would have been a hindrance, not a help.

With Douglass's explanation, we are presented with a choice. We can believe Kazin's accusation that abolitionists on their way to forming the Republican Party were mere "anxious opportunists" and his insinuation that Lincoln probably was not much different. Or we can accept the views of Frederick Douglass—that Lincoln, in his heart of hearts, "loathed and hated slavery." And that the compromises he made were strategic and essential for winning the war and ending slavery. In my view, Douglass's views are completely credible and demolish the idea that Lincoln was a mere opportunist being prodded or guided by radicals.

Bridging the Radical-Liberal Gap

Lincoln was a liberal, but pursuing the Civil War and freeing the slaves was radical. Let's take a moment to clear that up, because more radical liberals—Teddy and Frankin Roosevelt and Martin Luther King Jr.—will show up as we examine the next three fundamental social changes.

Historian Richard Hofstadter, who focused on American political history, was a self-declared "radical liberal." He was anti-capitalist yet considered the late-'60s radicals to be "simple-minded, moralistic, ruthless and destructive." His goals were radical, but he knew the road was long and difficult.

There's no contradiction between wanting vast social progress and realizing that getting there will take good strategy, painful compromises, and many decades of struggle. In fact, being a radical liberal—a strategic liberal with radical ideas—is the best way to keep making progress.

That's good news for radicals. They can keep their ideals, give up their starry-eyed utopian ethics, and become radical liberals who compromise strategically.

Douglass showed how Lincoln was a strategic compromiser but said he was "swift and radical." Lincoln was willing to fight rather than chance the likely expansion of slavery. That is more radical than the radical abolitionists' suggestion:

> Let the South march off with flags and trumpets ... Give her jewels of silver and gold, and rejoice that she has departed.

So proclaimed Wendell Phillips, the radical "abolition's golden trumpet," as soon as the first state declared it would secede. William Lloyd Garrison agreed.

The End of Laissez-Faire Capitalism

The Progressive Era ended laissez-faire capitalism. Before then, America had no governmental restrictions on business—monopoly was legal, there were no workplace safety rules, no limits on the workday or workweek, and no consumer protections. Working conditions were horrific.

The decisive turn against laissez-faire capitalism occurred during Teddy Roosevelt's first term, starting in late 1901. In the late 1800s, public sentiment had turned against monopolies and trusts. Some legislation had been passed, but it was only under Teddy Roosevelt that businesses began to feel the effects.

What makes this a truly fundamental social change is that it did not fade out at the end of the Progressive Era but continued to grow and mature to the present day. Of course, there have been mistakes and setbacks, but the increase in corporate regulation, which started at zero in 1900, has been phenomenal, and has made capitalism much more humane.

Was it the radicals? Kazin would like us to believe that radicals played a major role, but he finds little evidence. He dismisses the radical anarchist movement as meeting a self-inflicted "early death." He dismisses the Socialists, saying Eugene V. "Debs' great spirit could not obscure the futility of his cause." Even the Populists, who achieved 10% of the popular vote in 1892, quickly faded away, and Kazin doesn't even call them radicals.

So instead of these obvious possibilities, Kazin concludes: "The powerful critiques of monopoly ... voiced by radicals like [Henry] George and [Edward] Bellamy ... put an end to the freebooting capitalism of the nineteenth century." Really?! Two guys you may never have heard of ended laissez-faire capitalism in America?

Edward Bellamy wrote *Looking Backward*, which described a perfect communist utopia (the next step after socialism) in the year 2000. Problem was, it gave only one small clue as to how to reach this utopian state. Here's the clue: Bellamy's utopia was powered by "the final monopoly in which all previous and lesser monopolies were swallowed up ... The epoch of trusts had ended in The Great Trust." And this idea led to Roosevelt's trust-busting?! Not really. Bellamy's book was an extremely popular, but short-lived, distraction—nothing more.

Henry George was far more substantive and rather brilliant. A self-taught economist, he proposed a tax on land as the best and only necessary tax. But George tied his proposal closely to the *Bible* and Christianity, sure that his tax could end poverty and bring "heaven on earth."

He saw no need to reign in capitalism so long as only land was taxed. Again, Kazin seems not to have figured out how this led to trust-busting, corporate regulation, consumer protection, or the eight-hour workday. I'd like to suggest a different theory.

The progressive movement. Teddy Roosevelt filed suit against a massive railroad trust in 1902 and won the case. That was the first major antitrust victory, and it led to 44 antitrust suits filed during Roosevelt's two terms and twice as many filed under Taft's term as president. In 1903, Roosevelt also created the Department of Commerce and Labor with its Bureau of Corporations. That turned into the Federal Trade Commission, now in charge of consumer protection and the enforcement of antitrust law. He also passed the first consumer protection legislation, the Pure Food and Drug Act, and the Federal Meat Inspection Act.

Roosevelt was no radical. As he put it, nothing would be accomplished "if we do not work through practical methods and with a readiness to face life as it is, and not as we think it ought to be." That's the most succinct endorsement you'll ever find for using the strategic liberal approach instead of the utopian radical approach.

As always, the liberal politicians needed the backing of a popular movement. The famed Progressive Movement was driven not by radical dreams but by the shocking and visible consequences of laissez-faire capitalism.

Farmers were impoverished and bankrupted by railroad trusts and Eastern financial capitalists. Small-time oil producers like the parents of famous "muckraker" Ida Tarbell were bankrupted by the outrageous business practices of robber barons like John D. Rockefeller. Jacob Riis, a confidant of Roosevelt, published *How the Other Half Lives,* exposing the horrendous working/living conditions of immigrants. Stephen Crane described the life of young boys working 10-hour days in coal mines, growing up owing their souls to the company store until they were buried in the company 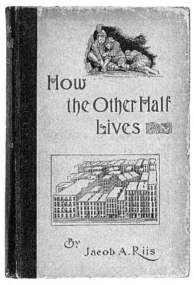 graveyard. Behind locked doors, 146 workers perished in a sweatshop fire. The company was absolved of responsibility and collected $64,925 in insurance damages. The families on average received $12 per life lost.

These atrocities drove progressive change—not radical, fuzzy-headed utopian novels or radical proposals for magic taxes. In good radical fashion, Kazin does not even consider the impact of the horrors of laissez-faire capitalism on the non-radical public, which he always sees as hopelessly ignorant, uncaring, and in need of the insightful moral guidance of radicals.

The end of laissez-faire capitalism was brought about by good-hearted people pushing for reforms that happened one step at a time with the help of good-hearted politicians who worked hard and strategically to pass these reforms. That's strategic liberal incrementalism. It's not incremental because we prefer slowness for its own sake; it's incremental because it's a hard process, and small, sure-footed steps prove quickest in the long run.

Launching Responsible Government

Progressivism aimed to make capitalists play fair and to level the playing field between labor and capital. But progressivism did not view the government as having much responsibility for those the capitalist system left destitute.

The Great Depression drove home the need for the federal government to take an active role in ensuring the public welfare. This led Franklin Roosevelt to create his New Deal. That was never intended to last, and it didn't. But it opened the door to a new view of government responsibility that was soon cemented in place by Social Security. In 1930, public social spending was half a percent of GDP; by 2016, it had grown to 19%.

The popular movement. There was enormous public sentiment during the Depression in favor of government action. Although this did produce radical activity among the intelligentsia and in parts of the working class, this radical activity did not have much impact on the Roosevelt administration, probably because the radicals' electoral base was far too small. When Roosevelt was elected in 1932, the Socialists got 2.2% of the vote and the Communists 0.25%. By 1940, the Socialists, too, were down to 0.25% and the Communists to half of that. Meanwhile, Roosevelt was winning by landslide margins. When Norman Thomas, the five-time Socialist Party presidential candidate, was asked if FDR was carrying out his socialist program, he quipped, "Yes, he is carrying it out in a coffin."

Huey Long, who by 1935 had organized 27,000 Share Our Wealth Clubs with more than seven-million members, had far more impact on Roosevelt, who actually brought him home to meet his mother. Roosevelt also called him the second most dangerous man in America. But Huey was no radical. He was a pragmatist who hated socialism. Kazin knows this and ignores him. Huey was another radical liberal.

Roosevelt listened to the popular movement, the voice of which was predominantly liberal and looking for practical solutions—mainly jobs. His longest-lasting programmatic contributions were the Wagner Act, which gave workers the right to form and join unions, and the Social Security Act.

The authors of these Acts, Robert Wagner and Francis Perkins, respectively, were both highly dedicated liberal reformers with lifelong records of service. They were not remotely like the opportunistic political-establishment hacks Kazin and other radicals would have you believe are only motivated by pressure from radicals. FDR's fundamental social change was brought about by dedicated, strategic liberals, not by radicals.

The End of Jim Crow

The end of Jim Crow laws in the South meant the end of legal segregation and of legal exclusion from the ballot box, as well as an end to defacto terrorist enforcement of White supremacist norms. In my view, this is the second most important social change after the ending of slavery.

It has not, of course, ended racism or done anything close to that. But breaking that system—the laws along with their enforcement by state-assisted terrorism—required a century-long struggle by Blacks that led to the most advanced political movement this country has ever seen.

But neither Kazin nor Black Power radical Stokely Carmichael nor the radical founders of Critical Race Theory (Ch. 36) agree with that judgment of the civil rights movement. Kazin includes a 10-page section that covers both the civil rights movement and the Black power movement. He begins with his only mention of the Civil Rights Act:

> The same elites who [bombed Vietnam] also sponsored the Peace Corps and the Civil Rights Act, hoping to mollify the discontented before they turned to revolution.

The word "subterfuge"—deceit used to achieve one's goal—comes to mind. According to Kazin, the Civil Rights Act was a deceit used to avoid genuine revolutionary change. That echoes what Stokely Carmichael said at a huge rally in 1966 at U.C. Berkeley:

We've said that integration was irrelevant when initiated by Blacks [he meant Dr. King] and that in fact, it was an insidious subterfuge for the maintenance of White supremacy.

That's a direct attack on all of Dr. King's work, and the work of every hero who risked or gave their lives in the civil rights movement. Kazin confirms his view that Black radicals, and not the civil rights movement, deserve all the credit:

Radicals like Carmichael and [Black Panther Huey] Newton had jolted millions of people to comprehend themselves and their society in assertive and candid ways ... This new understanding was an authentic kind of freedom.

In our first three cases, radicals try to take credit for an agreed-upon fundamental social change. But in this case, they disparage ending Jim Crow as a help to White supremacy and claim that instead, the fundamental social change was gaining an "authentic kind of freedom" via the Black power movement. The question this time is not who caused the change but which change was fundamental—the end of Jim Crow or some quite different "authentic kind of freedom" caused by millions comprehending themselves (whatever that means).

Which did more for the Black community, the Panthers' "authentic kind of freedom" or what Kazin implies is the "inauthentic freedom" to attend a good school, not be lynched with the sheriff's approval, and so on?

Because Kazin's sole claim for radicals throughout American history is their supposed far greater ability to "transform the moral culture," let us compare the sources of these competing moral transformations—the Panthers' leadership and the civil rights leadership. Which was a better source of moral culture?

Was Huey P. Newton really a better moral leader than Martin Luther King Jr.? That's Kazin's radical claim in a nutshell.

Black power. Stokely Carmichael, who launched the Black power movement and gave the Panthers their name, started out as a Freedom Rider and organizer of newly-enfranchised Black voters. But before that, he had been radicalized in high school by the son of the chairman of the Communist Party. Similarly, the Black Panthers were self-declared communist revolutionaries, following Stalin and Mao.

The Black Panthers' elementary school in Oakland, California, and their free breakfasts for poor children were widely acclaimed. But according to Erica Huggins (the school director for eight years until it folded in 1982) "Toward the end, paranoia and addiction and all these things [from] outside the school impacted everything." Huey Newton, who had a powerful cocaine habit, was charged with 33 counts of grand theft for embezzling $600,000 from the school between 1980 and 1982.

Before becoming school director, Erica Huggins had moved to New Haven, Connecticut, after her husband was shot and killed by a rival Black power organization. There, with Elaine Brown, she founded a new chapter of the Black Panther Party.

Soon, Alex Rackley, a 19-year-old member of Huggins's chapter, was suspected of spying for the FBI. So he was taken to the basement of the Panthers' headquarters and tortured for two days until he "confessed." A day later, they shot him. As it happened, they had the wrong guy. After admitting she was present for the torture but claiming she was afraid not to participate, Huggins was acquitted by a hung jury.

In 1974, Huggins and Elaine Brown were both back in Oakland, and Brown was leading the Oakland chapter of the Panthers while Huey was on the lam in Cuba, having murdered a prostitute. Brown hired Betty Van Patter, a Panthers-friendly bookkeeper. On Friday night, December 13, 1974, Betty was with friends at a bar when a Black man handed her a note. She left immediately and was soon seen at the Lamp Post bar, a Black Panthers hangout. Then she disappeared. Her body was found 35 days later washed up on a San Francisco Bay beach. She had been badly beaten.

Ken Kelley would later learn what had happened. He had once been the Minister of Information for the White Panther Party (Black Panther Party sympathizers), and when Huey Newton returned from Cuba in 1977, he began helping him with public relations. Kelley reminisced about his many encounters with Newton in an article he wrote for the *East Bay Express* three weeks after Newton's murder during a drug deal gone wrong. Kelley's concluding revelation was this:

> While he'd been in Cuba, he told me, he'd ordered the murder of a good friend of mine who had been hired to do bookkeeping for the Panthers. She'd refused orders to cook the books, to make them look legit, and had threatened to call the cops. Listening to Huey brought all the stupid, senseless bloodshed back home. It hadn't

been a simple hit—she'd been tortured, raped, shot and thrown into the bay.

I think about my dead friend Betty almost every day. I'm sitting in her office chair right now—her daughter gave it to me—as
I type out the words of what has to be the hardest piece I've ever
written in all my years in journalism.

There is no credible evidence that Betty threatened to call the cops,
but Elaine Brown does tell us, in *A Taste of Power*, that if any controversy leaked out, it would have damaged her campaign for Oakland City
Council. She lost anyway.

This glimpse of the dark side is, of course, a one-sided view of the
Panthers, but it is a view generally hidden from the broader left (for instance by Kazin), and it's a crucial piece of the radical puzzle.

It makes clear the damaging nature of the radical utopian ethic. As
Max Weber noted 100 years ago, if a radical takes a "righteous" action
that damages his own cause, the radical believes the fault must lie with
someone else. That's why the entire radical left blamed the torture-
murder of Alex Rackley on the well-known FBI infiltration of the Panthers. The Panthers were viewed as righteous, so any evil resulting from
their actions must lie with someone else.

Of course, most Panthers supporters, Black and White, were well-
intentioned progressives and just sucked in by Black power mythology.
Ken Kelley was once one of these, and I was on the fringes of this con
job for a while myself.

Civil rights. The civil rights movement could not have been more different from the radical Black power movement. It had radical goals—the
end of Jim Crow and decent jobs—but it did not follow the utopian radical ethics that shunned compromise. Equality with Whites was a dream,
but it was not a utopian dream—White America was no utopia. And every step in the civil rights movement was a compromise relative to their
goal.

The civil rights movement was a movement of radical liberals (liberals with radical goals) with a brilliant strategy developed over decades.
Strategic discussions of nonviolence began in the 1920s, and the first
direct contact with Gandhi was a note sent by W. E. B. Du Bois in 1929.
By 1936, King's mentor, theologian Howard Thurman, was meeting
Gandhi in India. Thurman was also the mentor of James Farmer, who in
1961 organized the first Freedom Ride. King himself spent a month in

India studying Gandhi's teachings. All of this was preparation for building a movement that would transform the moral culture in a vastly more positive way than radicals seem capable of recognizing.

The other half of the radical myth of moral transformation holds that political leaders like LBJ and Bobby Kennedy, who actually made change happen, are just morally-deficient opportunists. Let's take a look.

Bobby Kennedy, President Kennedy's attorney general, was the movement's door to political power. He was sympathetic and had potential, but needed education. His close watch over and interactions with the movement did the job, and Bobby became a committed advocate for civil rights. He convinced his brother, who delivered his "Report to the American People on Civil Rights," proposing what would become the Civil Rights Act of 1964.

Bobby's dedication was recognized by the Black community, as was made clear at the time of King's assassination. Bobby was on his way to a rally in the heart of the Indianapolis ghetto at 17th and Broadway. Fearing for his safety, the chief of police told Bobby not to go. But his assistant, who was Black, knew Bobby's reputation in the ghetto and said he "could sleep all night in the middle of 17th and Broadway and not be hurt." Bobby did not turn back. At the end of his short speech, the crowd went home, and Indianapolis stayed calm while 100 other cities erupted in riots.

When President Kennedy was assassinated, it was left to Lyndon Johnson to get civil rights bills passed by the Southern Democrats. They knew how to stop such bills—but so did LBJ, who beat their strategy. Not only was Johnson a brilliant political strategist, but he was also a highly effective moral strategist, as he once explained:

> Now I knew that as President I couldn't make people want to integrate their schools or open their doors to Blacks, but I could make them feel guilty for not doing it, and I believed it was my moral responsibility to do precisely that—to use the moral persuasion of my office to make people feel that segregation was a curse they'd carry with them to their graves.

After his freshman year of college, Johnson had taught at a segregated grade school for Mexican-Americans. He was quickly promoted to principal and organized all sorts of activities. He never forgot those kids, and when he signed the 1965 Higher Education Act, he said, "It was then that I made up my mind that this nation could never rest while the door to knowledge remained closed to any American." Radicals may paint him as a mere dealmaking opportunist, but that is only because of their own blindness.

Conclusion

The critical pieces are now in place, and we can see clearly how change happened. First came liberal movements such as political abolitionism, progressivism, Huey Long's Share Our Wealth movement, and the civil rights movement. As liberal movements, they employed strategy. They took steps they believed would succeed, even though this meant the steps were small. In other words, the movements made compromises when compared with their radical-liberal (not utopian) goals, but they were compromises that helped to gain momentum or gain a new foothold.

Second, liberal politicians are needed in positions of power. They can only do a little to create public sentiment themselves, so they wait for a social movement like the progressive movement or the civil rights movement to shift public sentiment and then climb on board. But it took Johnson, an acclaimed dealmaker, to finish the job. And the movement needed the brilliant leadership of Dr. King. Both the politicians and the movement leadership were essential.

Looking at the four most dramatic social changes in American history, we see the liberal approach working every time while the radical approach has had little influence except when it was negative: Radicals in the 1840s tried to stop those who formed the Republican Party. Radicals provoked Teddy Roosevelt's misstep against the "muckrakers." Radicals infiltrated FDR's administration to spy for Stalin, and the radicals of the late 1960s help drive 20 million from the Democratic Party.

Once again, I am using "liberal" to mean those who accept responsibility for the consequences of their actions, think strategically, and are willing to compromise for the sake of progress. The goal of the liberal is progress, not righteous purity.

Positive fundamental social change takes a social movement and good politicians working together with each side respecting the fact that they play very different roles. Both should have a radical vision of the future, but both should adopt the liberal strategic ethic and reject the radical utopian ethic of self-righteous purity. We should strive to follow FDR's model and be tolerant, radical liberals.

CHAPTER 39

Putting the Pieces Together

A house divided against itself cannot stand.
—Abraham Lincoln, 1858

Trump won. That should have been impossible by historical standards. Never before has a sociopath with no public-service record taken the presidency. This happened despite the Democrats running a top-flight candidate with an economy nearing full employment.

Something was fundamentally wrong with the country. Half the problem sits on Trump's side and lies out of our reach—Fox, Limbaugh, lingering racism, anti-intellectualism, and so on. But these forces were not able to stop the country from getting more liberal before Trump took power. Since 2007, we've elected our first Black president, reelected him, approved gay marriage, and legalized marijuana in many states. And even after Trump won, Obamacare went from neutral to 51%-to-40% in favor. On top of that, over the last 24 years, the electorate has gone from about 15% non-White to about 28%.

With the political landscape shifting our way both long-term and short-term, why do we suddenly have the most anti-democratic president in our history?

If we're honest with ourselves, we know we should have won—big. And if we change track, I'm sure we could. Carping at the Republicans will not fix this. It's up to us to look in the mirror and fix what keeps us weak.

The danger is greater than at any time since the Civil War. But it's political, not economic. Neither our Democratic Party nor our democracy is near collapse, but if Trump wins a second term, all bets are off. The Republican Party is now completely under his control. On the day the House voted to impeach him, the best multi-poll average of his net favorability reached its highest point since his first two months in office.

With another term, he'll pack the courts with far-right conservatives who will be in power for decades, and like any strongman, he is packing the government with sycophants who will follow orders, legal or not, since he can pardon anyone.

If Trump is reelected, the same forces that are polarizing and weakening our party now will likely tear the Democrats apart. That, combined with a corrupted Republican Party, is the danger we're facing if we lose the presidency again in 2020.

Our Polarization Helps Trump

Trump's strategy is polarization. First, he increased Republican polarization, which was already getting out of hand due to the Tea Party. With the nomination in hand, he went after the nation, and he's never stopped. He has no understanding of statesmanship or making the country great again. His one focus and only strategy is playing to his base and a few sympathizers who he hopes to recruit.

In this age of negative partisanship, the best way to rally your base is to make them hate and fear their opponents. That means polarizing his base, and that polarizes us. But we should resist that. When they hate us, we usually hate back. Which is exactly what he wants. Our hatred galvanizes his base better than anything he can say himself will make them vote in large numbers.

Now stop and think. If polarization has been a winning strategy for Trump since he entered the race in 2015, should we join him in polarizing the country, or should we fight polarization?

Of course, most Democrats want to fight it as do a great many independents and Republicans. They dislike the acrimony and know instinctively that a country full of hate does not favor democracy. But there's a faction of our Party that thrives on polarization, both internal and national, just the way Trump does. No, their politics is nothing like Trump's politics. But both extremes thrive on polarization.

Part 4: Mythology Traps describes a set of polarizing myths generated and believed by Democrats. The most transparent of these is the myth of the Overton Window (Ch. 27). It holds that extreme radical positions are all we need to create radical change. In fact, the popular, sometimes radical website Vox.com tells us that while extreme positions are good, "unthinkable" positions are even better. Well, of course. Everyone without a brain knows that.

But if that were correct, Trump's extreme views would be making Democrats more conservative. I don't see that happening, and the evidence is that extreme-left views push the left to the left and the right to the right. That causes national polarization.

A similar fate befalls the myth of the bully pulpit, even though it's far more believable. Presidents who use their bully pulpit to sway public opinion almost never succeed, and often have the reverse effect because they stir up the opposition. But the greater problem this time is internal. When radicals see that a Democratic president is not performing miracles from his pulpit, they conclude he is probably working for Wall Street. Similar delusions cause radicals to deprecate candidates who aren't the preachy type.

Another myth holds that anyone in the establishment—either because they're rich or have a position in the party—must be corrupt. Bernie Sanders, in particular, has pushed this myth hard, which is ironic when you consider his current hero. He claims FDR was a "great, great president," models his democratic socialism on FDR's Second Bill of Rights, and runs ads that imply they are almost twins. Yet FDR was well above the 1% cutoff financially and probably the most establishment Democrat ever. Sanders could not be more hypocritical on this score, and he is using the myth to tear down the Democratic Party.

Sanders is also promoting the myth that FDR's policies were "democratic socialism" in an attempt to distance himself from his true socialist past. This has led many if not most of his followers to believe socialism is just a nicer kind of capitalism. In fact, almost none of them seem to know what socialism actually is or that Sanders is still an honest-to-Marx socialist or that socialism is the most unacceptable political label for a presidential candidate.

This myth causes Berniecrats, almost none of whom are actually socialists (or "democratic socialists"—the same thing), to disparage Democrats who know what socialism is and therefore reject the label. And it tars the party with a label that conservatives have always used to attack Democrats. The Republicans are holding their fire, hoping Sanders will be nominated and salivating over the chance to use their horde of anecdotes concerning his past socialist missteps. One of these was cutting a deal with democratic socialist Hugo Chavez, who he later called a "dead communist dictator" (Ch. 5).

Delusions Rule

The more desperately we care about social change, the easier we are to fool. That's not the whole story, but there's a lot of truth to it. In the 1850s, the Xhosa people of South Africa were sorely oppressed by the British. In April 1856, 15-year-old Nongqawuse saw a vision and prophesied that if the Xhosa would kill all their cattle and live righteously, the spirits would sweep the British into the sea and replace their cattle with healthier ones. So they killed more than 300,000 head of cattle, and three-quarters of the tribe starved to death.

This was an extreme but classic millennial movement of which there have been hundreds. Desperation leads to gullibility. You may think that the fault lay with the unsophisticated Xhosa, but remember that the very sophisticated Germans of the 1920s bought the myth of the Thousand-Year Reich that would rule the world. That turned out even worse. But still, such things could not happen to sophisticated Democrats. Or could they? Part 2 shows how easily California's far-left Democratic establishment fell for Jim Jones, America's worst mass murderer. So it should be no surprise that many Democrats are falling for more benign millennial movements promising a quick trip to the Promised Land. The worse things look, the more attractive such myths will become.

Everyone seems to want rational explanations, usually based on economic problems, for why we are caught up in our present political malaise. Such real-world inputs do play a role, but their effects are filtered through something akin to mass psychosis. So logic and theories can explain a little when applied by the wisest among us. But that doesn't help those of us who get sucked into bogus explanations because we can't tell who to believe.

There are two partial escape routes from this predicament. First, learn that delusion is the dominant player in politics. Second, learn to be cautious and when to be most cautious.

The first escape route teaches us to fight polarization by cutting everyone some slack, at least until we really know who them well. Most people are trying to do what they believe is right, and when they fail it's simply because they've been deceived. They have "good intentions," even when they're on the road to hell.

Practicing this simple rule (cutting some slack) goes a long way to depolarizing us. It makes us see what seemed to be evil enemies as just mistaken adversaries. That applies equally to fellow Democrats and Republicans. And when we are less polarized, we stir up less polarization among our adversaries. Yes, there are some sociopaths, but they comprise only a small percentage of the population. Most folks want to do good.

Political and Moralistic Traps

The second route out of the predicament of mass psychosis is learning when to be cautious and when to be most cautious. So Parts 2 through 4 take a close look at the three most important kinds of Political Traps. As Part 1 explains, most of these can easily lead into the Moralistic Trap.

Political Traps, by themselves, lead to issue polarization, which is not helpful but not deadly. The purity trap, however, leads to emotional polarization—hatred for one's opponents. Political Traps convince people they know what's right. Moralistic thinkers believe that what's right is so obvious that it is *obvious to everyone*. That ridiculous assumption lands them in a purity trap: They think anyone who disagrees with them cannot possibly be mistaken, so they must be immoral. This causes them to see their opponents (quite often other Democrats) as evil enemies.

Political Traps come in a number of identifiable types. And looking at a sample of each of the three most common kinds will make it easier to recognize them as we encounter new ones. So Part 2 presents six charisma traps. The most important and surprising one of these is Donald Trump. Lacking appropriate skills, much of his popularity is based on his charisma. That's a valuable lesson because his charisma is invisible to most Democrats, so they fail to understand much of his appeal.

But charisma is not some universal property; rather, it is the ability to form an emotional bond with an audience. So any particular case of charisma depends as much on the audience as on the leader. Charisma traps are also important because they are the basis of the appeal of demagogues.

Part 3 looks at populism traps. Populism is one of the simplest ideologies, and it is particularly dangerous because it appears to the casual observer to be more democratic than our representative democracy. But as our Founding Fathers knew well, it is the vehicle of demagogues, and it fails to protect minorities. So they built in our checks and balances specifically to prevent populism.

The danger for those on the left is that they are predisposed to believe populism is progressive. Consequently, when Sanders supporters see populist tendencies in Trump's base, they become hopeful for a revolution based on a progressive merger of Tea Partiers and Berniecrats (Ch. 16). This is delusional. And in such times as these, chasing electoral delusions is dangerous.

In fact, there is an irreconcilable difference between right- and left-wing populism. Trump's right-wing populism is based on the culture war, while Sanders' left-wing populism is based on a crude Marxist economic analysis. In Trump's populism, liberals and progressives are part of the elite, and many of the one-percenters are hard-working rich who are part of "the real people."

Part 4 covers the Overton window myth, the bully-pulpit myth, and a few other examples of the third kind of Political Trap, the mythology traps. Because these were discussed above, we can move on to the new identity politics.

The New Identity Politics

The new identity politics started developing in the 1970s and grew out of the Black Power Movement and postmodernism. The former was explicitly based on revolutionary Marxism. The latter was based on a strange mixture of German and Italian neo-Marxism, Maoism, and a couple of philosophers associated with Nazism. All of that was filtered through an odd collection of elite French intellectuals.

Needless to say, the resulting ideology is completely foreign to American political thought. It shares virtually nothing with liberalism, progressivism, or even socialism, and it rejects outright the civil rights approach to identity politics. It even rejects the accomplishments of Martin Luther King Jr. and the civil rights movement.

In contrast to the civil rights movement, which would see freedom from police harassment as a basic civil right that should be extended to minorities, the new identity politics sees it as a White privilege that Whites should feel guilty for having.

While civil rights protesters were proud of their exceptional bravery when confronting the Klan and the Southern police, identity politics protesters typically demand protection even from sympathetic liberals—even minority liberals—who simply question whether their approach is helpful.

A central message of this new politics is that if any member of a minority group feels offended by a White person, then no matter what actually happened or what the White person intended, the White person has "perpetrated" an offense—a microaggression. This view has deep roots in French postmodern "philosophy."

Prioritizing the subjective over the objective has now been taken to such an extreme that all of science is discredited as "masculinist stories," and we now find the National Science Foundation funding feminist glaciology to the tune of $700,000. These grants produced a paper that claims that male scientists do not put up their satellites to measure ice loss in Greenland and Antarctica but rather to make "claims of objectivity" that are "akin to the 'god trick of seeing everything from nowhere.' "

This denial of science is actually part of a much broader denial of truth and the Enlightenment in general, all of which some postmodernists have now realized is very helpful to Trump. But an even worse effect of the new identity politics is that its many excesses are the most prized material of all right-wing "news" outlets. And there is nothing better for getting Trump's voters out to the polls come November 3, 2020.

Radicals versus Liberals

Polarization splits the Democratic Party between radicals and liberals. Radicals recommend policies that are further from the status quo. But recommendations (and demands) are a dime a dozen, so this attribute of radicals tells us little. A deeper view of the radical-liberal distinction can be traced to Max Weber, a founder of sociology. That view provides far more insight and also provides a compromise solution that gives us the best of both worldviews.

The radical "ethic," according to the noted radical Michael Kazin who is an expert in radical thought and history, and also according to Weber, takes a purist approach. The radical does what's "right" according to his utopian view, even if the outcome is harmful to the radical cause. For if there is harm, it is the fault of others. Kazin and Weber both compare this to a Christian form of thinking. Man should follow God's laws, and God will take care of the consequences.

The liberal ethic is strategic. A liberal should do what will produce the best outcome, taking account of the fact that Trump will play dirty. The compromise solution, which I recommend, is to be a radical liberal. Imagine the ideal outcome, but realized there's no magic shortcut, and getting there will require strategic compromises and a lot of hard work and patience.

Not the Time for a Hail Mary

If you've got the ball on your own 50-yard line and there are 5 seconds left in the game, you may as well throw a "Hail Mary" pass and say your prayers. But no one does that with a lot of time left on the clock. It makes sense only when failure will do no harm.

But even the radicals know that our political game will continue. What they don't know is that trying for a "political revolution" is like throwing a "Hail Mary" pass. They think that electing Sanders or maybe Warren will take us all the way to the "Promised Land," and failing will doom us to defeat.

They "know" that this time is different. There's never been such a dedicated honest leader before. But followers of every one of the hundreds of millennialist movements have thought the same things. And none succeeded.

So if you know someone who is hellbent on trying such a crazy experiment at the worst possible moment in the country's history, you might remind them of the words of Sanders' lifelong hero, democratic socialist Eugene V. Debs: "I would not lead you into the promised land if I could, because if I led you in, someone else would lead you out. You must use your heads."

It's time to resist Trump, not by being the noisy, toothless enemy he needs but by quietly doing the one thing he cannot abide—having us disengage from his polarizing antics. Teddy Roosevelt's favorite West African proverb applies: "Speak softly but carry a big stick. You will go far." Understood properly, that adds depth to Michelle's wise maxim, "When they go low, we go high."

Though our path has been rocky, we have followed it ever higher for more than two centuries. Now our progress has been blocked, and the path itself could vanish before our eyes. Ending the current catastrophe would reopen the door to progress. That would be miracle enough. We must work together, take courage, and grow stronger. That's what winning takes—nothing less.

Chapter notes can be found at: `RippedApart.org`

Bibliography

Alexander, Michelle. *The New Jim Crow: Mass Incarceration in the Age of Colorblindness,* 2010.

Bawer, Bruce. *The Victims' Revolution: The Rise of Identity Studies and the Closing of the Liberal Mind,* 2012.

Brands, H. W. *Traitor to His Class: The Privileged Life and Radical Presidency of Franklin Delano Roosevelt,* 2009.

Bronner, Stephen Eric. *Critical Theory: A Very Short Introduction,* 2017.

Butler, Christopher. *Postmodernism: A Very Short Introduction,* 2003.

Culver, John C. and John Hyde. *American Dreamer: A Life of Henry A. Wallace,* 2001.

Devine, Thomas W. *Henry Wallace's 1948 Presidential Campaign and the Future of Postwar Liberalism,* 2013.

Edsall Thomas B. and Mary D. Edsall. *Chain Reaction: The Impact of Race Rights, and Taxes on American Politics,* 1992.

Edsall Thomas B. *The Age of Austerity: How Scarcity Will Remake American Politics,* 2012.

Frum, David. *Trumpocracy: The Corruption of the American Republic,* 2018.

Goodwin, Doris Kearns. *The Bully Pulpit: Theodore Roosevelt, William Howard Taft, and the Golden Age of Journalism,* 2013.

Haidt, Jonathan. *The Righteous Mind: Why Good People Are Divided by Politics and Religion,* 2012.

Hochschild, Arlie Russell. *Strangers in Their Own Land: Anger and Mourning on the American,* 2016.

Jeffries, Stuart. *Grand Hotel Abyss: The Lives of the Frankfurt School,* 2016.

Judis, John B. *The Populist Explosion: How the Great Recession Transformed American,* 2016.

Kakutani, Michiko. *The Death of Truth: Notes on Falsehood in the Age of Trump,* 2018.

Kazin, Michael. *American Dreamers: How the Left Changed a Nation,* 2011.

Landes, Richard. *Heaven on Earth: The Varieties of the Millennial Experience,* 2011.

Levitsky, *Steven and Daniel Ziblatt. How Democracies Die,* 2018.

Lewis, Michael. *The Fifth Risk,* 2018.

Lilla, Mark. *The Once and Future Liberal: After Identity Politics,* 2017,

Long, Huey Pierce. *My First Days In The White House,* 1935.

Mauer, Marc. *Race to Incarcerate.* 2006.

More in Common. *Hidden Tribes: A Study of America's Polarized Landscape,* Oct. 2018.

More in Common. *Hidden Tribes: Midterms Report,* Nov. 2018.

More in Common. *The Perception Gap: How False Impressions are Pulling Americans Apart,* June, 2019.

Mounk, Yascha. *The People vs. Democracy: Why Our Freedom Is in Danger and How to Save It.* 2018.

Mudde, Cas. *Populism: A Very Short Introduction,* 2017.

Müller, Jan-Werner. *What Is Populism?* 2016.

National Academies Press. *The Growth of Incarceration in the United States: Exploring Causes and Consequences,* 2014.

Norris, Pippa. *Cultural Backlash: Trump, Brexit, and Authoritarian Populism,* 2019.

Oxford University Press. *The Oxford Handbook of Political Ideologies,* 2013.

Pinker, Steven. *Enlightenment Now*: The Case for Reason, Science, Humanism, and Progress, 2018.

Pfaff, John. *Locked In: The True Causes of Mass Incarceration and How to Achieve Real Reform,* 2017.

Rectenwald, Michael. *Springtime for Snowflakes: 'Social Justice' and Its Postmodern Parentage Paperback,* 2018.

Scurr, Ruth. *Fatal Purity: Robespierre and the French Revolution,* 2007.

Smith, Jean Edward. *FDR*, 2007.

Sokal, Alan. *Beyond the Hoax: Science, Philosophy and Culture*, 2010.

Sokal, Alan. *Fashionable Nonsense: Postmodern Intellectuals' Abuse of Science*, 1999.

Stone, Oliver and Peter Kuznick. *The Untold History of the United States*, 2012.

Sunstein, Cass. *The Second Bill of Rights: FDR's Unfinished Revolution—And Why We Need It More Than Ever*, 2006.

Wilentz, Sean. *The Politicians and the Egalitarians: The Hidden History of American Politics*, 2016.

Williams, T. Harry. *Huey Long*, 1969.

Wolin, Richard. *The Seduction of Unreason: The Intellectual Romance with Fascism from Nietzsche to Postmodernism*, 2004.

Woodard, Colin. *American Nations: A History of the Eleven Rival Regional Cultures of North America*, 2012.

Major Topics Index